AMERICAN ARTISANAL

AMERICAN
ARTISANAL

FINDING THE COUNTRY'S BEST REAL FOOD,
from CHEESE *to* CHOCOLATE

REBECCA GRAY

foreword by ETHAN BECKER

RIZZOLI
NEW YORK

FIRST PUBLISHED IN THE UNITED STATES OF AMERICA IN 2008
BY RIZZOLI INTERNATIONAL PUBLICATIONS, INC.
300 PARK AVENUE SOUTH
NEW YORK, NY 10010
WWW.RIZZOLIUSA.COM

© 2008 REBECCA GRAY

2008 2009 2010 2011 / 10 9 8 7 6 5 4 3 2 1

DISTRIBUTED IN THE U.S. TRADE BY RANDOM HOUSE, NEW YORK

PRINTED IN THE UNITED STATES

ISBN-10: 0-8478-2934-0
ISBN-13: 978-0-8478-2934-7
LIBRARY OF CONGRESS CONTROL NUMBER: 2007939127

TO MY GRANDMOTHERS,
CHARLOTTE CRAWFORD AND MARY ALLBRIGHT,
*who purchased few cookbooks, did little grocery shopping, rarely
cooked a meal, or spent time in the kitchen—except by necessity,
when it was cook's night off. Their food legacy wasn't recipes,
but a knack in finding people who could make good food.
They would have loved this book.*

CONTENTS

FOREWORD

DRIVING CROSS COUNTRY on Interstate 80 in July
makes it easy to understand just how incredibly well
America grows food in quantity. The grain crops in Ohio,
Indiana, Iowa, and Nebraska grow in orderly profusion as far as
the eye can see. Driving down California's Route 99 through
America's fruit basket, I am once again amazed at our country's
extraordinary ability to grow vast quantities of good food.

This abundance has resulted in a long history of artisanal
food in the effort to preserve and keep as much as possible. You
will find these artisans in pockets throughout America—such as
the wonderful garlicky sausages, salami, and other smoked
meats of the Pennsylvania Dutch Country. Then there are the
Southern salt-cured hams (reminiscent of Italy's prosciutto) that
are frequently made by small family producers with generations
of success behind them.

In this delightful and very personal search, Rebecca Gray
takes us on a journey of discovery of the new artisans of
America, often crafting nontraditional ingredients as well as the
traditional. While great food is a reflection of soil, sunlight, and
climate, it is also a reflection of the people who really give a
damn about making the most of what nature gives them.

Reading the saga of Chris Reed and his search for the most
perfect ginger to make his most excellent crystallized ginger, I
flashed on the memory of a good friend and outstanding deli-
master, Al Silverglade. Al often drove the back roads of Ohio's

Amish country looking for active smokehouses, stopping to taste and buy, and then working to keep his customers supplied with the best.

As I read each of the vignettes presented here, it is impossible to miss the obsessive quality that is required to meet Rebecca's standards. And she is so right, because without obsession, without passion, there are no great ingredients, no great chefs, and no great food.

I was delighted to discover some of my own finds among Rebecca's—such as the Santa Barbara olives and Reed's incredible crystallized baby ginger. Then there is Broken Arrow Ranch. As an occasional hunter and fulltime carnivore, I am extremely grateful that the Hughes family became obsessed with venison. Having heard Mike Hughes speak at an IACP (International Association of Culinary Professionals) meeting some years ago, I was captivated by the story he told about raising, harvesting, and bringing their products to market. I since have had the very real pleasure of devouring some of the Broken Arrow meats— not only at fine restaurants but also at home. The memories of a tender and tasty chunk of their antelope done au poivre over hardwood charcoal starts my mouth watering instantly. No need for any tenderizing marinade here, just a bit of high heat, salt, and pepper are all that is needed to bring out perfection.

The last thirty years have seen the beginning of a new culinary journey in America. This journey is partly an ingredient-driven one. We are now making wonderful foods we knew nothing of only a short time ago. We have gone from dire predictions of only a few brewers of mostly bland beer in the United States to a vast profusion of small, highly individualistic breweries. A celebration of heirloom tomato varieties known for their intense flavors and lovely textures has replaced the prospect of only one or two wretched varieties of tomatoes grown to accommodate mechanical harvesting. Yes, the factory farm will always be with us if we are to feed 350 million people, but the people and products profiled here are helping raise the standards of American produce, dairy, meats, and specialty items we have available to us.

Yes, we still and always will import ingredients from other countries, but using artisanal methods we are creating American wines, brandies, cheeses, sausages, even wasabi, that have few peers. By the same token, we will forever attract foreign-born chefs, but we are matching our artisanal ingredients and products with American-born chefs—some self-taught, and some coming from our increasingly fine cooking academies, such as the Culinary Institute of America in California and New York, as well as the Midwest Culinary Institute in Cincinnati.

These elements are fusing nicely with the opportunity we enjoy of eating other people's food in our country. By that I mean it is frequently difficult to find an Italian or Greek restaurant in Paris or a Mexican restaurant in Rome. Not so in America—the availability of and the exposure to all the world's cuisines has given us a taste and curiosity for *all* flavors and foods. This has contributed to our creation of a new cuisine that could become the most admired and imitated in the world. On the high end of culinary dining and artisanal ingredients, American cuisine may very well be there already.

A trip to California's Napa Valley will expose you to a microcosm of this revolution. You will find great American wines, olive oils, and artisanal products all within one small region. You can also experience what great chefs, some foreign born and some native, can do with those ingredients.

Rebecca Gray is ideally suited to bringing us the news about the people in this book and the artisanal foods they create. She and her husband founded and published *Gray's Sporting Journal,* an artisanal effort in every respect and always a pleasure to read and peruse—much like the book you now hold in your hands. Join Rebecca as she leads us in a journey of discovery of the new artisans of America—major contributors to the creation of our nation's own cuisine.

—ETHAN BECKER
Half Moon Ridge, Citico, Tennessee

INTRODUCTION

IONCE READ an article that had the rather gloomy title "Is Cooking at Home a Thing of the Past?" The author cited convincing research from the Food Marketing Institute in Washington, D.C., which reported that with each generation meal-preparation time is being cut in half, that our grandparents spent two hours, including picking their vegetables and killing the chicken, on the evening meal. Our parents spent an hour, we spend half an hour, and our children spend fifteen minutes on dinner prep—or sometimes less, depending on how much time speed-dialing for pizza delivery takes. What the author concluded from this was that declining minutes in the kitchen was a sign of an anti-cooking trend. We want to eat; we just want someone else to prepare the food.

Baloney, I say to the anti-cooking thing. Cooking is as basic and central to our being as the fire we use to accomplish it. And if we've really lost interest in cooking, then what's all that foodie stuff—a gadget for every kitchen task, the lessons in Tuscany, the explosive proliferation of food magazines and TV shows—helping us *do* in our kitchens? I don't deny that we're looking for quicker fixes for dinner—quick is part of the culture now. But beyond that we're searching for novel *cooking* prerogatives, innovative methods for building good meals—and meals that taste great. For better or for worse in America we no longer eat only because we are hungry. But there is a solution for fast and good that also gives us a chance to cook the meal. Somewhere between reconstituted mashed potato flakes and Julia Childs's *pommes soufflés* is a simple, delicious, and very flavorful plate of mashed potatoes—I'd use Wood Prairie Farm's Rose

Golds to get there. Yes, in a word it's about ingredients. And great ingredients, the people who lovingly produce beautiful food, and how they do it, their stories, is what this book is about. These artisanal food makers grow produce and raise livestock—or combine impeccable ingredients—to create superb foods that make it easier for us to create delicious, healthful meals. And they do it extraordinarily well.

I like to know a lot about what I eat and where it comes from, and I believe wholeheartedly that to know your food is to find great flavor in it. Certainly I'm not alone in this and it's a concept that has captured the imagination of many a foodie. It seems accurate to say that today we literally hunger for a more intimate knowledge of and involvement with what we eat—where it comes from, its history, who made it, its nutritional value and wholesomeness, the whole dynamic of a particular food. I'm lucky enough to have had a variety of opportunities to find out about some of the many different foods I appreciate. As a hunter, a fisherman, and a forager I have a great respect and wonderment for the animal, the fish, the plant that I take from the wild and prepare: it nourishes me. When you know what came before—long before—the cellophane wrap and the grocery store, your attitude about food is forever changed. There is a reverence that comes from being involved in the process from start to finish: it makes the meal more meaningful and makes it taste better.

Of course it is not completely practical to always follow food from its inception, but there are other kinds of intimacy that are useful and that produce a heightened eating experience. I was on such a rampage to get people back into their food that I once advocated, in print, the radical move of throwing away—giving up forever—forks. I find that forks just get in the way of communing with my food, a thoroughly useless utensil.

It's my contention that certain cutlery—particularly forks—can single-handedly wreak havoc on the ambiance and conviviality of nearly any decent dinner party. We need to bring back fingers and hands—and lots of napkins—to our eating experience, lest the pleasure, sensations, psychology, and, yes, even the very nutrition, be lost to those fork-tongued forks.

I don't condone throwing out all functionality at a meal, but the world really is full of fantastic foods that don't require—indeed are better without—silverware: barbecued ribs, chicken legs, asparagus, pears, new potatoes—the list goes on. So I advocate no-fork, Tom Jones–style meals: tiny scampi shrimp sautéed in olive oil, butter, fleur de sel, and a splash of Armagnac, sent out hot, ready to be peeled tableside and devoured. Apalachicola oysters, raw and at breakfast, with a dribble of fresh lemon juice, tipped from the shell for the satin slide down the throat. Lusty bread hunks pulled from warm loaves, with the resultant steamy, baked-bread aroma wafting around the dinner table. Yes, yes, yes! This kind of eating isn't about etiquette. It's about using all of our senses to maximize the experience of a great meal. Enjoy food, get into it. Okay, I'm a little crazed. Admittedly, forklessness may not be the complete solution to the fuller food experience. But it is this very desire to discover more—to become involved for the sake of flavor—that brought me to finding the folks who are just as wacky and passionate about food as I am.

For me what worked best, what pushed me down the path of discovery and toward wonderful-tasting food, was meeting and getting to know the crafters of the food in my hands. People whose lives are defined by their love of food, of their food. The stories I tell here aren't simply biographies, but accounts of these artisans' passion for the food they produce. But food is funny: recall the often repeated words of the nineteenth-century writer Jean-Anthelme Brillat-Savin, "Tell me what you eat and I'll tell you who you are." Yes, they were all kind enough to bare a bit of their souls to me, to involve me. Did they know what they were doing when they told me their life stories? Perhaps not, but they were generous, open, often humorous, always joyous, and always fun. They and their food were inspirational to me and always brought me back to my own kitchen happy to be using such wonderful ingredients to prepare a meal. They made it easy.

Yet this book is not *necessarily* about the best in the world—the very best, most perfect tomato, the best coffee, or the best crab cake. The best something-or-other—the authoritative hyperbolic food writing that rounds up all in a certain category and pronounces a king—smacks to me of arrogance or haste or both and often doesn't reveal the truth: that best can only be based on opinion. It's a matter of taste, of course. So this is only my opinion, my collection of best, the passions in my pantry. I have, however, tried in my selection to go beyond "Mmm, that tastes fabulous!" and to think about why each particular food is sensational. In so doing I hope I've transcended some of my personal biases and created a road map, found some grounds for commonality in artisanal foods and their makers, which will help you, the reader, bring great edibles—perhaps included here or found on your own—into your kitchen.

There are some obvious basic standards. Food is better fresh, of clear and critical importance to blueberries and tomatoes, and remains meaningful for bread, honey, chocolate, potatoes, apples, tea cakes, coffee beans, goat cheese, olive oil, and many more. Even frozen steak, sorbet, and crab cakes aren't made better by extended periods in the freezer.

And freshness can lead us, at least by implication, to another characteristic to consider when discussing good food—the proximity to its origin and producer. Again, with some foods proximity, like freshness, is more obviously important than with others. My father used to take a jar of mayonnaise from the fridge, go out to his kitchen garden, pick a cherry tomato hot from the noonday sun, and dip it into the cold mayo for a super-fresh and tasty lunch. We'd probably all agree that tomatoes are wonderful right off the vine, light years better than those "fresh" pale orbs grown to withstand shipping across the country—or the world.

Close proximity to the source of an edible can bring advantages other than freshness: it provides better opportunities to know the *terroir* of the food, the sense of place, the range of local influences—water, air, soil, weather, geography—that transmit to a food and create its character and goodness. And with nearness to the source also comes the possibility of knowing its genesis. For me so many of the products in this book were made better for having known where they came from—and it is perhaps why many originate not far from my New England home or the Midwest, where I grew up, and why all are made in the USA.

Of course there are those items—stuffed olives, dried mushrooms, and ginger ale—where freshness or proximity has little relevance. But trust me on this: to know and learn about Chris Reed is to better enjoy a bottle of Reed's Ginger Brew. And it is the very reason for a book like this. We are introduced here to keepers of quality, entrepreneurs or sustainers of a legacy, whose vision is very, very personal. They're either of the *terroir* or enthused artisan, maybe both. Often passionate, usually obsessive, some admit to being a bit crazy, but all are brilliant food people able to perform magic. Knowing about the devotion and attention to food, the flavor sensations food artisans make possible—and their marvelous stories—can bring joy to any meal. So what about that much-sought-after quick-prep meal? These folks make that possible too. But I'll bet time's passing won't even enter your head—not even a point to consider when such a fabulous meal is produced.

The food writer and former chef Anthony Bourdain asks in his book *A Chef's Tour*, "When was the last time food transported you?" I can honestly say that all of the foods here transported me. That is why they are included in this book. The ingredients took me to a specific place, or to a particular time, and often used that most powerful and magical of tricks: they evoked or, better yet, created a memory. I can ask for nothing more, and I say thank you, thank you, to these American artisans.

So welcome to my pantry, to my collection of passions, and to the lives of some men and women who make extraordinary food. May you read, learn, laugh, and, most of all, discover your own passions in your pantry.

HE FOUND HIS LOVE
ON BLUEBERRY HILL

{ BLUEBERRY HILL FARM }

I WAS IN college in Boston when my dad first mentioned he
was thinking of buying a blueberry farm in Michigan, some
twenty-seven acres of high-bush blueberries just south on
the Blue Star highway, and a few miles west, between South
Haven and Kalamazoo—and not far from Lake Michigan,
where I'd spent every summer of my life.

Michigan is renowned for its fruit—cherries, peaches, pear,
apples, and it even has a modest grape-wine industry. And this
particular southwestern corner of the state, with its sandy, acidic
soil, abounds in good small blueberry farms. Many are U-pick
operations, some machine-pick berries for processed foods such
as pies, blueberry jam, fruit "leather," or tarts and cookies, and
some combine processed berries with the fresh-pack business of
distributing pints of blueberries to grocery stores. It is an area
used to employing migrant workers, but it also has a sprinkling
of towns—long-ago stops on the Civil War's underground railroad—that are populated by the descendents of runaway slaves,
folks who for generations have made their living either as small
truck farmers or field hands picking the crop of the season.
Then fringing the fruit farms and hugging the beaches of the
Big Lake is a strip of resort towns and second homes—summer
refuges for city-dwellers from Chicago.

It was probably there, at our summer house in Douglas,
that as a little girl I first ate the best blueberries imaginable:
Michigan blueberries. Big, fresh, and flavorful, sweet, but never
with the sweetness of over-ripeness, my preference was to eat
them with a splash of heavy cream. It was one of the eating
pleasures my father and I shared. (Although now I note he's

switched to combining blueberries with soft vanilla ice cream.) So I wasn't unhappy when he decided to buy Blueberry Hill Farm, maybe just a little surprised.

Lou Crawford's expertise and experience in food technology is significant: an undergraduate degree in chemical engineering from Princeton, an M.B.A. from the University of Chicago; seventeen years of working for the family business in Chicago making meatpacking machinery. Then later he started a consulting business that took him to over a hundred countries—sometimes living away from home for months at a time—designing, building, surveying, and updating food-processing (primarily meatpacking) plants. Handsome, this daughter would call him, tall and brown-haired with truly green eyes and a ruddy complexion. I can't remember when he didn't wear a hat—back then it was a Stetson—and he completed the outfit with cowboy boots, wearing in his world travels what he knew to be immediately identifiable as American. He'd worked for the UN in Nigeria and the largest hot-dog/bologna maker in Colombia, but he wanted a more stable source of income, not so up and down as the meat-processing business. He also was looking for something to take him into retirement that didn't require such extensive traveling. "I don't want to die in some hotel room in a foreign country," he always said.

Admittedly, your dentist isn't usually the instigator of a life-changing event. Equally, it might also be difficult to see how blueberries could much affect you, except perhaps by causing a temporary blue stain on your teeth. But my dad is an unusual character, and odd things happen to him. Why not be influenced by a dentist from Chicago who wanted a new occupation as he, too, moved toward his own retirement? I can only imagine that first discussion in 1968:

"Ever think about what you're going to do when you retire, Lou?" the dentist probably said.

"Uv csi du," my dad would have responded.

"Yes, me, too. I've been thinking about buying a citrus farm. I understand they can be very lucrative," the dentist must have said.

"Iwodnt lvinflda, idrdrtkabt Mishgan," Daddy surely retorted.

"You're right, Michigan would be a better place to retire to, but what crop grows in Michigan and makes money? Rinse, please."

Spit. "Blueberries."

Maybe it didn't go exactly like that, but I do know a barter arrangement was made between Lou Crawford and his dentist: free dental work for a study of what was truly the best crop to produce in Michigan. Lou examined peach, pear, and cherry farming, but it was blueberries that seemed the most viable; wonderfully plump, sweet blueberries that, as my dad has come to say, are so "perfectly packaged."

Blueberries, a shrub of the genus *Vaccinium*, are one of the few fruits truly native to North America. Blueberries were held in the highest regard by Native Americans who believed that because the blossom end of each berry, the calyx, forms the shape of a perfect five-point star, the berries came from the Great Spirit—the Northeast tribes called them star berries—and were sent to relieve hunger in times of famine. Parts of the blueberry plant were used as medicine—the leaves made a tea that was good for the blood, and blueberry juice was a cough treatment— as well as a dye for baskets and clothing. Dried blueberries were added to stews and soup and even crushed and used as a rub for meats. The nutritional value and health benefits of blueberries— as with so many plants popular with the early Native Americans—are exceptional. A good source of fiber and high in vitamin C, blueberries—one of the few naturally blue foods— recently have been found to be a great source of antioxidants, those vitamins and minerals that may help increase immune function and possibly decrease the risk of infection and cancer.

The colonists, too, understood some of the nutritional value of wild blueberries, gathering them and drying them for winter use. And later, blueberries, in the form of a beverage, were an important staple for Civil War soldiers. In the 1880s, the first blueberry "businesses" were born, with wild-blueberry canneries developing in several areas of the Northeast.

But in 1911, Elizabeth White, one of a New Jersey cranberry grower's four daughters, changed everything about the business of blueberries when she decided to attempt their cultivation. In a taped interview in 1953, White recalled, "Father and I had talked about the possibility of adding blueberries to our cranberry crop... but we didn't know how to propagate the plant. At the time it was said among the farmers of New Jersey that blueberries could not be cultivated." Then White read a USDA publication by Dr. Frederick V. Colville entitled *Experiments in Blueberry Culture* and she immediately wrote to Colville and suggested a collaboration. He brought the scientific knowledge; she had the "laboratory" for solving the problems of blueberry cultivation. She asked the local group of "pineys"—a reclusive southern New Jersey community of people connected culturally to Appalachians and known for their great hunting and foraging abilities—to go into the woods to find wild blueberry bushes bearing large berries. They dug the bushes up and transported them back to the Whites' farm. It took five years, but finally the inaugural shipment of commercially produced, cultivated highbush berries was sold in 1916. The selection and breeding process continued in New Jersey, with Colville developing the original varieties know as the "big six": Earliblue, Blueray, Bluecrop, Berkeley, Herbert, and Colville. Several of the varieties were named after the "pineys" who first found the wild shrub ancestor and brought it to the Whites' farm. (There's also a cultivated, although often referred to as "wild," blueberry that is a low-bush variety. These shrubs are six to eighteen inches tall—versus four to ten feet tall for high-bush—and have a tiny, more tart berry. The drawbacks of the low-bush variety are that the berries ripen at just one time of year and have a much lower yield per bush.)

Today the United States produces 90 percent of the world's blueberries. High-bush berries now come in multiple varieties and grow in thirty-eight states and provinces, most significantly in Michigan, New Jersey, Maine, Washington, Oregon, New York, North Carolina, Georgia, Florida, and British Columbia. And international growers in general, and specifically in Central and South America, are increasing too.

After New Jersey, Michigan became the next state to enter the commercial blueberry business, in the 1930s. The Michigan Blueberry Growers Association, a marketing cooperative that grades the berries and distributes them, was started in 1936 by thirteen Michigan growers. Today the state leads the country in blueberry production, with 32 percent of the market share. My dad credits the association with first helping him learn the blueberry-farming business and then freeing him of the marketing responsibilities. In 2000, MBG combined forces with two other berry companies—Nutripe of California and Hortifrut, the largest bush-berry grower and shipper in Chile, Mexico, and Spain—to form a marketing company called Global Berry Farms. This has made it possible to provide customers year-round access to fresh ripe berries that are consistently good.

Like most commodities, the wholesale price changes from year to year, and with blueberries even week to week, depending on the crop's availability. The fresh-pick wholesale (about 50 percent of the market) range in recent years has been as low as $1.05 a pound in 2001 and as high as $1.73 in 2004. Happily, there's been a constantly expanding appetite for blueberries primarily because of their versatility, convenience (no peeling or pitting), and health benefits—now they come in the form of everything from beer to vinegar, syrup to salsa. The increasing market demand—the annual per-capita consumption of blueberries in the United States is approaching a pound per person—coupled with years of improved growing and irrigation techniques, globalization, and increasing volume leaves little doubt that blueberries can be a very lucrative business.

My father's dentist decided to forgo a new life with berries and in a rather impetuous move left his wife and family and went to Mexico to open a practice in orthodontics. My dad, meanwhile, had researched, initially through publications and trade organizations, the business of blueberry farming. Next he met with one of Michigan's biggest blueberry farmers. The son of a horticulturist, the grower showed up in a Cadillac. Although the guy didn't quite say that his expensive car was the result of his successful blueberry business, its presence didn't hurt, and probably helped convince my dad of the potential in blueberry farming. He saw an ad in a trade magazine for a farm near South Haven and bought Blueberry Hill in 1971.

It was to be the beginning of Lou's great love affair. "I remember that first spring, the smell of the small pinkish white, bell-shaped flowers—no bigger than a thumbnail—on the blueberry bushes. I'd spent my entire career in and out of slaughter houses, around death, and now I was standing in a field of flowering bushes watching the bees pollinate and awaiting growth of the beautiful blue berries. And it was home to so much wildlife; it was full of life. I fell in love with blueberries."

Lou came to the farm with two attributes of a farmer: a penchant for philosophizing and complete optimism. Both characteristics proved indispensable, as those initial years were fraught with bad luck and difficulties. During that first spring of 1972 there was a disastrous freeze (although Daddy chooses to recall that spring as when his blueberry love affair began) and nearly his entire blueberry crop was lost. But the following year was considerably better: the producing bushes brought in 137,000 pounds of blueberries—but that was a bit of an aberration. The next five years saw generally low total weights, dipping in 1977 to just 38,000 pounds. Then in 1979 Lou had a blueberry boom, 193,000 pounds—though of course the price wasn't very high.

But Dad's an optimist and so he bought additional acreage, an old pine farm, and planted Elliots and Bluecrop on it. By 1981, the nursery bushes he'd planted on the Blueberry Hill Farm in the early years were mature, and he brought into production an additional twenty acres of bushes. Things looked good— well, except for the big drought that year. A different person might have been disheartened, and even an optimistic person might have felt a bit discouraged. But no, something had happened; there was something about farming, about blueberries and the whole cyclical process, that had inspired passion within my father.

Like so many small farms, over the years a series of family members spent time and got involved on a variety of levels with the farm. My brother worked there during summers with a series of college friends, my sister's husband helped out during one picking season, and then later one of their teenage sons worked grabbing lugs off the back of the picker. I was out east and had but fleeting encounters with the business of blueberry farming, a small memory here and there. I remember when we took our children, all quite young, to the farm to see the berries on the bushes and pick a few for the morning's blueberry pancakes. I had difficulty convincing the kids to put the sweet, perfectly ripe berries into their buckets. It seemed that for every one in the bucket, three went into a mouth, then five for the mouth, and finally nothing for the bucket and handfuls for the mouth. In short order our daughter Hope's pink cheeks had succumbed to a lovely—although messy—blue hue.

Most of my association with the farm was to search in my New Hampshire grocery store for the Grand Junction, Michigan, label and report back to my father how much I'd paid for his blueberries. (I was never exactly sure why he needed this information. But it was always fun to imagine that the berries might have come from my dad's farm.) What the farm really gave me was my first real understanding of the need to be connected to what we eat, and the pleasure of that connection. And I learned from the Michigan farm about *terroir*, the importance of a sense of place and those range of local influences—water, air, soil, weather, geography—that transmit themselves to a food and create its character and goodness. I became convinced that if a bowl of blueberries tasted wondrous and special, of sweet summer sun, I didn't need a label to tell me they were from Michigan. Certainly I'm partial: I grew up on Michigan blueberries! Perhaps that's part of the concept of *terroir*. And of course my blueberry-farming father confirms that Michigan blueberries taste superior to others because of the generations of experience, the "good eye," intuitive agricultural sense, and TLC of the Michigan farmers—not to mention ideal soil and weather conditions—that all contribute to making the Michigan berries extraordinary.

On a blueberry farm every season brings a new and different beauty. Red-leafed bushes in the fall that drop and leave stark wooden limbs reaching toward a winter sky. By spring the leaves are back, shiny green and spattered with those millions of pretty little flowers that finally give way in summer to heavy clusters of blue fruit. Yet every season also brings a new phase of demanding, backbreaking work: fall starts with the cultivation of the land between the rows by mowing and then fertilizing the bushes; in fall and winter there's the continual and necessary pruning process; in spring there's hand-herbiciding and more fertilization. Two colonies of bees per acre (about forty thousand bees) are brought in for three weeks to pollinate the blossoms—with fingers crossed that there'll be no wind or rain to prevent them from flying.

Early July brings the beginning of harvest. Pickers are hired for the fresh-pack. And for the processed berries a huge dinosaur of a machine shaped like a large upside-down horseshoe passes over the bushes, long fingerlike rods inside lightly shaking each bush as it goes and making the ripe berries drop to canted trays, where they jiggle their way back to awaiting crates. Now the berries are brought from the fields to a picking shed, where they're "cleaned," twigs and stems removed by workers standing on a line as a river of blueberries passes before them. The berries then are trucked to the Michigan Blueberry Growers Association warehouse in Grand Junction.

Daddy once told me that one of the aspects he loves best about blueberry farming is "the very complicated food technology of it, the science—chemical and mechanical—of farming." According to Lou, very little has been actually written about it and he says that much of what he's learned about blueberry farming came from his fellow blueberry growers and neighbor farmers—who were eager to impart their knowledge to a newcomer and as farmers, those rural philosophers, quipped relevant advice such as "Good judgment is born of experience, and experience is born of bad judgment."

Trial and error is a good teacher, but Dad is inclined, too, to tinkering and making improvements. Over the years he invented many solutions for a blueberry farm's inefficiencies, some brilliant, some downright crazy. For example, he came up with a hair-brained (not to mention dangerous) scheme: he was going to build an ultralight airplane from a kit, strap a canister of insecticide on his back, and fly over the bushes spraying the berries. He figured this would save the large expense of hiring the less accurate crop duster. Fortunately, his plan was thwarted when the manufacturer of the ultralight kit stopped production and went back to the drawing board. It seemed the planes were frequently and inexplicably crashing. But Dad also devised an irrigation system that utilized water saturated with manure from the neighboring pig farm, thus adding good nutrients and natural fertilizers to the water and feeding the bushes.

I asked him one time what he liked so much about blueberry farming. "I have a great time at it," he said. "I get to mow the fields with the tractor, build sheds, pour cement, construct irrigation trenches, create more efficient pruning techniques, and adapt other fruit-sorting operations to blueberries. And I enjoy walking the fields in the early morning when the dew is still heavy on the bushes and the blue of the berries is tinged with a white hue. It's the ideal time to pick them. That's their most flavorful, perfect moment."

Dad's farm got bigger. By 1991, he actually owned three separate land parcels planted with bushes that yielded over 390,000 pounds of blueberries. He also tried adding another crop, first shiitake mushrooms and then chestnut trees, as financial backup in case of a bad blueberry crop. Neither the mushrooms nor the chestnuts proved very productive, but he hired a farm manager and had several other full-time employees.

He'd begun to realize that the joys of farming were also the drudgery of farming. Endlessly mowing fields with the tractor, building sheds, pouring cement, constructing irrigation trenches, creating more efficient pruning techniques, and adapting other fruit-sorting operations to blueberries were inescapable tasks and no matter how many employees he had, the responsibility was on his shoulders. Success came with a price: a staggering work load. So was this any kind of retirement?

In 1992, Daddy sold two parcels of the blueberry-producing land to his farm manager, Steve Hunt, and kept Square Root

Farms—the old pine farm—for his own farm tinkerings. He leased the blueberry bushes on Square Root to Steve—which meant that Steve did the hard labor of the farming—but Dad still stayed very involved in the managing, helping to make decisions and guide Steve. They did very well. All combined, the hundred producing acres set a record high in 2002 of some 688,200 pounds of harvested blueberries—more than triple the production of ten years earlier. And the fresh-pack berries, higher in price per pound than processed berries, had become 60 percent of the business.

In 2005, the summer before my dad's eightieth birthday, my brother and sister and I came to South Haven to talk with him about selling Square Root Farm. It was at his instigation, but I wondered how much he really wanted to give it up. He was very gray-haired now and had swapped the cowboy hat for a cap he'd bought in France. He spent his time in the winter on Jekyll Island in Georgia painting animals and oceanscapes, but still came to the farm for spring flowers and summer harvest. We drove to the farm in his big car—not a Cadillac, but in that price range—to meet Steve and talk with him about purchasing Square Root from Dad. We cruised the perimeter of the fields in the car looking at the bushes, then the irrigation ponds, the chestnut trees, and the house Dad had built just the year before for Jack, one of the farm's longtime employees. Harvest was over and the fields looked unusually dry and lifeless. It did seem like the time had come to sell.

Many years before this, my dad had hoped my brother would come back to run the farm. Like many farmers, Lou seemed inexorably tied to his land and fantasized that it could stay in the family. But when I asked him about whether he still harbored such a hope he said, "I realized that I'd just probably get pissed off at anyone who took the farm over from me, so better not to have it be a family member. I've gotten everything I ever wanted out of the farm, every dream I had for it came true, and then some. It gave me a philosophy and a life."

To me this sure didn't sound like a man ready to sell it all. But I was wrong. We struck the deal with Steve to buy the last of my dad's blueberry farms that afternoon. And when we returned to his house in town he dished up bowls of blueberries with vanilla ice cream. As we ate, I suddenly realized that one of the reasons he was able to comfortably sell the farm was in my mouth. He didn't need the land or the bushes, he'd always have the fabulous taste of Michigan blueberries, the *terroir*, to remind him of the magic and to sustain the passion. Amazing, actually, what a food can do.

{ BLUEBERRIES WITH CRÈME ANGLAIS }
Serves 4.

4 egg yolks
¼ cup sugar
⅛ teaspoon salt
½ cup milk
½ cup heavy cream
1 tablespoon orange liqueur (Grand Marnier is good)
    or vanilla extract
4 cups Michigan blueberries, washed and picked over

In a saucepan, whisk together the egg yolks, sugar, and salt. Combine the milk and cream and whisk that into the egg yolk mixture.

Cook over medium-high heat, stirring constantly, until the mixture thickens—it will thicken quite suddenly. Remove from the heat, pour through a fine-mesh sieve, then whisk the crème anglaise until cool.

Add the liqueur, spoon the crème anglaise over the blueberries, and serve.

{ BLUEBERRY BOUNCE }
Yields 1 gallon.

2 cups Michigan blueberries, washed and picked over
1 cup sugar
Enough vodka to fill a gallon jug with the berries in it

Combine the blueberries and sugar in a bowl and let them sit overnight.

Put the sugared berries in a clean gallon jug with a tight-fitting lid and pour in the vodka. Put the lid on and turn the jug upside down to distribute the berries. Place the jug upright in a cool, dark spot for a week, inverting it several times a day.

Pour into smaller, more manageable containers and store with your other liqueurs. Serve in small glasses as an aperitif or drizzle over ice cream or sorbet for dessert.

PRIME TRADITIONS

{ ALLEN BROTHERS }

I DEFINITELY DON'T care for chicken," Todd Hatoff said with conviction. Because Todd is co-owner with his dad of Allen Brothers, purveyors of exceptionally good premium beef, his dislike of chicken was not particularly a revelation. "But beef *is* my favorite food, and believe it or not hamburger," he said. I was a little surprised at the hamburgers since fabulous steaks are what have made the 114-year-old Allen Brothers the stuff of legend. Not only is the quality of Allen Brothers' beef famous, it's also a classic: *Chicago* steak. With a legacy of my own founded in Chicago beef, I admit a bias, but it's an educated bias. Allen Brothers really does procure, process, and provide incredible-tasting steaks—my mouth waters as I think about their dry-aged T-bone—and surely being in Chicago and part of the Hatoff meat heritage has something to do with their talent for bettering beef.

I've lived in the East, away from the city I was born and raised in, for two-thirds of my life now. Yet still, when asked where I'm from, in some sort of fit of overzealous literalism and much to the chagrin of my husband, I blurt out: Chicago. It *is* where I came from—where four generations of my family lived—so it is my heritage, part of me. Call me crazy, but Chicago's massive flatness and powerful sprawl I find beautiful, even thrilling, and remains more comfortably familiar than the White Mountains of New Hampshire that are so close to my home now. I still think of Chicago as Sandberg's City of the Big Shoulders and understand: "proud to be Hog Butcher, Tool Maker, Stacker of Wheat, Player with Railroads and Freight Handler to the Nation."

Perhaps it's the butcher pride I relate to best since my father, grandfather, and great-grandfather all worked in our family-owned meatpacking-machinery business. And in the 1950s when I was growing up there, the city still clung to its century-old reputation as meat capital of the world. Our company was located on Western Avenue, not far from the Union Stock Yards, and just a few miles from Halsted Street—the longtime address of Allen Brothers.

Memories of that old industrial district—wide Midwestern boulevards lined with old-fashioned, near-windowless factories—surfaced in my mind's eye as Todd talked: "The last slaughterhouse in the City of Chicago was across from us," he said. "We have a couple different facilities, actually, about fifty thousand square feet all total. Our catalog facility is about two blocks away from the office, which is on top of the processing center. The wet-aging, large cutting room, all the processing are in a big, red-brick building about twenty minutes away from the main limestone arch that marked the entrance to the old stockyards."

You can't talk about meat and Chicago and not mention the Union Stock Yards. Built in the 1860s by a consortium of nine railroad companies on swampy land in southwest Chicago, by 1900 the stockyards had grown to 475 acres, contained 50 miles of road, and had 130 miles of track.

After all, at that time Chicago processed 82 percent of all the meat consumed in the United States. It was the heyday of big, city-centered meatpacking companies—Armour, Hammond, Swift, Morris—when Chicago's slaughterhouses were tourist attractions and actress Sarah Bernhardt would remember her visit to the hog butchers as "a horrible and magnificent spectacle." Henry Ford was inspired by the meatpackers' "disassembly" line and a decade later configured his Model T's "assembly" line after it. As early as the 1893 World's Columbian Exposition, visitors took day excursions to see the Union Stock Yards on the southern rim of the city. The stockyards' ultimate boundaries were Pershing Avenue, Halsted Street, Forty-seventh Street, and Ashland Avenue. Yet there were many other meat-related

enterprises—like Allen Brothers and my family's company—
that lived on the perimeter of the stockyards. The Union Stock
Yards closed in 1971, and the ancillary meat companies are all
gone now too. Only the giant arch, and Allen Brothers, remain.

I asked Todd about his family's Chicago meat lineage.
"Well, it's complicated," he said. "In my direct bloodline, I'm
four generations in the meat business."

Todd's great-grandfather owned Oakland Meat Company,
which was one of the biggest hamburger makers in Chicago in
the early part of the twentieth century. Todd's grandfather, in
the 1940s, took the company in a different direction by getting
heavily into steak. Oakland Meat Company sold to all the insti-
tutions in Chicago—and out of town, too—and eventually
merged with United American Food Processors.

"My grandfather not only supplied beef to steakhouses, but
was big in pork," Todd said. "The rib craze was on and he was
the one who really pushed it. He sold a ton before the rib craze
died—and he passed away. That was in 1983."

And although United American Food Processors had been
the king of private meat companies in its day, the business col-
lapsed less than a year after the death of Todd's grandfather.

So where did the original Allen brothers fit into the story, I
wondered: There were actually two brothers, last name of Allen,
correct? "Well, yes," Todd answered, "but it's complicated, as I
said." He hesitated, clearly trying to decide how much of the
complexity to get into:

"A couple years before my grandfather died," Todd continued, "my family established a relationship with Melvin
Solomon, who owned, at that time, Allen Brothers. Mel's
uncle had bought out the original two Allen brothers within
six or seven months of its start in the early 1900s. Ten years
down the line, Mel joined Allen Brothers. And Mel is actually
like a distant cousin to us, and he's still living. As a matter of
fact, he's currently in a relationship with my grandmother—
they're girlfriend and boyfriend—she's eighty-seven and he's
ninety-two years old. Yes, it's always so close in this industry—
and as I said, complicated."

After the United American Food Processors demise, Allen Brothers continued with Mel, Bobby Hatoff, and eventually Todd—who joined the company in 1992—as partners.

"But that partnership ended after a good twenty-seven years when my father and I purchased Mel's half of Allen Brothers," Todd said, "six days before nine-eleven. Uh-huh, that was an interesting time. A scary thing because after nine-eleven, fifty percent of the food service business—and Allen Brothers's largest customer base—disappeared. Nobody was going to restaurants after nine-eleven. Yet we're here today and we're really a completely different company. We've had milestone after milestone year in both divisions—both direct to consumers and food service, proving my father's strategic direction was right. His whole ride he's made the right decision."

Bobby Hatoff's ride had included seeing a need to shift directions—to sell direct to customers, not just to restaurants—even back before the partnership with Mel. But as in most success stories, Todd's dad may also have been blessed with some good timing, too—despite 9/11.

During the 1980s, steak was placed on the health god's list of top ten foods declared tantamount to Satan's fare. The average annual beef consumption by the early 1990s had reached an all-time low of sixty-five pounds per person—down from eighty pounds in 1973. The fat, the meat, the very protein was considered bad for you. Personally, I was very depressed during this period until, as with all real food extremes, there was a change.

Beef consumption started increasing in the mid-1990s, most measurably in restaurants. Dollars spent in upscale steakhouses jumped 25 percent in four years; a thousand new steakhouses opened across the country in 1994 alone. Existing steakhouse chains grew too: by 2000, Morton's of Chicago had expanded from thirty-six restaurants to fifty-two. And since 80 percent of the steaks served at Morton's are from Allen Brothers, business was good for the Hatoffs.

More boosts for beef came with the growing acceptance of the Atkins diet, which promised healthy weight loss through a low-carbohydrate, high-protein diet, and then also from John

C. La Rosa, a doctor and former chairman of the nutrition committee and task force on cholesterol for the American Heart Association. Rosa reported in 1996: "It turns out you can eat anything you want once a week, and it won't really matter."

So if you could have beef just once a week, why not make it a doozy of a steak? Yes, and this then speaks to the real reason Americans began to return to their steak-eating ways, to the *steak*houses. The short answer is taste.

Of course, taste is complex and basically subjective. But with steak it's pretty clear that, at least partially, it's fat that makes for flavor. Certainly Americans, while they understand the risk factors, are all a little hooked on the taste of fat. As *New York Times* food columnist Molly O'Neill said in her article "The Morality of Fat," "The preoccupation with fat has become a struggle between good and evil, between the baseness of human instinct and the glory of rational restraint. . . . Americans remain wildly divided by how they battle dietary fat, meal by meal, snack by snack."

Steak is classified into three categories—each tied to a level of fat—by graders from the USDA: prime, choice, and select. The grades are also an indication of the eating characteristics—taste, tenderness, and juiciness—which are determined, to a large extent, by the meat's fat content. Prime is the most "marbled," with 15 percent more fat than the next category, choice. This is the most widely sold grade and has 15 percent more fat than select. Select, as the newest, is the leanest of the three grades, and the classification was developed and promoted in response to our fat/beef health worries.

Only about 1 to 2 percent of the meat in this country is graded prime, with the vast portion being sold to restaurants or exported; rarely is it sold through grocery stores. According to Molly Patterson of the National Cattlemen's Beef Association, prime used to be readily available, but in response to our concerns over fat in the 1980s cattlemen changed feeds for their cattle in order to produce leaner meat. "American beef is twenty-seven percent leaner today than it was twenty years ago," she said. "As a result, the highest level of prime isn't even produced anymore."

This isn't exactly true. Wagyu cattle—which genetically come from the Kobe beef region and are now raised outside of Japan—translated means "white beef" because it is so marbled with fat. It is certainly prime—at $150 per pound it better be—and is produced in the United States. Wagyu cattle are fed beer and liquor mash, and their growth is slow—often they aren't slaughtered until they're over 550 days old—and hormone-free. But this ultimate in premium beef is rated prime not because of what the steer eats, but because of how intensely marbled it is and its flavor and texture characteristics—which is superior to most other types of beef.

Diet and hormones in our meat supply have, for decades, been an issue. But of late the controversy has centered on the relative importance of grass-feeding, and organic and natural feeds. These categories of diet overlap and aren't always clearly defined, especially to the consumer. For example, all cattle are grass-fed to some extent, but what the grass-fed movement advocates is a diet that is at least 99 percent grass. And as much as the new grass-fed and organic beef movement would like, it's extremely difficult for these herds to ever produce meat at the prime grade. Grass-fed steers don't produce the same quality of fat or flavor profile as do corn-fed steers. Or as Todd put it, "It's hard enough to get premium prime from grain-fed cattle, even harder from the natural meat, and it's impossible to achieve the quality with all grass-fed beef."

What Bobby Hatoff must have realized by seeing the significant increase in his food-service business was that people love good prime beef and will pay to eat it—and maybe even at home for that once-a-week fix or for special dinner parties. His "change in strategic direction" for the business was to supply great prime directly to the consumer. Since you basically can't get prime in a grocery store, mail-order was the way to go. The kind of customers who order prime beef by mail can be extremely demanding, expecting only the very best. But Allen Brothers was in a position to provide the best prime beef, and when Todd graduated from the University of Wisconsin he came to work for his dad in order to run the catalog business.

"Now direct sales are twenty-three to twenty-five percent of the business," said Todd. "And it's the more profitable side, with better cash flow than the food service. But the two are very important for each other. Catalogs are seasonal, but we don't have the problems that go along with being a seasonal business since we have the food-service piece. They really complement each other very well. And I'll tell you a little secret: because we're bringing in all this premium product for our restaurant accounts, we do get to see what this country has to offer for prime beef. I wouldn't be able to do this without the food service. I have all this selection *because* I'm in the food-service business. No one else has that."

And he is supplying some very high-end restaurants. I remember that in 1997 when the Allen Brothers' website listed the company's restaurant customers the list included Ruth's Chris, the largest chain of upscale steakhouses in the country. Yet when I looked recently it was gone. I asked why.

"We used to have Ruth's Chris," Todd explained, "but unlike Morton's, they're spot buyers. Morton's controls all of their purchasing from Chicago. Ruth's Chris has forty different franchises and different suppliers; nothing is consistent. Ruth's Chris has a different market. We're too costly for them now. And always watch when anyone is putting butter or other stuff on a prime steak. Question that because you're ruining it. Why pay for prime if it has to be slabbed with butter?"

I asked Todd how he could always be certain he was getting his pick of top-grade prime. He manages to get premium selection not just from his small Wagyu-producing cattle ranch but from mega meat processors such as Iowa Beef Packers (IBP).

He was silent for a moment—as if he was trying to comprehend why I'd ask such a silly question—and then said, "Well, the meat is checked as we receive it, but we've been in business over one hundred years and our suppliers know exactly what we want and will accept." In other words, to try to sell Allen Brothers—that stronghold in the rarified air of magnificent prime beef—anything other than the best would be meat-business suicide.

Honest assessment of quality—and grade—is almost a point of honor in the meat world, where a good reputation is still a real basis for business dealings. Since the grading process is entirely voluntary and also visual, it would seem to be very subjective and arbitrary. Not really, according to my father, who spent nearly twenty-five years in the family meatpacking-machinery company and his own consulting business. He claims that grading is relatively straightforward and uncomplicated, "much like determining the beauty of a woman, there are certain key elements that make it so you simply know at a glance." What problems there are with the grading system derive more from the very wide range within the grades. The difference between a high-grade and a lower-grade piece of prime meat can be significant and requires a very experienced eye to determine.

So Allen Brothers does a lot of "hand-selecting." They have a range of different specs depending on the customer, and as the prime comes in they choose the meat in order to meet those specs. "Even within prime there's a wide range," said Todd, "and we give the catalog customers the highest grade within prime. So the meat comes into Allen Brothers in what we call primals—like the short loins that contain the rib eye, strip loins or tenderloins—and then we do our own aging of the meat."

All beef in the United States is aged in some fashion. Aging meat makes it more flavorful and tender and, depending on the method, dry or wet-aged, it can also add to the cost. Dry-aging is the older, traditional, and now more costly method used by only the very high-end steak purveyors: the carcass or large pieces of meat are hung or placed on drying racks with cool, circulating air and ultraviolet lights for three weeks or so.

Wet-aging is relatively new, born out of the change in shipping and buying practices: the meat is bagged in vacuum-sealed plastic pouches, allowing the meat's juices to age it. Usually aged for less time than the dry-aged, it also shrinks less. Allen Brothers does mostly wet-aging now. According to Todd, just a very few of their restaurant customers request dry-aged meat. Dry-aging is best suited to cuts that have a bone or a wide trim of fat on it—like a porterhouse—so the range of available cuts is limited. Also, those who grew up on wet-aged beef usually don't like the taste of the dry-aged, which often has a stronger, more intense flavor.

For me, dry-aged meat hits exactly the right high note and then the flavor lingers there to remind you for a while of its perfection. (Perhaps I also prefer it because dry-aged beef is what I grew up on and because now I've become a devotee of another dry-aged meat: our own venison. We hang the entire deer in the open, cool autumn air, for at least a week, and the distinct, robust flavor is fabulous.)

"Hanging the whole beef carcass is a thing of the past," Todd told me. "We have very modern methods now in the U.S. I went to Europe—went to their finest—and saw what they do. Americans don't know how lucky they are! They were intermixing chicken and beef, juices were flowing everywhere. They'd put me in jail and throw the keys away if I had that going on."

At Allen Brothers, after the meat goes through the aging process it's trimmed up and portioned out again, according to specific specs. For example, a strip steak has on the sides what's called the cover fat. At Allen Brothers they cut a one-eighth-inch cover, just enough to maintain the form of the steak.

"We have forty to forty-five butchers," Todd explained. "All start off as a trimmer and train for three and a half years before they're a master butcher. Some of our butchers have been with us forty years. But it's a dying skill. A lot of butchers can't butcher the whole cow anymore. Even though in our business we don't really do that anymore, we still have eight people here, including my father and myself, that can still do the whole cow. We'd be a little rusty because we haven't done it in a long time, but we could do it. At Allen Brothers, we train everybody because we think we train them differently. I can bring in a butcher from a grocery store or other meat-processing company and it's a problem because they've been *culturized*. I tend to like people who haven't been trained, so we can train them the way we want them to do the product. We're very strict. A lot of places leave heavier covers and you're paying for fat. Not in my house! And I don't leave the tails on either; I take off all that stuff and I give the person the meat. When you're paying these kinds of dollars—well, my customers appreciate getting the meat."

I asked Todd who he felt was his competition.

"When we first talked, in 1997, we did have several competitors in the food-service area. But nine-eleven killed a lot of companies and others consolidated. I'm the last premium independent, and that's sad to me. The soul is gone in the consolidated companies. On the retail end my competition is far fiercer because of the web. Little butcher shops all across the country manage to get a hold of Holstein—which is the wrong prime, not my type of prime—and ship it across state lines. It's illegal to ship across state lines unless federally inspected and USDA certified, and that costs millions of dollars to do. It's not competitive to me when it comes to quality—I have all the quality—but it is competitive in just selling meat."

What about a place like Lobel's of New York. Do you consider them competitors? "Not really." Todd seemed irritated by the question. "They're just a butcher shop on Madison Avenue. They don't compete in quality against us. They get a lot of press, though."

Indeed, Lobel's is butcher to the stars and gets tremendous press. They are quick to tout: "your order is shipped FRESH and is never frozen."

Allen Brothers ships both fresh and frozen, but prefers to ship frozen. Because they use massive freezers that can flash-freeze instantly, the blood stays in the meat and doesn't leave the muscle or get into the bag, so the meat retains its integrity. According to Todd, "If you ship fresh, no matter how much blue ice you put in there, meat purges. People think it's better, but I've done surveys and people have never been able to tell—most of the time they'll think the frozen, the properly frozen and thawed, is actually the fresh. I think the press pushes fresh as being better. But my reality is that the majority of my customers buy frozen; only five percent are buying fresh. And this is true with all our meat products—lamb, pork, duck—all of it."

I knew that Allen Brothers had, since the beginning, carried lamb and pork, but Todd was taking on more: "Now we have some interesting stuff coming up. We're launching a whole new array of fish—as well as lobster, stone crab, and other shellfish—in a separate catalog, but mailed together with our regular catalog. It'll be coming from all the freshest sources. My food-service connections helped there. They have pointed me in the right direction for what's the best. I've been working on it for two years and finally locked all that down. Finding it all, going and seeing—Nova Scotia, Hawaii, Australia—finding people I believed in and trust."

Having a vision for a company is good, and Todd clearly inherited his father's capacity to find expanding markets for Allen Brothers. But the business skill must go beyond vision for the operation to work—especially if it's going to last 114 years.

Todd said, "We all started out—my father started out, I started out, my grandfather started out—having to wash the floors, stack shelves, cut the meat, clean every inch of the plant, deliver meat, and carry it up the stairs when the elevator is broken because it has to get to the kitchen on the third floor. I had it far better than my father or my grandfather or great-grandfather—it was far rougher for them."

But it goes beyond hard work, too. In the office there's a picture of Todd, who's now president of Allen Brothers, and his dad, Bobby Hatoff. Formal, both men dressed in dark suits and silk ties, French cuffs clipped with understated cufflinks, a white handkerchief in Bobby's coat pocket, a pin in Todd's label, they both seem relaxed and happy and for a second you think they must be brothers.

"I'd come into the plant in the summer or on weekends with my dad. It was very family-oriented, and I feel that it is that way now. My team has been with me forever; I have worked with my top management since I was a little boy. I'm not married—always traveling—and my sister isn't in the business, although she's a chef. I do have my cousin working here with me. We grew up together and have a very close relationship. And of course, my dad's right in the next room. He's my dad, my partner, and my best friend. I can't imagine walking up these stairs and not seeing my dad."

So there is the legacy and all that goes with it, but we know that there is still more.

Todd said, "I love this company with all my heart and I am very, very proud of it and everyone who works here. And they feel the same way. I never wanted it to be the biggest, only the best, and we are getting bigger and bigger. But I want to make sure that I cannot fail at being the best. I don't know how big I can go before I lose control of that. That's going to be my trick, that's going to be the thing I have to watch. I don't need the whole world. I just want to make sure I maintain the integrity of what we are, the soul."

Not long after my conversation with Todd, Ed and I grilled an Allen Brothers dry-aged rib eye. As always, we cooked it rare. I served it with salad and a baked potato, because that's what my family served it with back in my Chicago days. And the taste? A steak with tooth, yet buttery, it was rich in flavor—it was quintessential. And it brought me home again.

{ HOMEMADE BURGERS }
Serves 4 to 6.

1 pound ground beef
3 Italian sausages, hot or mild, removed from casings
1 small onion, diced
½ small red bell pepper, diced
2 teaspoons Worcestershire sauce
Salt and freshly ground black pepper

Mix all the ingredients except the salt and pepper well and form into 4 large patties or 6 smaller ones.

Season with salt and pepper and grill (or fry) over medium-high heat for 8 to 10 minutes for medium-rare, or to desired degree of doneness.

{ HERB-CRUSTED TENDERLOIN TAILS }

Serves 4 to 6.

6 (5-ounce) tenderloin tails
3 tablespoons olive oil
Salt and freshly ground black pepper
2 cloves garlic, minced
$3/4$ cup mixed fresh basil, chives, parsley, and rosemary

Preheat the oven to 400 degrees. Lightly brush the tenderloin tails with the oil, season with salt and pepper, and then roll in the garlic and herbs.

Place on a baking sheet and roast for 8 to 10 minutes for medium-rare, or to desired degree of doneness. Let rest for 5 minutes and serve hot, or let cool and slice for steak salad.

BREAD AND THOU

$\left\{ \text{CLEAR FLOUR BAKERY} \right\}$

DRIVING THE STREETS of Boston—those meandering pathways set down by seventeenth-century cows—is not easy, not intuitive, and often not the most expedient method for getting through the city. So instead of a car ride to Clear Flour Bakery, I rode the Green Line of the MTA—the mass transit system made famous by the song and Charlie's inability to get off it. Out Commonwealth Avenue toward the town of Brookline, my travel first was subterranean. The subway car then lurched up into the sunshine of Kenmore Square to become trolley, carrying me by old haunts: through Boston University and the journalism school, past the left turn to my first apartment—and on to Brookline. There's an imperceptible melting from the bigger city into the smaller one and, to my way of thinking, Brookline could never be considered a "suburb"—it is fully urban here. But since its beginnings in the 1600s, when it was farmland parceled out to Bostonians for their cattle and crops, it has serviced Boston. Embracing the city's overflow, Brookline became home to everyone from wealthy Bostonians seeking land for their summer estates, to multiple and rotating ethnic groups, to yet more colleges and their students. It became a town of distinct areas—enclaves of the diverse populations— and wonderful, vibrant neighborhoods.

Coolidge Corner was the Brookline neighborhood where in 1975 Ed and I first lived together, just up the street from the offices of our publishing company, in the old S.S. Pierce building. Our apartment was a block from Myron Norman's fabulous—and now renowned—Harvard Wine & Liquor, where we were taught which Cabernets and Valpolicellas accompanied wild duck. We could lunch on chicken Veronique—a chicken, grape, and walnut salad—at the French restaurant across the street or walk to the Jewish delicatessen for blintzes. Or we could go a little farther down Harvard Street for hot, hot vindaloo or Thai green curry. There was a real Chinese laundry, a fabulous bookstore with a comprehensive newsstand. And it was still a place where little old ladies stopped you on the street to tell you the baby you held in your arms was beautiful.

Brookline was the place—and the time in my life—where I began to learn about cooking and baking my own bread. And although Clear Flour Bakery didn't exist when I lived there, it fits my cosmic sense of order that the artisan bread bakers of choice for me now are the extraordinarily talented Christy Timon and her husband, Abe Faber, at Clear Flour Bakery, located just blocks from Coolidge Corner in Brookline.

On a warm March day I walked the few short blocks from the MTA stop, down Thorndike Street, to find Clear Flour Bakery on a rounded corner of short, one-story brick storefronts. A few concrete, half-Doric columns were distributed across the face of the building, some 1920s idea of facade decoration and a clue to its vintage. Above a door a large blue sign with white lettering identified the bakery and marked where to enter, and as I did so the soft, warm air of dough and pastry and bread-baking surrounded me. A small counter and cash register stood in front of tall, wrought-iron shelves piled with bread—coburgs, baguettes, crinkle loaves, bloomers, split-tin loaves, and more. Certainly there was every shape of hearth bread—and every color, too, from purple-black to golden. The morning's production of loaves stood tall, at attention, a bountiful tribute to the baker's art. The bread display divided the room, but through the baguettes I could see two bakers at work making cinnamon rolls. One of them left her post to find Christy and Abe for me.

Christy is small in stature, with graceful lines and a lovely pink-blush complexion. With short, brown, perhaps once-blonde hair, and a smile that came readily, she spoke in a gentle voice. Abe is tall and dark-haired and wore square-lensed glasses as opposed to Christy's round ones. He spoke fast, in New York-minute style, and often made Christy and me laugh.

"Well, you started the bakery, so you start," Abe said.

"I grew up around Chicago," Christy began her story, "and went to college in Virginia for a year and then the University of Wisconsin. It was in the early 1970s and I got a job to support myself at a restaurant in Madison named the Ovens of Brittany. The focus was on French food so they made their own bread and pastries. I didn't go to culinary school, but we worked our way through Julia Child and baked everything we could—we threw out a lot of stuff—and we made a variety of cakes and tarts every day. There were two levels of the restaurant—more casual and sort of fine dining—which meant I had a chance to do some fancier stuff; it was fun. So I graduated with a degree in dance—that really pays well. I was flush!"

She grinned at her sarcasm, then went on to say, "I did baking because I liked it, but it also had a paycheck attached. Bread work can be scheduled at all times of the day and I could arrange my work schedule and be free for class or rehearsal."

After graduating, Christy was offered an opportunity to dance in Boston. She moved, but continued to work for restaurants and catered in order to support herself. "You couldn't make money dancing," she said. "You just danced, you did that for free." So she decided to go into partnership—catering hors d'eouvres and meals—with a woman she'd met. "Creating meals and menus was really fun," she said, "but schlepping everything to the site was not. I wanted a place, a kitchen to control everything, and so we rented this space."

When was that? I asked. Abe answered, "Nineteen eighty-two. I'll give you dates; she doesn't know dates. She doesn't know when we were married! And we got married in the bakery, with no heat, on Thanksgiving because that's the only time we could close the bakery."

Christy smiled. "So we rented just half of the current space—it was very raw—about six hundred square feet, no hot water, a trough in the bathroom, one one-ten outlet. It was not nice."

She found an old ten-burner stove at a church and bought it for $100 and eventually built her kitchen. Then she went to restaurants: "Because the bread thing was just beginning in New York, like Dean and Deluca's and others doing hearth breads, and I wanted to do that kind of thing here." She also wanted something steady to pay the rent and thought if she got regular bread orders, and then had the catering on top of it, it could work. "I started making bread," she said, "and then the restaurants started saying, 'Can you make this variety?' I was mixing it, shaping it, baking it, and driving it around and then I met him."

"Wait," Abe said. "She's not telling the story dramatically enough."

"Not dramatically enough?" Christy said, speeding up. "Okay. I went through a stage when my partner and I had a difference in what we wanted to do. She wanted to keep the catering and I wanted to do bread and the bakery, so we split up. I kept the shop and she took the catering clients and did that out of her house. And then I met Abe because I then really needed a driver."

"That's *why* you met me?"

"No, no," Christy said, "I knew you, but you were a starving artist."

"Wait, back up," Abe said. "Let me tell her side of story. She had a friend—a microbiologist named Carey Phillips—who, back before it was a popular thing to bake at home, messed with sourdough. He had a sourdough starter he gave her, and she started to play with that."

Christy learned to make bread mostly by trial and error. Using a variety of methods, she'd make her own starters or occasionally experiment with a recipe from a magazine. "I remember the first time it worked putting a sourdough together," she said. "I went out for a run and when I came back it had risen and I was just like, 'Wow, this is *so* great!'"

In the course of doing the catering, Christy had begun to realize that it was very fascinating to her to make bread, and an avenue she wanted to pursue. Abe returned to telling the story: "So for a catered event when people asked for bread, she didn't just bring bread. She worked another eight hours to make her own bread from scratch. And people noticed that and asked, 'Where'd you get that bread?' and she'd say, 'Oh, that's just something I've been playing with.' I think I'm not making this up, but it was never in her mind a definite thing that she was going to make mostly bread forever. Then at some point, when it didn't fit into the Hobart 25, she bought a 1928 Hobart from Dinky Donuts for fourteen hundred dollars and got one more warmer oven. She'd started with sourdough, but then when she was delivering it she realized there was this terrible French baguette being passed out. It was all pumped up with chemicals and lots of yeast and tasted like sawdust. She wanted something good next to her bread so thought she'd start making a French bread, too."

Then one day someone called and asked Christy the name of her bakery. A friend had given her a book on bread-making that was sitting on the counter. Since milling terms had always appealed to her, she quickly flipped through the book and answered, "Clear Flour Bakery, how about that?"

"So she was doing what interested her and what she wanted to do," Abe said. "It wasn't like she said, 'Oh, I'm running a bakery so...I need a mixer.' And basically, she was doing everything herself—baking the bread, delivering the bread, billing for the bread—and she was working all the time. When she started the bakery and trying sourdough, I was a baby—no, not really. She's ten years older than me, so I was twenty and she was thirty when it started in 1983."

Abe grew up on Long Island and finished high school early "because I was smart at that time. Since then I've lost brain cells or something, and I'm not as smart." He went to college for a year, left, and moved to Boston to find work. "I just wanted to see what work was like, and I found out: you work very hard and get kind of bored. So I decided to go back to school."

He went to Massachusetts College of Art and created, as he explained it to me, "Big installation art, like you put a quarter in the machine and fire comes out and then a ball would come through a waterfall and it fills the room and cameras start projecting a film on sheets of water."

"Really economically feasible stuff," Christy teased.

Abe continued, "I started having art shows, but it was a lot of work. You had to really promote yourself. I began to realize it was going to be a long haul of working sixty, seventy hours a week to earn four dollars and fifty cents an hour to spend money on motors and paint. And you would have these shows that ended up in pieces and very large objects you'd have to store all over town in places like my friend Christy's bakery basement. So I would come by and visit."

"Because it was free food," Christy laughed.

"She had this desk," Abe kept on, "and all these receipt books were piled up on it and I would flip through them. I said, 'Are these all bills that people owe you? People owe you thousands of dollars!' and she said, 'Yeah, I don't have time for that because I have to make the bread and deliver the bread.' And I said, 'I could make some phone calls and collect some of these for you.' She said, 'What I really need is someone to deliver the bread for two hours.' And that was it."

Abe delivered the bread in a Chevy Nova that belonged to Christy's grandmother and despite the car's finicky carburetor he would make it back in time to collect bills or mix up dough. "I'm not sure exactly when this was," he said. "All I know is we kissed on my car in front of the bakery the summer of 1983."

"There you go," Christy laughed. "There's the benchmark."

"You were hot, you still are," Abe grinned. "And you had an amazing energy level. What time did you get up every day, two, three, four o'clock? There wasn't a whole lot of sleep there. Pretty soon I was working some intense hours too. Not like her, but I continued doing my art thing. Then it became clear to me that being involved with bread *was* art. We were just scratching the surface of a huge wealth of traditional information—mostly from other countries—about bread. Making food with your own hands and serving a community of people—after years of feeling frustrated working in the arts—and then realizing, oh, but this is art, this is my expression. And it happened in a happenstance meeting with her, who I fell in love with and married."

Christy had started the business as a wholesale bakery and initially wasn't licensed to sell retail. But when people began coming to the back door of the bakery asking for a baguette, she'd hand them bread and tell them to leave fifty cents. The bakery got licensed in 1985 but Christy and Abe remained casual about their retail customers. They'd put a few baguettes out on a little table and people would leave seventy-five cents on the counter.

"We had a reputation for being snooty," Abe said, "because for a long time we turned down person after person who wanted to buy our bread retail. Then even after we were licensed neighbors called the bakery 'Sorry, Sold Out,' because we had that sign out all the time."

Christy added, "They'd go, 'Do you want to go to Sorry-Sold-Out and see if they have anything?'"

They had learned from their wholesale restaurant business that it wasn't worth trying to do more than what could be done well. "Somehow we had the sense to see that's the mistake in business: it gets big, and the quality goes like this." Abe turned his thumb to point to the floor. "Christy was smart—we were smart—to say, 'No, I'm not going to do more than I can control.'"

"You have to continue to be involved and actually like the work," Christy said. "I don't want to run a bunch of places and sit at a desk. I want to bake!"

"The reason it's so good is because we're so involved," Abe said. "And she was in demand because no one else was making a bread with crust and taste. We were just smart enough to see what was being lost. In the beginning Christy could sell anything—what we were selling then we'd be embarrassed to sell now—but we were the only show in town. Nowhere could you go in this country and find—except just a few things in Harold Field's cookbook and in ethnic parts of cities—how real bread is made. Somehow, through industrialization, something was lost and moved into Wonder bread."

Ah, Wonder bread, for so many of us our first and favorite bread. I recall sitting cross-legged in front of the television with

a sibling on either side of me. We always snacked on our preferred form of very white bread while watching TV. My sister's
would have been an airy slice, just defrosted and still cold, eaten
crust first, peeling it off the second-course white stuff. I
removed the crust too, but instead discarded it. I would squeeze
the white part into a doughy pancake, roll it, play it first for a
cigarette, and then chomp it down. And my brother would have
used his slices as small edible trays to support huge globs of
peanut butter and jelly. All of our slices were snatched from a
package decorated with red, white, and blue balloons, and called
"Wonder." It was just that, an all-American wonder. The brand
name of Continental Baking's white loaf was, and remained
through the 1980s, the best-selling bread in America. For those
of us growing up in the 1950s it definitely was the stuff of our
bread memories.

Not even a distant cousin to Christy's sourdough, the
Wonder. But bread, all bread, really plays a big role. It is so central, an integral part of our spiritual and actual nourishment, and
as such is threaded with constancy through many different
social and economic histories. Bread, more than any other single
food, is, and simply always has been, our most basic, fundamen-
tal sustenance—truly the staff of life.

Of course, wheat is at the core of any bread saga and is
thought to have been the product of an accidental crossing—
someplace in western Asia—of two wild grasses. Grains are
known to have grown in Europe some eight thousand years ago.
And among the excavated remains of a Swiss lake, *crushed* cereal
grain was discovered, evidence of an advance toward true bread
and away from soaked and pressed cereal cakes.

During Rome's 360 years of occupation, Britain developed
into one of the great granaries of the Roman Empire. But that
would change when in 1565 Conquistador Pedro Menéndez de
Aviles and six hundred settlers established the first European set-
tlement in North America. The early settlers introduced wheat
bread to the New World and found the crop to flourish beyond
their wildest dreams. By the end of the eighteenth century,
Britain was importing most of its flour and wheat from America.

The land was not all that made the New World fertile ground for bread. American ingenuity—the science of food and labor-saving inventions—brought innovation to the bread world: the first successful threshing machine, the McCormick reaper, and a more refined milling process for better-quality flour were invented here; the United States began exporting pearl ash (potassium carbonate) to Europe for use as a leavener, and by 1850 there were over two thousand commercial bakeries in the United States.

Scientific thought not only inspired bread-improving inventions but brought attention to the health and nutritional value of various foods, including bread. In 1869 sisters Catherine and Harriet Beecher Stowe described the real scourge of society: *commercial* white bread. They wrote, "Light indeed, so light that loaves seem to have neither weight nor substance, but with no more sweetness or taste than so much cotton wool." Yet commercial bakeries continued to grow and prosper. Distribution of fresh baked goods became possible with greater urbanization, and thereafter were an important and expected convenience in the new industrialized society. In 1924 only 30 percent of all U.S. bread was still baked in the home. And along with the wheat and flour production—one billion bushels of wheat harvested that same year—America was fast becoming the world's bread basket.

With our drive to make more bread, to make it faster and to feed the world, we did lose something, as Abe Faber suggests. As productive a crop as American wheat was, the modern milling process of rolling the grain, as opposed to stone-grinding it, all but denuded wheat of its food value, stripping it of both germ and bran and consequently the fiber. In addition, flour was also bleached and bromated, which eliminated its natural vitamin B content. (These chemicals are used to whiten and also "mature" flour faster, making the commercial bread-baking process easier and faster.)

The founding of Pepperidge Farm Bread in 1938 marked a departure in commercial bread. Maggie Rudkin, a Connecticut housewife, discovered that one of her sons had an allergy to the preservatives in commercial bread. She began experimenting with baking her own preservative-free bread, a whole-wheat loaf made of all-natural ingredients that also was high in vitamin B. It was so beneficial to her son that his physician asked Rudkin if she would bake loaves for other patients. She did so from her Pepperidge Farm home, of course eventually selling her bread through grocery stores.

The nutritional quality of American commercially produced bread was also challenged by military physicians when they found that an extremely high percentage of World War II draftees were malnourished. President Roosevelt convened a National Nutritional Conference in 1941, and two years later the USDA released the first recommended daily allowances (RDA) for nutrients. By 1944, all yeast-raised commercial bakery products were to be fortified with vitamin B and iron by order of the War Food Administration. What was taken out of the flour was to be replaced, at least in terms of vitamins.

But what about fiber? The importance of dietary fiber in lowering cholesterol and as a cancer preventative began to be confirmed in the late 1960s and has remained a critical element in a healthy diet. The nutritional value of fiber and grains has always been stressed in the U.S. Department of Agriculture's "Food Guide Pyramid," both the original 1992 version and the newer pyramid introduced in 2005. But the newer pyramid also emphasizes the importance of whole grains—half of our daily grain intake should be whole. This clearly endorses the bread-eating habits of those of us who indulge in the new-old breads: homemade or artisan breads, those choc-a-bloc with unbleached, unbromated flours, often high-fiber whole-grain and organic flours. But the popularity of the new-old breads isn't only because they occupy a favored place in the nutritional pyramid but also, much more important, they offer fabulous flavor.

The bread renaissance probably got at least an embryonic start at the same time natural foods were being popularized in the 1960s. In Paris, Lionel Poilâne took over his father's bakery in 1970, and began improving recipes and techniques. He interviewed ten thousand traditional bakers in France and identified eighty distinct regional varieties of bread, and in 1981 published a book famous among bakers, *Le guide de l'amateur de pain, The Bread-Lover's Guide.* He said, "What many bakers don't realize is that good wheat can make a bad bread. The magic of bread baking is in the manipulation and the fermentation. What has been lost...is this method. I utilize the most sophisticated material, the most extraordinarily complex machine: the human being." By 1984, he was exporting his bread to the United States.

Also in the mid-1980s, several great American bread bakers were getting their start. Daniel Leader traveled throughout France and Italy, and corresponded with bread bakers in Denmark, California, Vermont, Michigan, and New Hampshire, to learn what he could about bread making. He had his ovens built by a mason who came from France—carrying with him the bricks and ironworks! Leader's Bread Alone Bakery, nestled in the Catskills, became a tremendous success and supplied many of the trendy restaurants of New York City. Manhattan's Amy Scherber of Amy's Bread, too, found affirming success in New York; and in California it was Joe Ortiz and his Capitola bakery, Gayle's Bakery, that would forge the bread way on the West Coast. In 1980 there were fewer than a hundred shops in the United States that specialized in baking fresh bread daily, but by 1995 there were more than a thousand.

In many of these artisanal bread bakers you find common characteristics: independence, a desire to strive toward perfection, satisfaction in producing an honest and pure product, reverence for flavorful European-style breads. The exceptional artisans, like Christy and Abe, strive to bake better and better bread.

"We knew that there was something else out there," Abe said. "We are a hundred percent self-taught and thought we might not be doing something right."

So in 1990 and in 1992 they traveled to Europe. "We went to find bread," Christy said.

Except to visit their parents they had never been away from the bakery. But with finally enough staff in place they took a month, rented a Fiat, and drove all over Italy and France.

"When we returned," said Abe, "we had this slide show that we would put people to sleep with because we had a thousand images of bakeries and close-ups of bread. People were horrified that we didn't go to the Louvre and that the only thing we did for fun was visit wineries. We had only about ten sentences in French, but the feeling of friendliness was there. Boy, did we have a good time, and it was an eye-opener to all sorts of tiny little things: the feel of the dough, the taste, the hydration, how to handle a sourdough. There was this crust from a little bakery in the south of France, made by this super-pure guy, and we were fighting over this tiny last crust left in the bag a week later. It was just flour and water and salt and it tasted like hazelnut and honey to us. You can only be inspired for so long by what's in your own brain."

"When we finally got to travel," Christy said, "and got to see all this stuff that we hadn't even thought of, it put images in our heads of what bread could be. I came back and all I wanted was a hearth oven. I told him, 'I don't want a Mercedes. I don't need any diamonds or anything. What I really want is a hearth oven.'"

Abe explained they'd always been fairly risk averse. Christy had borrowed $5,000 from her parents and another $3,000 from a friend—only $8,000 to start the bakery. They'd worked really hard, but not made much money in those first years. They knew the proper oven was something you really needed in order to make real hearth bread and, despite their aversion to risk, they decided when they came back from France in 1992 to order a $70,000 hearth oven.

"Every penny we'd saved," Abe said, "we put into the oven, plus we went into hock. But we were feeling a little more stable than before. We had a manager for the first time to answer phone calls, pay bills, and we decided, because Christy was like forty, to have kids. We wanted to do that, so Christy got pregnant. We weren't telling anyone, but then after our manager returned from her vacation we said—"

"—I'm pregnant and leaving," Christy finished his sentence. "And I delivered my kids, twins, the day the oven came to be installed."

Abe smiled, "I came running over from the hospital to sign the papers. It was the final piece. You can take it only so far, monkey-ing around with an oven that was built in America to bake turkey. It's not a hearth oven."

Hearth ovens are notorious for being tricky and difficult to set up and it's critical to have a good mason. Abe told me about a bakery in San Francisco that actually installed an extra back-up oven because one particular guy, a master mason from Spain, was going to retire. Christy and Abe bought a Vanguard oven, which has a metal rather than a masonry firebox. But still it took two years to get their hearth oven working properly.

"We had trouble with the burner," Abe said. "And the local guy kept monkey-ing around with it and then finally they brought a guy over from France—great guy with big thick glasses—and he took one look at the burner and said, 'Oh, you need another twenty feet of stack. You need more draft with all those buildings around.' So we called the sheet-metal guy and put on a bigger stack and it did work better. But frankly, I think the whole oven thing is a little overdone. It's the appliance the bakers use, it's just a tool. You can make phenomenal bread at home. Ninety percent of what we do has to do with handling and fermentation."

So by 1994 they'd been to France twice, their kids were born, and they'd installed the hearth oven. Next they decided to go around the country and visit the bakeries making long-fermentation hearth bread. Back then there were only about ten of them, but Christy and Abe came back impressed by how much the other bread bakers didn't know and how out of control they were. And Abe and Christy were even more convinced that they wanted to remain a small bakery.

"We wanted to be the village bakery," Christy said, "have contact with our customer. When we started selling out the back door, it was clear it was a lot more rewarding, just in terms of the interaction, than selling wholesale. The only time you hear from a hotel is when they need more or when they don't want to pay for something. And we're so lucky to be in Boston—the area is so international."

"On this corner alone," Abe continued, "is German, Italian, Russian, Japanese. With wholesale there's a lot of stuff on the market so chefs can call and say, 'I really like your bread but up in corporate they say I can only spend seven cents rather than twenty-five a roll.' Frankly, three or four restaurants go out of business every year and more and more we're dealing with a community of people who, more likely than not, are going to go into bankruptcy. It's hard for a bakery to have that exposure every year and to do business with chef-owners who come and go. We'd never think of dropping the wholesale because you do need a steady business during the week."

Christy said, "On weekends there are lines and on holidays people wait two hours in line. I'm not proud of the waiting, but they come from all over, and it's sort of a community event. Because we're doing something real and it's gratifying to know that it's noticed."

Abe had fidgeted at times during the conversation, clearly anxious to get some idea across, and then he suddenly said, "Now, well, I don't know the kind of timeline you're on, but I just wanted to tell you about the Bread Bakers Guild of America—how it came to be. I'm on the board, vice-chair. So there was a person named Tom McMahon who owned a big bakery in Philadelphia and he realized that a lot of hearth-bread bakers in the U.S. were reinventing the wheel. In 1992 he formed a nonprofit called the Bread Bakers Guild of America. One of the central ideas was to demonstrate that bakers were not just the guy dropping the dunkin' donuts in oil."

I had actually spoken with Tom McMahon back in the late 1990s. I knew that Tom, perhaps not unlike Abe, viewed artisan bread making almost like a cause. He was on a mission to make American bread real again and help our bakers make that honest loaf. In an effort to accomplish this, Tom hoped to change public perception of bakers from just that donut guy to true artist. So Tom lobbied the French for over a year to allow Americans, along with teams from twelve countries, to compete in the Coupe du Monde de la Boulangerie, the very prestigious, once-every-three-year bread-baking contest. The French kept saying we'd embarrass ourselves. But Tom persisted, and at their first competition, the United States placed third, which secured the team's eligibility for future competitions. Now the United States has had five teams and has won the competition twice.

"But even if it's not a winning team," Abe pointed out, "the team gets an education, gets to work with some of the best bakers, and there's the trickle-down effect."

Tom McMahon had great vision and went on to build a state-of-the-art baking center and then, perhaps as important, approached the millers about altering the profile of U.S. flour to better suit the long-fermentation styles of the artisan bread makers.

"Not little ones," Abe explained, "but huge ones like General Mills. He never approached ADM because they're trash millers. But he went to big people and said, 'We're starting this organization of bakers and more people are going to start baking like this.' And a core of people at General Mills is now committed to supporting the guild, working with bakers, and asking what they want."

True enough. Abe put me in touch with Tim Huff, who is technical manager for the Bakery Flour division of General Mills. Tim told me that even though the guild was a very small portion of the industry, "there seemed something fun about them." When Tom McMahon opened the National Baking Center, he and Didier Rosada—the center's head baking instructor—invited the General Mills people to visit. They showed Tim what artisan bread was all about, redefining quality, showed him that it had a more open crumb, irregular cell structure, and different color.

"The flavors of those breads we'd never been exposed to before," Tim said. "Didier showed us that the lower-protein winter wheat has a tolerance for longer fermentation, develops a nice balanced elasticity, and has a warmer golden blush on the bread rather than the amber rust color from summer wheat. Flours for artisan breads need to be capable of longer and cooler fermentations and are gently mixed. Processed breads are produced at higher speeds, with a more abusive mixing of the dough, and a faster-developing gluten structure. And there's basically no fermentation time, because that may cost money.

The flavor difference we would not have believed before that day: the complexity of the flavor note—not sweet, but not bitter, just a tannic note on the back of the tongue. We also pretty quickly heard from our artisan friends that we just didn't need the additional treatment on flour of bleach and bromate. So we tried to find the best domestic flour to match the artisan bread bakers' needs and ultimately came up with General Mills's Harvest King. And now Harvest King is our third-largest-selling brand of bakery flour."

Harvest King has until recently only been available to bakeries and to West Coast grocery stores, so it was not a flour that I'd ever used in my more than thirty years of baking bread weekly. For me, King Arthur Flour had always been the flour of choice.

"King Arthur used to be the only people doing unbleached and unbromated flour," Abe said. "Of course, now General Mills has worked on the profile of their flour and created a product that is suited to long fermentation. Historically, the relationship has been that to bakers, millers are cheats shafting you and pumping up the moisture—and there are still vestiges of those old relationships. But we're halfway there to making better connections. And it's really great, because it wasn't Nabisco calling up the millers and asking about the fermentation. Now the guild has thirteen hundred bakers around the country getting information from a newsletter, master classes at the baking center, and all kinds of snippets came out about baking bread."

Christy added, "Some of this stuff that came out finally made it all have sense to me, like fermentation, which took me two years to understand. It was so helpful to me I thought everyone has to have this. Baking bread was done as a ritual, as opposed to done scientifically, and there wasn't an understanding of which parts were important even within your own bakery."

"In the beginning we were like doctors taking the approach: 'You cut this out and you either live or you die.' Now we have a textbook and an organization," Abe said.

I could see in Abe's description of the genesis and significance of the bakers guild that this community of bakers provided a mechanism for learning and support that specifically affected Clear Flour Bakery.

"We started spinning off bakeries," Abe said. "We didn't want to start more bakeries ourselves. But we must have had ten to twenty people who'd worked for us, got bored, and went off to other parts of the country to start their own bakeries. In our narrow world we're committed to this tiny little section of Brookline, serving as the neighborhood bakery. That's very important to me. I don't want to be big. On the other hand, we're lucky enough to have professional relationships with hundreds of people around the country who are on the cutting edge of being traditional bakers. If it's a holiday and you've never made this ethnic bread you can call or email someone in this incredible fraternity. We do less trial and error, like with the German breads we introduced recently. That took a year of experimentation to bring out three or four products—instead of a five-year trajectory—because it's all science, which is what we know now."

We'd talked for nearly two hours. Abe and Christy had taken me from their start and into the larger context of their place in the world of artisanal breads in America. So as the conversation began to wind down and move in the direction of their plans for the bakery and the future, it seemed the right time to ask my favorite question: What are your dreams?

Christy said, "I love the location, but if I won the lottery I'd put in all new everything, I'd put in all new equipment. I'm tired of piecing it together every year."

"I call it sensuous decay," Abe laughed. "People like that. Plus it's real and you see people make the connection. In this society where food comes from someplace else, that's important. People say, 'You're making that right here, you're *making* food here?' We think of bread as something like the rice in sushi: it plays a subservient role; it's second to the main course. I want to make it complement the salmon. To me bread is very subtle—the crust, the thinness, does it taste acidy or of grass seed? We'll make breads for the holidays that have gorgonzola cheese in it, or cranberries, and people go gaga so instantly. The funny thing is that *that's* easy. She'll work tirelessly for X hours to figure out something that will make a slight difference to the texture or aroma and even if no one notices it, she still gets off on it, and so will I. And there will be someone who notices. They may not know what it is, but they know it is different."

Was this a business they wanted their children to go into, I asked?

"Only if they want to," Christy said at first. Then: "No, because it's very hard work. They keep saying, 'Mom and Dad, why do you have the bakery because you fight so much about it?'"

"We do carp about it in front of the kids," Abe said. "But I think what's more significant is that after twenty years she comes home and says, 'I think the poolish went a different way today. It had this really lively feeling.' It's like having a garden—you plant a seed and the plant comes up—and there's that absolute childlike wonder for me of life coming from a seed. It's incredible, and it's the same thing from bread. You can tell how good an employee is going to be if after a few weeks he says, 'Well, I think I learned everything here. What's next?' And then you have someone like Christy, who says after years, 'It's a living thing, it rises! Look at the way it opens.'"

Abe admitted that he, too, would like to build the ultimate bakery, made so it could be cleaned easily. "And was a simple, but perfect environment where we could make the bread that we like to make," he added. "There's so much crap out there. I like money, but the compromises people make for money is gross. If I win the lottery, I'd like to have three-day weekends to spend time with my kids. And to make what we want, make what currently is turning our crank."

"There are things I want to do still, make different kinds of bread," Christy said. "I'd love to just bake, not have employees. Just bake what I want to bake and when I want to. It takes a while to get something right, to develop it. And the customer is not always right. I gave my German bread away for two years. People who'd never been to Germany would say to me, 'It's stale!' And I'd have to answer their questions. But there was this one German family who bought six loaves every week. What I'd like to be able to do is just offer it to people and if they want to pay money for it, then great!"

There was a pause and then Christy laughed and said, "You know we're all a little crazy, don't you?"

ED PICKED ME up at Clear Flour Bakery so we could make our clean getaway to New Hampshire. Christy had loaded a strong-handled, brown-paper shopping bag with breads and pastries and given it to me as we walked out the door. I stuffed it in the back seat as we motored north. But it was noon, we were hungry, plus I need to "test" Christy's products. Soon we made the heft of the bag less so, first by a little, then by a lot. We divided a plain croissant to eat—utterly divine—then a chocolate one, better still. I returned to the bag and pulled out a French champignon with lemon juice—a roll shaped like a mushroom and brushed lightly with lemon juice—and devoured it only just slow enough to realize its perfection. Next we tore off hunks of the buckwheat walnut bread—actually Ed was driving and I was tearing—then the baguette, and, finally, the pinnacle: Christy's sourdough bread. Happily eating more bread in one sitting than I can remember eating in two weeks, we were positively giddy from our bread orgy. But what was so very curious about our bread frenzy was that not only did the bread taste incredible, fabulous, and like nothing I'd ever eaten, it also had an uncommon ability to satisfy completely, not overfill, and gave great contentedness. They may be crazy, but I'd be blissful joining them in their insanity.

These bread artists understood the tradition, the art form, made it their own, and remained intently focused on working hard to achieve perfection. And they continued to revel in the joy of making something extraordinary. They'd taken from the best of European breads, and made the best of American bread. And they'd been doing it well for a long time. These are the things that count.

Sadly Clear Flour Bakery isn't my neighborhood bakery, but faraway, and its bread is an edible that loses something with each passing day—maybe even each passing hour.

So at home I knead the dough as I always do, mesmerized by the rhythm of it, and musing. Sometimes I think about who the loaf will feed—once my small children, now just the two of us or sometimes friends. Or for how long baking bread has been a part of my life, both in sickness and in health, and filled the role of my ultimate food for the soul. Or sometimes I think about nothing at all. This time Christy's bread was on my mind, not just as an extraordinary food worthy of craving, but perhaps as something more. Her breads are inspired—and inspirational—certainly, yet at the same time confirm the value of my own honest loaf. I can't ask for anything more. Indeed, this is a perfect passion.

{ WHOLE-GRAIN IRISH SODA BREAD }

Christy Timon wrote me the following about Irish soda bread: "Because the Romans never extended their reign as far north as Ireland, the early magic of yeast as a leavening of bread never found its way there. Instead the use of chemical leavenings developed as a way of making the daily loaf. This whole grain version is more like what was eaten and made every day, not the fancy holiday bread that has eggs, raisins, and sometimes caraway seeds. Though I work daily with yeasted breads, all the fine qualities of flour that make leavening possible must work here as well, and this is a delicious bread that has the advantage of being faster, without compromising taste. The techniques needed to make this bread also demonstrate the use of a 'soaker,' moistening the coarsest grain before mixing it into the final dough. This ensures that the grain softens completely and becomes 'neutral'; it doesn't absorb water that the flour needs to take up during the bake."

And Abe added to the bread directions: "It would be great if it still can fit into the final formatting to leave it in the gram measurements . . . Working by weight almost ensures success, whereas working by volume is almost certain to cause something short of total success." I did try to convert the measurements to cups and tablespoons for those home bakers who don't own a scale with grams. But the conversions were imprecise and so the results, I'm sure, would be less than satisfactory.

Makes 2 (684–gram/1 ½-pound) loaves.

For the whole-wheat soaker:
38 grams cracked wheat
38 grams boiling water

For the final mix:
265 grams white flour
283 grams whole-wheat flour
76 grams whole-rye flour
38 grams rolled oats, plus more for coating the loaves
10 grams wheat germ
10 grams salt
19 grams sugar
10 grams baking powder
7 grams baking soda
95 grams cold unsalted butter
479 grams (½ quart) buttermilk

Preheat the oven to 400 degrees. Make the soaker: Place the cracked wheat in a heatproof container, pour the boiling water over the wheat, and cover. Let stand for 30 minutes; all the moisture should be absorbed and the grain plumped.

Make the final mix: Measure with a scale all the dry ingredients into a mixing bowl, sifting the baking powder and baking soda to eliminate lumps, and stir together to thoroughly combine. Thinly slice the butter and add it to the dry ingredients. With a heavy-duty mixer with the paddle attachment, cut the butter into the dry ingredients on low speed until the butter is reduced to pea-sized bits.

Switch to the bread-hook attachment and with the mixer on medium-low speed add the buttermilk. Mix for 3 minutes, or until all the ingredients are incorporated and moistened, and some elasticity of the flour is evident. Add 76 grams of the soaker and mix until fully incorporated.

The softer the dough, the larger the volume of the loaf; adjust the hydration by adding small amounts of water, if necessary. Different flours absorb very different amounts. This dough will become firmer as it sits, since the flour will continue to hydrate. The dough out of the bowl should be softer than you think you would be able to shape.

The ideal temperature of the mixed dough is 65 degrees. If it's colder than 65 degrees, the flour has trouble absorbing the moisture, but warmer is okay. If it is colder than 65 degrees, you may want to let the dough rest at room temperature a bit until the flour is more fully absorbed.

Turn the dough out on a lightly floured surface and immediately portion it into two 1 1/2-pound round loaves. Roll in a dish of rolled oats to coat the loaves on the outside. Press each loaf so that it's flat and wider, to about 1 1/2 inches thick. Place on a baking sheet and let the loaves rest for 20 minutes after shaping.

Using a sharp serrated knife, cut a cross into the top of each loaf about 1/2 inch deep. This will allow the dough a place to expand while baking. Bake in a 400-degree oven for 35 to 45 minutes, until the loaves are golden brown with the cuts pushed open. Let cool to room temperature before slicing. Serve with butter.

DANCING WITH SALMON

{ DANCING SALMON COMPANY }

IN THE 1980s, Ed and I traveled to Alaska to fly fish for salmon and rainbow trout and to forget our urban selves in Alaska's powerful and pervasive wilderness. The strength and magnificence of that country is blatant, and unforgettable, and perhaps, once inside you, inescapable. We returned every year from 1984 to 1988. I went back to Sitka, in southeastern Alaska, in 1995, and then in 2006 we went together to the Bristol Bay region, to Dillingham and the Nushagak River. Each time we fished for Pacific salmon. And on this recent trip we discovered how to extend our Alaskan visit beyond our two weeks: we took home with us the wonderful taste of smoked wild fish— Dancing Salmon's smoked fish, to be precise. The two-year-old company processes local Bristol Bay fish and, from family recipes, creates fabulous smoked king and sockeye fillets, a coho or halibut roulade, salmon spread, and more. Flavors that, for us, always bring Alaska back.

It *is* a long, long journey from New Hampshire to Alaska. But the east-to-west plane ride is the better direction, made so by the notion that we were going toward the land where summer has almost never-ending daylight. And in our sixteen-hour travel day we actually out-ran the sunset, arrived in lightness, and had a chance to see some scenery along the way. When Washington passed below us, we recognized it as sort of the prelude to the final eruption of Alaska. Next and abruptly, the blisteringly bright white of the mountaintops came into view. They stand hard-edged and pointed and nearly always snow-capped, reaching grandly to the sky while sinking into fathoms of cold-blue ocean. Alaska is all about new, beautiful, and unrelenting mountains, thousands and thousands of miles of new mountains, from the Fairweathers in southeastern Alaska up to Anchorage and the highest point in North America, Mt. McKinley. It's hard to pay attention to the jet's landing when McKinley and Cook Inlet are out your window. But now it would be just two more plane rides to go before we'd reach the Nushagak River, and fishing.

From Anchorage to Dillingham and then by float plane across the tundra to the camp, where we stayed for a week, immersed in fishing. We returned to Dillingham for a day and a night before adventuring on to Seward.

Dillingham is like all of the Alaskan towns I've visited—it doesn't stand up well against the staggering natural beauty of the mountains, waters, and land. Certainly the geological structures overshadow anything manmade. Acquiescence to nature seems the only possible plan, and so the town is little more than messy encampment, a handful of buildings flung with relative impermanence along rivers and into the woods. Old junk lies where it fell, and nothing looks new. Everything shows marks of being victimized by the hard Alaskan weather. It seemed a subdued, dull place until we went to visit Pearl Strub, co-founder and one of the family partners in the Dancing Salmon Company, and whose energy and enthusiasm for her new business were palpable.

We walked down the dirt road just outside the Beaver Creek Bed and Breakfast until we could turn left onto Aleknagik Lake Road—the main highway—and where a train of heavy semis rattled by, each delivering a punch of wind to us as they roared toward Dillingham proper. The Trinity Lutheran Church, gravel berms, then evergreens, a trickling stream, and a long-abandoned wreck of a car were the roadside sights. We kept going for about a mile until we found Bea Street and then saw the sign—a school of 3-D fish carved in wood leaping around painted words: Dancing Salmon Company. The short driveway took us past an outside cooler, a boat, a pile of logs, and several outbuildings and brought us in front of a low and long building, a plain brown section attached to a one-story log house. The access ramp, lined with flowers, indicated the company entrance, and once inside we were greeted by Pearl, her three-year-old grandson in tow. A pretty woman who seemed too young for grandchildren, Pearl was dressed in jeans and a lavender shirt. Short in stature with black shoulder-length hair, she'd arranged the front locks so they were pulled back and clipped. Pearl smiled, pulled her grandson up to sit on her hip, and showed us to her office. A connector—maybe once a hall-way—from the retail operation to the house, it was barely big enough for three chairs. I could see past the rack of rifles on the office wall into her living room, and to where an elderly woman sat watching TV. A very tall, thin man with gray hair and wire-rimmed glasses came from the living room to take the small boy from Pearl.

"This is my dad, Ray Kase," Pearl said. "Dad and I started the business together, but he kind of forced the issue by going out first and buying the smoker. That was a major investment because it's a forty-thousand-dollar piece of equipment!"

Pearl was born in Dillingham, as was her mother, who is half Aleut, a quarter German, and a quarter Swedish. Her dad had moved to Dillingham from northern California as a young man and worked in heavy equipment construction. Ray's father had smoked salmon commercially in California in the early part of the twentieth century. "So it was part of the family history," Pearl smiled. "I still have one of the original labels from my grandfather's smokehouse, along with a letter that he wrote to the state in order to get licensed."

After graduating from high school, Pearl went to the University of Hawaii, then the University of Alaska, but never got her degree. She came back to Dillingham, married Bob Strub, had three kids, and was a stay-at-home mom until the kids went to school. Then she went to work for the Bristol Bay Native Association, and eventually became director of their Workforce Development program. She managed twenty-five people, had oversight of a $3 million annual budget, and did a lot of traveling. "That got real tiring," she explained, "especially when the kids were gone and my husband was home alone. But I went from a very, very good salary to nothing. I actually cashed

my retirement in to invest in this, and my husband keeps looking at me like, huh? I just kind of got tired of that whole scene.
And Mom's health condition played a real important part. We
realized she needed more care."

Pearl added that the low price of salmon also contributed
to their decision to start the company. "My husband's been a
commercial fisherman for years, and it's been real frustrating to
give our fish away to the cannery for basically nothing."

When Pearl referred to her husband having to "give his fish
away" to the cannery she was talking specifically about salmon.
Alaska is home to the world's largest wild salmon runs, and the
Bristol Bay area is one of three top regions in Alaska—along
with the Copper River and Sitka—where very fine, quality
Pacific salmon is found. Salmon are anadromous fish and live in
both the Atlantic and the Pacific Oceans. There are five species
of Pacific salmon: the coho (silver), pink, Chinook (king), chum,
and sockeye. And although each Pacific species has its own set
of unique characteristics in size, shape, and coloring, they all do
two things differently than the Atlantic salmon. They live in
Pacific waters, and when they travel from their ocean homes to
spawn in the rivers, they die there. The Atlantic salmon returns
to the Atlantic after spawning time and time again.

Despite the fact that the Pacific salmon fisheries have long
been managed, dams and other habitat degradation, especially
in the Pacific Northwest, have caused dramatic declines in the
salmon population in the last decades. And for the same reasons, the commercial harvesting of Atlantic salmon in the
Northeast has been illegal for many years now. Actually it was
the severe shortage of wild Atlantic salmon that in the 1980s
first gave rise to the development of the farmed salmon industry
in Maine. Abundant, a renewable resource with year-round
availability, farmed salmon seemed an ideal solution for replac-
ing the diminishing wild stocks. Fish farming flourished in the
lower forty-eight, and by the 1990s nearly all smoked and
canned salmon came from fish farms.

But Alaskan wild salmon hadn't experienced the same dec-
imation. So Alaska's canneries—although seasonal operations

and in competition with the farmed salmon prices—could continue to pack wild fish. The cannery might not pay Bob Strub a good price for his salmon, but a company that produced a superior-quality "value-added" salmon product might be able to buy the fish at a better price.

So in the fall of 2004 Pearl and her dad started their business by smoking just silver salmon. "Pretty much we spent that first season trying to replicate my dad's recipe," Pearl said, "taking it from a little home smoker and trying to do it in a commercial smoker. We wanted to come out with a product that was very similar to our home-smoked while still taking it through the process that we're required to—to meet the regulations that ensure a good, safe product."

They started their first full season in 2005 by purchasing halibut, then king, sockeye, and then in August the silver salmon. "Last year we ran the whole season," Pearl said, "and we also concentrated on developing some additional products. So we kind of expanded and instead of just smoking we applied to do a formulated product, a roulade. I made up a stuffing and took either fresh salmon or halibut and rolled it into a roulade. And that has been quite, quite popular. I figured out the recipe from my husband's uncle, who has a business down in Utah. He showed us something similar that he did with a bread stuffing. I really like to cook and I thought you could take that recipe and make it a lot better. So just like with the smoked salmon, we did a taste testing. I developed five different stuffings, made the rolls, and we let people around town try them and then vote. This one particular recipe was like ninety-nine percent the favorite. This has spinach, a cream cheese base, and mushrooms. It's pretty tasty and been pretty popular even locally. We never thought we'd have a local market. But it's easy because it's in individual servings and people can just take them out of the freezer, put them in the oven at three hundred and fifty degrees, and fifteen minutes later have a nice dinner."

Dancing Salmon has concentrated marketing efforts on another "local" market, the area fishing lodge clientele. Pearl works with the lodge owners to do custom processing for the sport fishermen. The lodge clients bring their fish in and it's smoked, packaged, and frozen, and ready to ship in a matter of days.

"With the smokers in Anchorage it could be weeks," said Pearl. "And we make sure the fishermen get their own fish back—it's all tagged; there's no mixing. This one guy called and said he was very concerned because last year he had his fish processed in Anchorage and when he got his smoked fish back, it was all tails. He said he didn't want all tails, and I said, 'You're going to get whatever you give me. You give me all tails, that's what you're going to get back!'"

Of course, the custom smoking for sport fishermen is only a portion of their business, and in addition to retail, they sell wholesale product. At the beginning of the season, they make sure to have a small inventory of smoked king for the retail business, and then concentrate on putting all the rest of the fish that comes in into fresh-frozen.

"It makes our product more versatile if we can just pull that later and smoke it," Pearl explained. "We do our initial freeze in one freezer. Everything is vacuum sealed, put on trays flat, and put into one freezer van overnight until they're frozen solid. Then they're packaged and put into a master carton and transferred into another freezer van. So we do a lot of shuffling. We do have to concentrate on the efficiency, because there's only four or five of us down in the plant at one time, and a couple of them are just kids. I think we have got it down."

In their first full year they processed about twenty-five thousand pounds of fish, but there were problems the second season. I got a glimpse of how perfectly the fish season must go for Dancing Salmon to be fully productive—it's a thoroughly unpredictable resource in a very volatile environment. In that 2006 season, the halibut run came in early. It started May 15, which in and of itself wasn't bad, but there wasn't enough ice available for the fishing boats to cool their catch. The city ice plant hadn't repaired the water lines they'd let freeze during the winter. And the local cannery, Peter Pan, wasn't buying fish yet so hadn't started making ice. Plus canneries aren't keen on selling their ice to another fish-processing operation. The kings came in very strong in June but they were jack kings, which means they were very small.

"The problem with that," Pearl said, "is the cannery pays sixty cents a pound. I pay two dollars and fifty cents a pound, and by the time you fillet the fish, the recovery yield is not there. Plus when you smoke the smaller kings up it's just not the same product as if you had the nice big kings. So we had to be real careful in our purchasing. Then the sockeye came in real strong, but again small. We had two-pound sockeye, which is a good canning fish. But it made it real difficult for an operation like ours. We have to be real particular with the product."

They found a set-netter, who would pick out good fish for them and, in his last set before coming back into town, would ice his load, sell everything else to the cannery, and then ice another load for Dancing Salmon and bring it in for them. "We pay our fishermen really well," Pearl explained. "We've actually asked our fishermen to handle the fish in a manner that's what *we* want. We want our fish bled live and then gutted and iced out there and brought in on the same tide. So we're getting real fresh, good-quality fish. The problem is that the Bristol Bay salmon run is very short, and when the fishing is heavy the fishermen can't take the quantity they need [to make money] and handle the fish in the manner I want them to. They're getting much better—using slush bags [bags filled with water and ice, which chills the fish down quickly since it's colder than just ice] and stuff like that."

Bob Strub provides about half of the fish Dancing Salmon uses, but during the peak of the run he delivers everything to the cannery—over one hundred thousand pounds. He's an engineer who simply likes commercial fishing. Originally from Washington State, he came up to Dillingham and met Pearl in 1977. The twentysomething-age Strub kids each fished with their dad, and all three are also partners in Dancing Salmon.

"My dad made the investment on behalf of the kids," Pearl said. "They're partners, and I have one nephew who this month will become of legal age to add into the partnership. Then the last will be my grandson here, Julian. He's actually been out there working. And my oldest daughter not only works in the plant, but during the peak of the season jumps on the boat with her dad, comes back in, and processes. My son, Chris, fished with his dad but now he's trying to become a commercial pilot. And my middle daughter, who's a structural engineer in Anchorage, contributed the Dancing Salmon label and website design."

There hasn't been much formal marketing of the Dancing Salmon products yet; the business relies on mostly word-of-mouth sales. According to Pearl, "People just come by and buy our product, and know someone back somewhere who'd like it. Like now someone in Boston is buying our smoked king—labeling it something like Red's Best—and selling it to high-end restaurants. And in Virginia there's someone who's buying the smoked sockeye for their winery."

They try to sell out of all product—except some to make roulade—after each season. If any smoked product is left over from the previous year, they give it to the lodges to serve early season at the beginning of the fishermen's week. "The product is still really good," Pearl said. "So the lodges tell their clients where they can get it. It is good promotion for us and it helps them out too."

Also, Pearl takes advantage of a particularly Alaskan sales opportunity: the Dillingham hospital puts out an RFP for halibut and salmon that the last two years has been awarded to Dancing Salmon. Their bid is competitive, but they're willing to also process some king salmon bellies and heads, which the older native people prefer.

Marketing, Pearl points out, is just one of her many jobs: "We're doing it all, smoking, selling, shipping, doing the federal and state paperwork. And we have to do that when we're in our aprons with our boots on! What we're trying to do is this whole big process. What other bigger companies do with a whole lot of people, we do with just a few of us. So it can be real chaotic at times. We are trying to figure the marketing thing out. We had an intern this year, and I said to him, 'You're not just going to be on the slime line, like if you were at the cannery; you're going to have to help market our product.' And he did. But we have a lot of fun; our intern actually went back and told the company that he worked for that he really liked working for us."

For Pearl it's more than fun; it's about the interesting people she meets. She tells a great story about when Togiak Outfitters called and asked if Dancing Salmon could send over samples of smoked fish. "So I rushed it over to the airport. What I didn't know is that they usually smoke their clients' fish for them right on their own grounds. But they had this one guy who didn't like what they were doing. So it was for this *one* client from Austria who came every year for two weeks to fish for silvers. Then before he and his son got on the plane to leave for Austria, they came in carrying duffle bags and bought as much smoked king as they could pack into those bags to take with them. So this year, after fishing a week he's going to charter another Beaver to carry over his fish so we can smoke his fish and he can take it back to Austria with him. He said, 'This is how real smoked fish tastes!' That makes me feel really good. Our fish has gone to Austria, Ireland, England, South Africa—the only place I can't get it into is Canada."

The smoked-fish industry in Alaska is filled with small mom-and-pop operations that are in every town, but don't ship great quantities out-of-state. But in the lower forty-eight, the smoked fish that you buy from Zabar's or Balducci's in New York—in fact, probably in most of the good grocery stores on the East and West Coasts and in the Midwest—are from one source: Acme Smoked Fish. Acme has been curing, smoking, filleting, and packing fish in its Brooklyn, New York, facility for more than fifty years. Acme still uses almost exclusively farmed fish, despite the recent negative publicity concerning farmed fish and the resulting resurgence of wild salmon products. While there are lots of good ecological and economic reasons to support and eat farmed fish, the rap on farmed salmon is that it's prone to disease, the farming system is bad for the seabeds the fish are raised in, and the farmed fish can harm the wild stock. Not to mention that the flavor of farmed salmon is decidedly blander than that of wild. In Alaska, where the nearest salmon-farming operation is in British Columbia, there is great pride in the quality of Alaskan wild fish—in the *terroir* of its waters—and in the quality of its smokehouses, too.

"We don't use any preservatives or flavorings," Pearl said. "Some people have asked us if we could use pepper, and we haven't even wanted to go in that direction. We wanted to keep our product simple. We actually harvest our local cottonwood and make our own chips."

I asked Pearl how, beyond trial and error, she'd learned about commercially smoking fish. She said she'd gone to a two-week processing class given by Doug Drum, another smoker who owns Indian Valley, and gives classes during his slow season. He not only instructs but generously shares his recipes. "It's a really a good experience," Pearl said. "We did everything right from the beginning: we did our fillet halves and they checked our recovery to see how we'd improved. There were about a dozen of us in the class—we even had someone from Egypt! Doug puts us up right there at his place in a bunk house where in the summertime he puts up his crew. It was pretty intense."

Pearl said she learned a great deal, including that many of the larger smokers inject liquid smoke into the fish. "I could taste the difference," Pearl said. "Even though they say it's actually made from real smoke, it still is a different taste. They use nitrates and nitrites, and we just stayed away from all that. We label all of our product as a frozen product."

Pearl plans to enter Dancing Salmon's smoked fish and roulade in Alaska's Symphony of Seafood new-product contest and perhaps also attend the Boston seafood show. "But I'm kind of worried about it," she admits. "We have to make a decision if we're going to get bigger. Do we go for higher volume, buy a fillet machine, and get more freezer capacity? We have to decide if we concentrate on doing a quality product to a targeted market, or go for high volume? Like I told the kids when they want to take shortcuts: Are you a Peter Pan processor or are you a Dancing Salmon processor? And I kind of woo them back in line. Although when we're packaging, my nephew—I swear he has wimpy fingers—would drop pieces of fish and I'd say, nope, it's gone. But he decided, well, it's gone to sell, but not for me to eat!

But I feel really good because the DEC inspector brought his own fish to us to process, so that's a good sign. I do like doing it, but it'll be nice when it becomes profitable, that'll make it easier. It's very rewarding to see people enjoy what you've done and take time to email you back to say they like your products."

Pearl said her immediate goal was profitability, but her dream for Dancing Salmon was for it to become something the kids would be proud of, and want to continue and keep as part of their own heritage. All three kids tell their parents they don't want to live in Dillingham. So there's talk of doing just the initial processing in Dillingham and then shipping it in bulk to someplace in the lower forty-eight to pack and ship. "Only problem is uprooting my husband," Pearl said. "He doesn't even see that as an option. But then the kids could play a bigger part. We'll see. The oldest, Nicole, is real interested in all of it. Even the engineer daughter, Katrina, who works for Kaufman Engineering, likes it when her company has its monthly get-together and she can have me send our salmon for the meeting."

Wherever the Strub kids were, their parents always brought them salmon. Even when they were in college, Pearl and Bob brought fish and invited all the people from Alaska over for a barbeque. "One time," Pearl laughs, "we brought a big king with us when we flew into Phoenix. We got it into the car and drove to an inn, but got in there and had no place to keep our fish. So we put it into the bathtub with ice from our cooler. We had to scour out the tub the next day before we could take a shower and then we had to go convince the chef that it was okay to allow it into his refrigerator."

As Pearl talked, I could see Ray through the office window behind her. He was in the parking area and going in and out of a small wooden building. As my conversation with Pearl finished, I asked what her dad was doing out there: "Right now he's got strips going on out in our traditional smokehouse. We can't sell the traditionally smoked salmon because our smoked products have to be brought up to a hundred and forty-five degrees and held there for thirty minutes. We've experimented to see what we could come up with, maybe like a jerky, but we couldn't come close. So we just do a batch for ourselves. It's really funny after we get done doing all the commercial stuff then all of a sudden we do fish for ourselves!"

Ed and I wandered outdoors to peek inside Ray's little smokehouse and then have a look at the $40,000 smoker, the fillet tables, salt and brown sugar dry-brining area, and where the packaging takes place. Stainless is the hallmark of the commercial operation—the large monster of a smoker with many, many racks and a row of fillet knives mounted in readiness on the wall above blue-top tables, all very bright and clean. By contrast, the traditional smokehouse was dark inside—but for the red-pink salmon strips—and filled with gray smoke, a standing electric fan there to push the cottonwood fumes everywhere.

Seeing, smelling the salmon strips suddenly made me hungry for salmon, and Pearl was happy to take us back inside to sample her wares. She'd thawed smoked king and silver for us to try—both sublime, although to my mind there's a culinary reason the king is dubbed so—and handed us a plastic container of her spread and a box of crackers to take on our trip back through Alaska. We wished for those empty Austrian duffles to fill with smoked salmon, but knew we'd have to savor the flavor, eat the spread slowly down to New Hampshire, and order more, much more, from home.

I called Pearl to check on my order of multiple pounds of smoked king, the roulade, and the spread. A young voice answered and said to hold on while she held the phone up to Pearl's ear, "because she's up to her elbows in brown sugar." They were trying to fill a special order for the Nature Conservancy annual meeting and were trying to scrape together all the product they had left to complete it. Could Pearl detect my panic? "I'll call you when I'm shipping your order, to make sure you'll be there for it," she said.

Whew! I'd just need to be patient. But clearly I was hooked, captivated by dancing with the salmon, to cottonwood and brown sugar, to the Bristol Bay waters, and to the purity of the taste. And, of course, I'm addicted to Dancing Salmon's ability to bring Alaska back to me.

{ DANCING SALMON PÂTÉ }

Yields approximately 2½ pounds.

1 pound cream cheese, softened
6 tablespoons unsalted butter, softened
Juice of ½ lemon
1 ½ pounds smoked salmon
1 small jar of capers, drained

Either by hand or with an electric mixer, whip the cream cheese, butter, and lemon juice together until light and fluffy.

Remove the skin and brown fat (and any bones) from the salmon. Crumble half of the salmon into the cream cheese mixture and whip. Gently fold the remaining salmon and the capers into the cream cheese and salmon mixture. Enjoy with crackers or on baguettes.

IN PURSUIT OF GREAT VENISON

$\{$ BROKEN ARROW RANCH $\}$

I HAVEN'T ALWAYS known about game cooking. A culinary confrontation with a piece of venison in the late 1960s got me going; a white-tailed deer steak that mysteriously appeared at the Tufts University fraternity house where a boyfriend lived and where I spent a lot of time. This was back before college-age men thought it was cool to be a good cook, and so the task of preparing food unquestioningly fell to the woman on hand—in this case, me. I recall there were deer hairs on the steak, a clear sign that the last person who'd handled the meat knew even less than I did about venison prep. But while I carefully picked each hair off, I noticed something else: despite whatever it had been through, it was absolutely beautiful, rich lean meat. I don't remember—likely because it was pretty unmemorable—how I actually cooked it or even how the venison tasted. Fraternity evenings have a way of provoking forgetfulness, but still this void in my culinary knowledge, and probably some vague sense that venison could be spectacular eating, piqued my curiosity: How *do* you prepare venison?

The fraternity venison incident also foreshadowed what was to come—initially a necessary learning process, but eventually a life-long passion. In 1975 I married a hunter and fisherman, and the same year of our marriage Ed and I started our publication, *Gray's Sporting Journal*. Suddenly I was faced not only with game in my kitchen but with editing a cooking feature for our hunting and fishing magazine. And quickly I was again faced with the conundrums of venison preparation. This time, however, it wasn't just a cooking problem; I had to help tackle the job of butchering a whole deer carcass. Our first dead deer together appeared before me late one night atop our Jeep, look-ing especially awkward parked in front of our Boston Back Bay apartment. I was thrilled by Ed's hunting success, but as city-dwellers the best I could do was exclaim at the wonder of the marvelous animal before it was whisked away to a friend's sub-urban home—with attached garage—for "hanging" and future processing. I was into it now—if only for the imperative moral and ethical rationale that you eat what you kill—and committed to learning everything about venison, every subtlety of prepar-ing and cooking it.

The word *venison* is derived from the Latin verb *venari*, to hunt. And in Robin Hood-type olden days, venison actually referred to all game-meat of an animal killed in the chase. Now we're more explicit, defining the meat of the deer species as venison. So although it seems less obvious, we include moose, elk, and caribou in the venison group. These are three of the five species of Cervidae (antlered, herbivore, of the Artiodactyla order) that are indigenous to North America. The other two are mule and white-tailed deer, whitetails being the dominant and oldest of the North American deer species.

Deer were indispensable to the early Native Americans. Influencing the spiritual, cultural, and economic elements of tribal life, venison was also a substantial portion of their diet. At an archeological site in West Virginia, excavation showed that about 90 percent of the meat being eaten there was venison. And venison wasn't just everyday fare. At the 1623 wedding of Plymouth Colony governor William Bradford, the Wampanoag Indians brought gifts of deer. "We had about twelve pasty veni-son [meat pies], besides others," wrote one of the guests, Emmanuel Altham, "[and] pieces of roast venison and other such good cheer in such quantity that I could wish you some of our share."

There was such heavy deer harvesting in colonial times that by 1800 the herds had been reduced by 35 to 50 percent from pre-Columbian estimates. Between the years of 1776 and 1850, the population of Americans increased from 1.5 million to 23 million, all of them consuming vast quantities of wild game.

Plus, venison was inexpensive, which added more pressure on the resource. In 1868 venison was actually cheaper than beef or pork, and by the 1890s more deer were harvested—often by market hunters—than at any other time in our history.

By the early 1900s, the entire deer population in the United States numbered only five hundred thousand. And deer were not the only game being slaughtered: ducks, geese, turkey, grouse, quail, and buffalo all faced near extinction from overharvesting. In response, a federal regulation, the Lacy Act, was passed, which prohibited interstate commerce of game taken in violation of state law. The act basically ended the practice of market hunting, thus saving much of our wildlife. So for most of the twentieth century virtually the only way to eat American venison was if you, or a sharing friend, could successfully hunt deer.

The history of venison in Europe was quite different: venison was the stuff of kings; no democratic freedoms for the masses when it came to deer hunting or consumption. Hunting was strictly controlled by the ruling class, who limited the number of deer harvested and initiated habitat management to secure herd size. But eventually, in the process of colonizing other parts of the world, the European colonials not only discovered new species of deer, but exercised their freedom to hunt them.

In the mid-1800s the British transplanted red, fallow, and sika deer to New Zealand, primarily for recreational hunting, and the deer found ideal habitat. They prospered to the point that their exploding population all but denuded the hills of vegetation—causing extensive erosion, habitat loss, and near extinction of some ground-feeding birds. Within a little over a hundred years the deer grew so pervasive they were not only hunted extensively but poisoned as pests. Then some enterprising hunters decided that instead of letting the plentiful deer carcasses just rot, they would sell them to restaurants. This caught the attention of New Zealand farmers, and in the first true domestication of a wild species in over ten thousand years, farmers captured and then propagated deer. By 1987, there were 3,500 deer farms in New Zealand and over 860,000 pounds of Kiwi venison being served in U.S. restaurants.

There'd been a growing desire and interest here in new cuisines and all things culinary, which got its start when World War II troops returned from Europe. First it had to be French, then Italian, then ethnic, then any exotic or gourmet foods. The trend was fueled in the 1960s by the TV show of Cordon Bleu-trained Julia Child, and later in the 1980s it was redefined by Alice Waters's emphasis on artisanal foods. Certainly this progression helped drive the demand in the United States for Euro-exotic venison. From 1990 to 1994, our venison consumption doubled. Sure, venison's popularity was due in large part to our blossoming appreciation for gourmet foods, but it also had to do with the burgeoning emphasis on healthful, more natural foods. Venison is high in protein; contains iron, zinc, and many of the B vitamins; and it's raised naturally—devoid of growth hormones, antibiotics, and dyes. Venison is also very lean, with one-eighth the fat content as beef and less cholesterol than a skinless chicken breast.

With an increasing demand for venison here in the United States, the opportunity door was open for a domestic supply to find its way into the marketplace. During the twentieth century there had been an incredible rebound of wild American deer, from a total population of half a million in 1900 to 25 million in 1997. And in 2006 the white-tailed deer population alone was estimated to be close to 20 million. Despite this, the Lacy Act has remained intact, preventing any commercial use of wild game. But the Lacy Act has no jurisdiction over farm-raised animals.

Are there differences between wild and farm-raised deer? Of course. Farm-raised deer are fenced in and more sedentary than their wild counterparts. The constancy of their diet and the slaughterhouse approach to processing the meat all make for a different flavor—farmed venison is a bit flatter, less, well, flavorful than wild. In general, we've domesticated the taste right out of most of our meat, and farmed venison seems headed in that direction.

I admit bias here. Since my early deer days, I'd seized the challenge, grabbed the gauntlet, and spent decades learning how to prepare game. And included in my venison knowledge are strong opinions about processing—proper bleeding, cooling, aging, butchering techniques. It was always wild deer, and I was picky about it, downright snooty, shuddering at the very memory of my two first attempts at venison preparation—the fraternity hair-flecked steak and the car-top deer. Now I knew what made great venison—its wildness, which gave it complexities and subtle nuances of flavor that were simply unparalleled. And the way we handled it, I'm proud to say, encouraged that nuanced and fabulous taste.

But dealing with wild game requires extreme attention to detail. And worse, wild game isn't always available. I'd occasionally been driven to farm-raised venison, to test recipes or in desperate cravings after a deer-less fall, but I was always disappointed—until one of my chef friends, Jesse Perez, from San Antonio, told me about the venison from Broken Arrow Ranch in Ingram, Texas.

Broken Arrow Ranch supplies primarily high-end restaurants and produces what is arguably the best commercially sold venison. Its venison comes from free-range, wild deer, not those raised in fenced-in areas or provided feed. And it is *field-harvested*—a harvesting method unique to Broken Arrow, which mimics how wild deer are felled—with an instant shot to the head—and then immediately cooled and hung in a portable processing trailer. This is wild deer, harvested in a perfectly controlled manner, to produce the best possible venison.

Thirtysomething Chris Hughes is president of Broken Arrow Ranch, which was started by his parents, Mike and Elizabeth Hughes, in 1983. Mike had started a commercial diving company in the early 1960s and built his Houston-based business into what eventually became a publicly traded, multimillion-dollar business in underwater technology, Oceaneering International. He and his wife purchased the ranch in the late 1970s, initially for recreational purposes, but in 1982 Mike retired from Oceaneering and moved the family out to the ranch.

"When I say Dad retired," said Chris, "I mean he's not the kind of man that would retire and not do anything. He stepped away from the day-to-day operation and from being CEO and president of Oceaneering, but remains to this day on the board. They moved out here and I don't think they had any intention of starting a business. I don't know if he knew what he wanted to do, but this idea formed fairly quickly. On one of their trips to Europe, they recognized that venison and game meat were pretty prevalent on the menus throughout Europe. But back here in the U.S. it was almost nonexistent. They coupled that with the recognition that here in the Hill Country there's this large overpopulation of exotic wildlife—axis, sika, fallow deer, things like that. They kind of put two and two together and said here's this overpopulation of animals that need some management and here's a market in the restaurant industry that certainly we can tap into."

Sika and axis deer were introduced to Texas between the 1930s and 1950s, primarily for hunting purposes. They thrived in the central and southern Texas environment and although the native white-tailed deer is today still the prevalent species, there are now huge herds of sika and axis. These non-native species can compete very successfully with the whitetails. They forage for leaves and forbs just as the native species do, and once the natural herbs are gone the exotics can turn to grass—unlike the whitetails, which can't digest grass. The ranchers—realizing there was a danger the white-tailed deer could get pushed out—adopted a population-management program to keep the exotics in check.

Chris explained that the ranchers have several different options for managing herd size. One option is to just shoot the animal and let it lie. Or they can sell hunts to sportsmen. But since this has only a minor impact on the herd, and because most hunters prefer trophy bucks over the does, this isn't a real solution. A third option is to trap the animals, take them to auction, and sell them on the live market. This method involves additional time and cost—the trapper fees, loss of animals when transporting them, auction fees, and so on.

"And then there's us," said Chris. "The ranchers can utilize us as a way to keep their exotic population in check. It's a very, very easy thing. They just have to call us and we set up a time that fits into our schedule. We come out there, we harvest the animal, and then we send the rancher a check. We work with about a hundred and fifty different ranchers, who all view it as a good relationship. It's done on a completely voluntary basis and we pay them per pound, based on the animals we take."

Chris explained that the area—an hour or so north and west of San Antonio—around Broken Arrow isn't suited to any type of agriculture. So the deer haven't been exposed to pesticides and fertilizers. "These are wild animals," said Chris. "There's not a lot of difference between these animals and what people were eating six thousand years ago. The animals are not farm-raised and they're not being raised on artificial, supplemental feed. They're eating the grasses and the forbs, a wider and varied diet. Even if the deer is grass-fed, yes, it's natural, but it's only one type of grass. It might have a nicer flavor than a feedlot animal, but it's still only one flavor profile. Our meat is much more complex; it's very subtle. It's what is attainable out in the wild, but it is perfectly processed. We do a lot of things that either hunters don't do or they can't do. So it's what you can get in the wild if everything is optimal. Plus the axis deer is recognized by a lot of people as being the best tasting. You see a survey of hunters—you know, guys who have eaten everything from antelope to rhinoceros, everything under the sun. Hands down, everyone talks about axis being one of the best-tasting venison. And I think it's because it has a very lean meat, clean meat, kind of like veal."

One of the issues that Mike Hughes faced initially was who actually owned the wild exotic species. Whitetails, even though they may roam a specific property, are technically owned by the state and subject to Lacy Act protection and hunting laws. But ownership of the exotics was unclear; after all, they'd been *introduced* by the ranchers. In collaboration with the Texas legislature, Mike was able to get exotics classified as livestock, which made them the property of the landowners.

The exotics weren't subject to the laws, but Mike believed hunting methods were the most efficient way to harvest the animals and that they also produced a better quality meat than other methods. "Exotic species," explained Chris, "and axis in particular, are not animals that lend themselves to domestication. And if you trap axis deer and transport it, you'll lose anywhere from a third to a half from the stress. They get so stressed and tense that the meat muscle is actually bruised, and this creates a very gamey flavor. Field harvesting is the best way to get the quality, and it is also a very humane, stress-free way to kill the animal."

Additionally, Mike recognized that whoever bought the meat, especially restaurants, would want it inspected. And he wanted to be able to assure people that it was safe. "So he called the USDA," Chris said, "to see what he had to do to get somebody to come inspect it. USDA told him that because venison is not named under the federal meat act—which names beef and pork and poultry under the poultry act—that it wasn't considered meat and not under their jurisdiction. Anything not under the jurisdiction of the USDA defaults to the FDA. So he called the FDA, and they said that they weren't an inspection agency, they were a reactionary agency. So as long as you don't get anybody sick, you'll never hear from them."

But Mike thought having the meat inspected was critical. So he next checked the local codes and the municipal laws. "What they say," Chris said, "is something along the lines that meat must come from an approved source, which comes full circle to say it has to be inspected." In the end Mike worked with the Texas Department of Agriculture and their meat-inspection program to get a voluntary inspection. The state inspector inspects the product and puts a State of Texas inspection stamp on it. "So that's kind of an example of the hoops he had to go through to make this program work," Chris laughed.

Once through those initial hoops, Mike started marketing Broken Arrow venison to restaurants—through trade shows, wine festivals, and conventions, and by calling on chefs. "One of those good timing circumstances," Chris said, "was that our early customers were chefs like Robert Del Grande of Café Annie, Dean Fearing of Mansion on Turtle Creek in Dallas, Mark Miller of the Coyote Café, all of these guys that sort of invented the Southwest cuisine back in the mid-1980s. Venison was a perfect match for what they were doing. We found the right guys, during the right movement, that required the right ingredient. I think that helped all of us grow."

In 1983 Broken Arrow harvested a total of 230 animals. By 2005, they were harvesting seventeen hundred deer, eight hundred antelope, and seven hundred boar, and selling about 160,000 pounds of meat. "We're still focused on restaurants even today," Chris said. "We tried retail a little bit back in the early nineties—went into Whole Foods when they were just getting started and a couple other local retailers."

But the economics of retail just didn't make sense for Broken Arrow and eventually fizzled out. Consumers could always call the ranch and order product, but it came only in industrial-size packaging. "When I got here a year and a half ago," Chris said, "I revamped the website and identified the consumer market as a growth area for us. Especially with the advent of the Internet and the Food Network, it didn't take a visionary to see growth in the foodie culture, and it's real easy to repackage and make it more consumer-friendly. It's been a really nice growth area for us—in the year and a half we've seen probably three hundred percent growth in our consumer business—and it's been nice to offer our products to consumers as well as restaurants."

Born in Houston, Chris was in first grade when the family moved to the ranch. "I grew up running around the ranch with my younger brother and having a good time. When we were little, Dad had us do stuff around the ranch, mow the lawn or take the big rocks out of the road. It's a great place to grow up."

Chris's initiation into working for the business was at trade shows when he was about nine years old. "We had this covered wagon at the shows, and I'd slice up the venison sausage and pretty much give the same spiel I give today," Chris remembered. "And my brother and I would make up the gel packs for keeping the meat cold during shipping. Every summer we'd also help do the inventory."

Inventory meant that the brothers would have to get dressed up in insulated clothes and go into the big zero-degree freezer. They could only work about a half hour in there before they'd have to come out and get warm. The ranch is on a highway, Chris explained, and I was beginning to get this very funny picture of the trucks rumbling by and these two kids in winter garb, standing on the porch, in hundred-degree Texas weather. The truckers must have really wondered what was going on.

As a teenager, Chris got more involved in the marketing side of the business. He'd identify new customers and figure out what restaurants had opened or closed. Since there wasn't any Internet back then, he'd order up—from the chambers of commerce—restaurant guides from all the major cities across the country.

"We got junk mail from that forever!" Chris said.

Chris got his engineering science degree, with a minor in business, from Vanderbilt. "I got to school and was talking to my dad and said I didn't have any idea what to study. He said, 'Go into engineering, you won't go wrong.' We have a strong history in our family of getting an engineering degree and not actually becoming an engineer. He did it, my older brother did it, and now I've done it."

Chris married right out of college. And through his wife's work as a civil engineer at Kellogg, Brown and Root, they heard about opportunities to work overseas with the military support contract.

"My wife got hired first and was sent to Kosovo," he recalled. "I got hired two months later and sent to Macedonia for three months and then was sent to Bosnia."

Chris and Maeve Hughes returned to Houston, and she worked at Halliburton while he did projects for Oceaneering and applied to business school. He went to Wake Forest and got an MBA in entrepreneurship and marketing. "We liked Wake Forest because it was in North Carolina, but also because they had a strong program in family businesses—that was a nice feature. I kind of went to business school thinking I might come back to Broken Arrow, but I wanted to keep my options open. About halfway through, it cemented that this was what I really wanted, or at least wanted to give it a try. It's funny because if you'd asked me when I was eighteen if I was going to live in Ingram, Texas, I would have answered with a resounding no! It's a great place about ten years from now (everybody wants to come back), but when you come back when you're thirty you're a little ahead of the curve."

Chris and Maeve have infant and toddler sons, so Maeve works only peripherally in the business, mostly doing market research. "Right now she's more focused on chasing after the kids," Chris said. "She's a very, very smart, capable woman—she'd be very successful at any career—and she'll be a very successful mother. But I can't wait for her time to free up so she can help us out here at the company."

Chris's role at Broken Arrow is primarily management. "Just keeping the thing going," he said. "Certainly when I got here, I put my hand in every basket: went out on the harvest with the guys, spent some time in the meat room. I continue to pack boxes. I love it when they come in here and knock on my door and say, 'Hey, we need your help packing some boxes. FedEx is coming at three o'clock and we still have a lot of orders to pack.'"

Basically Broken Arrow has two different harvesting operations, one in the Hill Country around Ingram for axis and sika deer and the other in south Texas in the big open area of the King Ranch. This is where they harvest the south Texas, or Nilgai, antelope. Both operations employ a portable processing trailer to use in the field, which was designed by Mike Hughes in collaboration with the state. It allows for sanitary processing and immediate refrigeration of the meat.

From a range of fifty to two hundred yards, the shooter kills the animal instantly with a single shot using a high-caliber rifle with a sound suppresser. "They'll next approach the animal," Chris explained, "and bleed it right away. We use a technique called electro-stimulation, where a current is run through the animal, causing the muscles to contract and squeezing any blood out of the muscles. This will also tenderize the meat forty to sixty percent more than unstimulated meat. You know, there are a lot of things that cause meat to be gamey and tough. Improper bleeding and processing is certainly one of them."

The animal is then taken back to the processing trailer, where it is skinned and eviscerated, receives an inspection stamp, and is put into the cooler. Next it's transported to the central plant and unloaded into another hanging cooler to dry-age. The carcasses are dry-aged whole, bone in, for three to five days. This causes about a 6 percent moisture loss, but it helps to intensify the flavor. After five days, the product is cut into primals, vacuum packed, and put into another cooler, where it wet-ages for a total of twenty-one to twenty-eight days. Wet-aging stops the moisture loss but allows the enzymes to continue to break down muscles and tenderize.

"It's expensive to hold on to inventory for thirty days," admitted Chris. "It's expensive to double-handle the product, but it's what produces a superior product. And that's what we're trying to do here."

Chris acknowledged that there is a lot of good venison out there, especially from New Zealand. "Many restaurants have New Zealand venison on their everyday menu," he said. "Then when they have a special occasion, some dinner party that they absolutely can't screw up, they call us."

Broken Arrow is "a work in progress," he said. "I know there's a place it can go. There's a business model here that works. It's been working for twenty-three years. I certainly don't need to come in here and change that just to put my stamp on it. But when I was thinking about whether or not to get into this business, I saw that no other family member showed an interest in it. So I knew that if I didn't do it, it was probably just going to go away. I just really thought what a shame it would be to have this company go out of business and not be able to provide this quality product. I think it was a driving factor for me."

IT HAD BEEN a long time since I'd had wild venison—for a couple years we'd been in a big-game wasteland. And even the last, a New Hampshire white-tailed deer, wasn't ours, wasn't given the care, the attention, it was due. So I was very excited when the Broken Arrow box came, palpably so. Chris's note read, "The antelope roast should be a nice flavorful treat—we both know that all the flavor is in the working muscles." And very flavorful it was. But then there was the axis boneless loin—was I drooling? Yes, yes, yes, I was lost to its wonderful taste! Cooked rare, of course, the gentle essence of wild herbs, textured tenderness, and clean, true flavor—all validating that this was unmistakably perfect, wild venison. Indeed, it would have been a *monumental* shame if Broken Arrow had just gone away.

{ SOUTH TEXAS ANTELOPE CHUCK ROAST } WITH CHILI SEASONINGS

Serves 6.

1 (2-pound) antelope chuck roast

Montreal steak seasoning (see Note)

3 tablespoons vegetable oil

1 onion, chopped

1 (14.5-ounce) can beef stock, plus enough water to make
    2 cups

2 cloves garlic, peeled, or more to taste

2 jalapeños, seeded and diced

2 green chiles, canned; or fresh chiles such as habanero (if you
    prefer hot) or poblano (if you prefer mild), roasted and
    peeled (optional)

1 (14.5-ounce) can diced tomatoes

2 tablespoons tomato paste

1 $\frac{1}{2}$ teaspoons dried oregano

2 tablespoons New Mexico chile powder

1 teaspoon ancho chile powder

1 tablespoon ground cumin

$\frac{3}{4}$ teaspoon salt, or more to taste

$\frac{1}{8}$ teaspoon freshly ground black pepper

Season both sides of the roast with the Montreal steak seasoning (see below note) and pat it into the meat. Heat the oil in a
skillet and brown the roast on both sides. Remove the roast from
the pan.

Add the onion to the pan and cook until slightly browned. Pour
in a bit of the stock to deglaze the pan. Add the garlic and pep-
pers and cook for 1 minute. Place the meat in a a heavy flame-
proof roasting pan with a lid. Pour the onion mixture over the
top of the meat and add the tomatoes.

Combine the remaining stock with the tomato paste, oregano,
chile powders, cumin, salt, and black pepper. Pour this mixture
over the roast. Cover and simmer over low heat for 3 to 4 hours,
until the meat is very tender and falling apart. A fork inserted into
the meat should twist and "shred" the meat easily. After 2 hours,
watch to make sure there is enough liquid in the pan to keep the
juices from burning. If necessary, add a little water, but don't add
too much. The mixture should become a thick, rich sauce.

Serve over Mexican rice, with flour tortillas, salsa, and cubed
avocado.

Note: Montreal steak seasoning is a combination of garlic powder, ground coriander, black pepper, dried dill, paprika, salt, and
red pepper flakes. It is available from the McCormick brand, but
you can also make your own mix at home.

{ ROASTED VENISON WITH BLACKBERRY SAGE SAUCE }

High-quality meat does not require complex seasonings, which can often mask its true flavor. We prefer to prepare our venison simply and serve it over a complementary sauce.

Serves 4.

For the sauce:
2 cups Zinfandel
1 ½ pints blackberries, rinsed and well drained
2 cups brown veal demi-glace, or low-sodium veal or beef stock
     that has been boiled until it's reduced by half
2 tablespoons unsalted butter
Salt to taste
Juice of ½ lemon, or to taste
2 sprigs fresh sage

For the venison:
1 pound axis venison or antelope boneless loin
Salt and freshly ground black pepper
3 tablespoons oil

Make the sauce: Pour the wine into a medium-sized saucepan and bring to a boil. Add the blackberries and cook, stirring occasionally, for about 10 minutes, until the berries are soft. Add the demi-glace and bring to a boil. Lower the heat and cook, stirring occasionally, for about 10 minutes, until the sauce coats the back of a spoon.

Strain the sauce through a sieve and whisk in the butter. Season with salt and lemon juice. Place the sage in the sauce and let it steep for 10 to 20 minutes, or until ready to use. Keep warm. Remove the sage before serving.

Meanwhile, roast the venison: Preheat the oven to 400 degrees. Season the loin with salt and pepper. Heat the oil in a skillet and brown the meat on all sides. Remove the loin from the pan and let it cool for 10 to 15 minutes.

Place the loin on a broiling pan and then into the oven. Roast until the internal temperature reaches 125 degrees on a meat thermometer for rare, or 135 degrees for medium-rare, 10 to 15 minutes. Do not cook past medium-rare, or the venison will become tough and dry. Let the meat rest for 10 minutes.

Pour a little of the sauce onto serving plates, slice the loin into ¼ -inch medallions, and fan them on top of the sauce.

FOR THE LOVE OF
EATING TOMATOES

{ LONG WIND FARM }

IN 1989 WHEN we moved to Lyme, New Hampshire, there
were six farmstands within an eight-mile radius of my
house—Cotton Stone Farm, Crossroads, River Valley
Farm, Killdeer Farms, Cedar Circle, and Long Wind Farm.
Long Wind was the closest—only a four-mile bike ride for me
round-trip—just down the hill, across a steel-arched bridge over
the Connecticut River, and into East Thetford, Vermont. Long
Wind Farm is a thin, ten-acre strip of land that lies on the old,
pre-dam flood plain and is sandwiched by the banks of the
Connecticut on one side and train tracks on the other. Back
then, Long Wind's front acre had a two-room, plywood structure on it facing Wilson Road. The stand was plain, unembel-
lished save for the many clusters of purple irises outside and the
display of beautiful fruits and vegetables inside. Each of my
neighborhood farmstands seemed to specialize in one or two
distinguishing products: Cedar Circle had fabulous strawberries, Cotton Stone great flowers, and Long Wind's produce was
all organic. Plus, it had the most incredible-tasting tomatoes I'd
ever eaten, so much so that there became little reason to include
tomato plants in my home garden. Why bother to grow your
own when someone is doing it better just two miles away?

"People get really excited about certain vegetables and
fruits, like tomatoes, sweet corn, peaches, strawberries, greens—
early and late but not in midsummer," Dave Chapman, Long
Wind Farm's owner, said in the first of several conversations I
had with him. "Consumers will pay more for something that
tastes good. I'd pay twice the money for a good peach, wouldn't
you? Maybe I wouldn't buy as many in a week, but I'd pay a
lot more. Tomatoes are probably my favorite vegetable to eat—

definitely not my favorite to grow—but I probably eat tomatoes almost every day."

Dressed in a soft aloha shirt, full trousers, and round wire-rimmed glasses, David didn't fit my mental picture of a Vermont farmer—more a parrot-head stopping by to fill up on organic foods. And except for the slightly graying sandy hair there was no hint that he'd already passed his half-century birthday.

Dave grew up on a dairy farm in Lancaster County, Pennsylvania, but had no intention of becoming a farmer. "I never dreamt this is what I'd be doing," he said. After high school he spent time in Washington State and Colorado, and in 1976 he moved to Norwich, Vermont. Seven years later, at the age of thirty-two, he and his future wife, Claudia Henrion, bought the land in neighboring Thetford. They planted mixed field vegetables, grew them organically, and sold them at their farmstand and at the local farmers' market. One June—early in his farming career—at a Saturday farmers' market, Dave noticed a purveyor in a nearby stall selling greenhouse tomatoes. They weren't organic but something else about them caught his eye.

"I saw that people were very excited about these green-house tomatoes because they came in so much earlier than field tomatoes. That was back before grape, cluster, or even hydro-ponic tomatoes—when tomatoes were out of season, you were basically out of luck for anything that tasted any good."

He asked his neighbors in the stall next door if they thought growing organic tomatoes in a greenhouse was possible, and they said they thought it actually might be easier to do organically. Yet then, in the 1980s, the only organic greenhouse tomatoes being grown were in Europe. There were none here in the United States.

However, one of the advantages David Chapman had as a Thetford, Vermont, organic farmer in the 1980s was his proximity to a great resource, Eliot Coleman. Eliot is a master organic farmer who'd followed in the shoes of the original pioneers, Helen and Scott Nearing, of the back-to-the-land "good life" movement. In 1965 Eliot purchased land in Maine from the Nearings and for ten years grew and sold organic food for a living. He then spent fifteen years as an organic farmer at other farms, including the Mountain School, where Eliot maintained the boarding school's gardens, fed the faculty and students organic produce from the school's fields, and taught the high-school-age kids how to farm organically. The Mountain School is located in Vershire—one town over from Thetford.

Eliot shared with David a 1975 article about European greenhouses that, in addition to the farmers' market conversation, was the inspiration for building Long Wind's first twenty-by-fifty-foot greenhouse and planting tomatoes in it. Dave's initial crop was a disaster. The compost was too hot. Dave called Eliot, who suggested adding carbon to the compost, which David did, and the compost was still too hot. He added more, and then more, but by so doing eliminated the nitrogen in the compost. David was treading on new territory here with greenhouse tomatoes—territory that Eliot had not yet thoroughly traveled either—yet fortunately for generations of tomato lovers to come, David was really intrigued by the complexity of the problem. As Dave described his first attempts at growing organic greenhouse tomatoes, I was beginning to totally appreciate why he'd said tomatoes were not his favorite to grow.

This good-to-eat but bad-to-grow disproportion is just one of the many disparities that seem just to be integral to the nature of tomatoes. Botanically tomatoes are truly a fruit, or at least they fit most of the criteria for the definition of a fruit. A tomato is the mature ovary of an angiosperm, meaning it has the reproductive system of a flowering plant, and the fruit itself has a "fleshy" body and seeds. Yet despite botanical facts, in an 1893 decision the tomato was classified by the U.S. Supreme Court as a vegetable. The decision was based on the fact that the tomato is *used* as a vegetable, theory being since it is eaten with the main course rather than afterward it can't be a fruit. Although it may seem trivial to worry about whether the tomato is a fruit or a vegetable, the vegetable classification had a significant impact on the tomato business: it made tomatoes subject to the same import tariffs as other vegetables, thus protecting domestically grown tomatoes and allowing for significant growth in the U.S. tomato industry. Today the United States is second only to China in the world's tomato production; the annual per capita consumption of fresh tomatoes in the United States has increased steadily to eighteen pounds—an increase of 15 percent between the early 1990s and the early 2000s. Interestingly, it is also more widely grown in home gardens here than any other vegetable.

But tomatoes were not always so popular. The Spanish explorer Cortez returned to Europe in the sixteenth century with tomato seeds he'd acquired from the Maya, whose plants were thought to have originated in the Andes. Unfortunately, when Spanish herbalists determined that the fruit was part of the nightshade family, it was presumed to be a poisonous plant. In 1597 English botanist John Gerard wrote that the tomato was "of a ranke and stinking savour," although he seems to have admired it as an ornamental; and later in 1752 Philip Miller, "Gardner to the Worshipful Company of the Company of Apothecaries at their Botanick Garden at Chelsea," doubted that tomatoes were even edible.

Yet at the same time, and as part of another of those tomato ironies, the vegetable was considered an aphrodisiac. This may have been because of the exotic origin and sensual appearance of the tomato, but another story suggests that it came about through either a foreign-language misunderstanding or a hearing problem: a Frenchman was visiting friends in Italy and was served tomatoes; when he asked what the new dish was, he was told *pomo dei Moro*, or Moor's apples— Spaniards were often called Moors—but the Frenchman, being French, thought he'd heard *pommes d'amour*, or love apples.

Despite the love connection, tomatoes weren't really accepted in France as edible until the beginning of the nineteenth century. Napoleon's chef introduced them into French cuisine in 1800 with a dish concocted to celebrate the emperor's victory at Marengo in Italy. The recipe ingredients included Marsala wine, chicken, and tomatoes and is still around today and called chicken Marengo.

At about the same time, Thomas Jefferson was traveling extensively throughout Italy and then lived in France. With

Jefferson's return home, America was reintroduced to the tomato. According to Peggy Cornett, director of the Thomas Jefferson Center for Historic Plants, "From 1809 on, Jefferson sowed tomatoes in his vegetable garden [at Monticello] and noted this in his Garden Book 'Kalenders.'...He described his Spanish Tomato, which was likely akin to the Large Red, as being 'very much larger than the common kind.' Tomatoes in Jefferson's day weren't of the Beefsteak caliber. They were more deeply lobed and had more seeds than pulp." The Creoles in New Orleans incorporated tomatoes into their jambalayas and gumbos, and others, too, began promoting tomatoes. Less prominent than Jefferson but more flamboyant was Salem, New Jersey's Horticultural Society president, Colonel Robert Gibbon, who defied predictions that eating a tomato would cause instant death by consuming one in front of a crowd on the courthouse steps in 1820.

Amazingly, it took just thirty years to convert the tomato from poisonous decorative to delicious edible; by 1850, the tomato was the most eaten vegetable in the United States. And by 1872, Massachusetts horticulturist Luther Burbank had started "improving" the biotechnically amenable tomato and produced disease-resistant hybrids conducive to trucking north. In 1929 the bad rap on tomatoes appears to have vanished entirely as the Bureau of Home Economics published their ideal diet, which included fifty-five pounds of tomatoes a year per person. From 1920 to 1978, per capita tomato consumption in the United States (including processed tomatoes) would rise from eighteen pounds to fifty-five pounds.

And that which had been so maligned and dubbed poisonous was, rather ironically, now determined to be a health necessity. Tomatoes do pack real nutritional value: one medium-size tomato provides 40 percent of our daily recommended amount of vitamin C and 20 percent of vitamin A, and is a good source of fiber, potassium, and iron. It's low in fat, sodium, and calories (thirty-five calories). Best yet, tomatoes contain an antioxidant called lycopene, which has been shown to reduce the risk of prostate and colon cancers, and also contain another antioxidant, beta carotene, which is what gives tomatoes their red color and even more anti-cancer power.

Then in our exuberance (another of the tomato paradoxes) to fulfill the great demand for the healthful and delicious vegetable year round, tomatoes actually started to become less healthful and less delicious. Picked green (devoid of the beta carotene red) and "gassed" for preservation during shipping, tomatoes arrived in the supermarket an anemic pink shadow of the real thing; tasting like, well, not really tasting at all. Perhaps this is why tomatoes have remained so popular in home gardens.

This adulteration of the tomato would initiate a small but continuing revolution to bring back the tomato as it had been: tasty and brimming with nutritional value. Some of the smaller growers could respond to the tomato taste issue by revitalizing the old varieties, heirloom tomatoes. Heirlooms are "open-pollinated"—as opposed to being hybridized—tomatoes that have been in existence for at least fifty years and often have been handed down through families or communities. Heirlooms tend to be more flavorful than hybrids and come in a wider range of shapes—including scalloped, lobed, and heart-shaped—and different colors, too, such as striped, chocolate-brown, black-red, purple, and yellow. They have wonderful names that often tell their history: the Radiator Charlie's Mortgage Lifter variety was developed by Charlie Byles, who kept a radiator repair shop in West Virginia in the 1930s and, yes, paid off the mortgage through revenue derived from the big tomato's transplants.

Lifting mortgages they might have done, but unfortunately heirloom tomatoes often became history for very real reasons. Almost by definition, they don't have the shipping durability of their picked-green distant cousins; and since they are field tomatoes they are confined—at least in the northern climates—to a short growing season. And, as Dave Chapman points out, heirlooms also don't do well in greenhouses—once a field tomato, always a field tomato.

After Chapman's initial greenhouse disaster, it was as if the gauntlet had been thrown. "It took ten years to get it down," Dave said. "Farming is *very* unforgiving." First he tried expanding the farm. He'd built the greenhouse, continued with the roadside stand, still had bedding crops (such as flowers), sold produce at the farmers' markets, and owned four tractors for working the fields. He did have some success.

"But the business was very complex. I carried a clipboard more than a hoe," Dave recalled. "Then when my son arrived I wanted to cut my work schedule from eighty hours a week. I saw that father farmers weren't very involved with their kids—a field operation can be okay for older kids, but babies don't integrate well into a farm routine. So that first year with my son, when I cut my work week to sixty hours, that was my next disaster."

David thought that perhaps an organic greenhouse operation could provide the solution to his father-farmer dilemma. Organic greenhouses for just tomatoes would be less complex— a lot of responsibility, but easier to manage, with a simpler annual routine.

The seedlings come from Holland in October. They're put into compost plugs for ten days, then grafted onto root stock and planted in six-inch pots. The plants get pinched back and then planted in the ground around Christmastime. So from the end of December through March the plants grow, and then by early spring the tomatoes begin to be harvested. This schedule provided employees nearly year-round work—there'd be no stopping and starting up again or having to retrain green crews every year. So Chapman decided to give up the stand, the field operation, and switch to an entirely greenhouse operation. That was in 1995. It was a bit like starting all over again: "It rendered so much of what I knew—and had been doing—obsolete."

He went to Holland on a Working Land Fund grant to see how big greenhouses worked. There the average-size greenhouse operation is ten acres.

"It was a steep learning curve," he said. He went on to say that taste was not particularly an issue for many commercial organic growers. "I had to pick my way through the seeds that could be grown in a greenhouse on a large scale organically and still produce a flavorful tomato. If you did ten things right but two things wrong, you'd have a disaster. Every year you'd learn a lot, but you'd worry it'd be like the old saying: 'By the time you learn to swing the scythe well, you're too old to be able to swing it.'"

That was ten years ago. Now Long Wind Farm has one acre under glass and two-thirds of an acre under plastic. It maintains a work force of fifteen people year-round, with a general manager, plus greenhouse, marketing, and packing managers. Long Wind is one of the largest organic tomato greenhouse operations in the country. And the business can thrive in Vermont, where the organic classification is more stringently upheld than in many areas of the country.

Long Wind ships boxes of tomatoes to warehouses in Massachusetts and Connecticut, and now 99 percent of the farm's business is wholesale. Legal Seafoods, a restaurant chain on the East Coast, actually approached Long Wind directly— the owner is a real tomato fan—and distributes the Long Wind tomatoes to all Legal Seafoods restaurants, from Boston to Washington, D.C. According to Dave, Long Wind built its wholesale business mostly by word of mouth.

"Having a genuinely good product makes it easier to talk stores into taking it. Another selling point is that greenhouse tomatoes are often sweeter than field tomatoes. The challenge is to be consistently good."

For me, Long Wind tomatoes have definitely stayed consistently good. I can no longer buy them, of course, at a farm-stand or at the farmers' market—now they have little stickers that say "Long Wind Farm" and are in the organic food section of the grocery store. But there are certain times—when it's late summer and the greenhouse tomatoes are plentiful and so, too, are tomatoes in general—that a hand-scrawled sign goes up in front of Long Wind's boarded-up stand that reads: "Canning tomatoes for sale. Compost for sale." I know then I can stop and get a box of tomatoes for five dollars.

I drive down the dirt side road, passing by plastic greenhouses and sheds, and enter a wood building attached to the big glass greenhouse and see the packers working at tables. They are talking and laughing and occasionally hold a tomato to a five-inch square grading device—a Dave Chapman invention—made of masonite with two different-sized holes in it.

Behind the packers is a curtain of plastic shielding fifty-two rows of tomato plants that are being quietly tended. Vines are bunched together, forming a long, fat, leafless cable that runs along the baseboard of the greenhouse wall. Then on a staggered basis, each vine is carried on a string upward so the top of the plant is about twelve feet high or more, floor to ceiling, and the plant resembles Jack's beanstalk. Lower trusses and leaves are pruned to help aerate, keeping the plants healthy, while truss clips are used to hold the heavy fruit tight and firm to the vine so it doesn't break off. A rail runs between each row that serves both as heating element—via hot water—and as a track for a battery-run trolley that carries the pickers and plants' caretakers not only down the row but aloft to the glass ceiling and to the uppermost fruit. The tomatoes are hand-picked daily according to their color. There is netting draped in the areas where the tomato leaves don't provide enough shade. And an energy cloth for holding heat in is neatly folded around the perimeter of the glass ceiling, close to the louvered vents. A mist of water can be released up high while irrigation pipes run down low at near-compost level. Here and there among the leaves and fruit are boxes of bumblebees left to pollinate at will, and then an occasional sulfur pot to prevent mildew from developing. I know, too, there must be a snake or two in there to keep the rats away. It is humid and has the nice, earthy smell of sun-warmed tomatoes.

On my most recent visit to talk with Dave Chapman, I drove past the big greenhouse, past the field with mounds of compost, to the very end, where the road turned into a short driveway that curved to a stop in front of a wood-shingled house, the Chapman-Henrion home, with porches side and front. I was early and sat in a rocker on the porch to wait. I watched the cats saunter about the various outbuildings and listened to a dog bark randomly from somewhere inside the house. A light breeze first gently blew my hair and then pushed on to rustle the leaves of the weeping willow trees at the front of the house. I saw David Chapman walking down the road, coming from the greenhouses toward me.

It had been five years since I last spoke with him, and he was quick to remind me of his wariness of journalists.

"I have mixed feelings about publicity; in fact, I actively avoided publicity," he said. "It's because Long Wind fills a tiny crack in a big market, a crack that can easily be filled. It's the art of the possible, you know: if he can do it, I can do it too."

Fortunately, this guarded beginning to our conversation was interrupted by an alarm, which was actually the telephone ringing. Dave picked up the cordless:

"Yes, go ahead and close the vents in Rolling Thunder and then go to a computer and disable the Rolling Thunder rain alarm." He hung up.

"Rolling Thunder?" I queried.

David explained that Rolling Thunder greenhouse was so named because originally the whole house was on rollers—actually on golf balls—and could move back and forth, and as it moved made a noise like thunder. The purpose was to rotate the soil, but as the greenhouse became larger it became impossible to move, so rotation is now accomplished with a shovel.

"And how did you come up with that concept?" I asked.

"I saw it in a book that Eliot lent me; it was an old glass moving greenhouse in Holland. Knowing how to use mentors is a key skill for learning—Eliot Coleman, Dave Ryell, a hydroponics grower, and a Dutch consultant were my mentors and provided me with lots of information. And information, after all, is what drives every enterprise and innovation."

But David also talked about learning from mistakes. In 1998 Long Wind had a major white fly infestation and he had to pull his crop early.

"We don't have a chemical safety net like our hydroponics brethren, who when they get in too deep can just 'nuke' 'em. Biocontrol means a totally different paradigm." David explained, "Hydro folks can tolerate a certain amount of white fly. That's not possible for organic growers; the threshold is different. We had to come up with a strategy—a written strategy—so it never would happen again. Everyone told me what I'd done should have prevented white fly from occurring, but you can't really follow the advice of someone who has a chemical safety net. You have to draw your own conclusions. So I wrote a twenty-page strategy that maintains a balance and basically stops the problem before it's a problem. White flies have a lot of predators, but if you have to buy a million predators, it's too late. It's really very simple. Around here we call it the 'sheep suit' solution."

"The 'sheep suit' solution?"

He smiled. "There is a Gary Larson cartoon that pictures two wolves standing in gorilla suits, gorilla heads in hand, watching as the herd of sheep runs away. One wolf says to the other: 'I got it. Sheep suits!'"

As Dave suggested, and Gary Larson illustrated, some solutions are blindingly obvious and simple: like wearing a disguise that makes the hunter part of the hunted pack. You want to be able to get close to the sheep, not frighten them away with a gorilla suit. Dave's solution for white fly was to never tolerate *any* flies and certainly never get to the point of needing predators.

"But," he added, "it's not that obvious unless you understand the problem and can immediately transform. Our strategy has worked: we've had no disasters since the white fly problem. At least with farms you get totally clear feedback: Are we in business next year?... Actually, I'm quite conflicted. Some days I like Long Wind Farms, some days I want to give it up. I really don't feel like most other farmers; I'm not as focused on the farm. I spend a good amount of time with my family and have a lot of other interests. Claudia is a Tai Chi instructor and I'm very engrossed in Tai Chi. But Long Wind has been more interesting in the last five years. Businesses all have problems, but the sign of a good business is if the problems are more interesting—good problems. Long Wind's problems are good now because they're less about putting fires out and more about improving the system and production. They're more about how to make things better. I've been thinking about building another greenhouse. It's good to expand the business, but risky. At age fifty-three, I have to ask how much energy—juice—can

I give to the business. I hope it doesn't lay waste to our lives. But I can do it."

I realized as David talked about Long Wind Farm how much he really was like other farmers—or at least the artisan farmers I know. He said the source of the superior flavor of Long Wind tomatoes is determined, of course, by plant variety and then by soil, water, and light level. Like other artisan farmers, he's a bit of a philosopher, an optimist in his own way, and, most important, he understands the value of *terroir*, the sense of place and the range of local influences—water, air, soil, weather, geography—that transmit to a food and create its character and goodness. It is the concert of those elements, their control and management in an artful way, that produces fabulous flavor.

David's one break from his fellow growers is that—unlike Lou Crawford (see page 7) or Steve Wood (page 127)—he really doesn't like the process of growing and has little passion for the plant itself. Much of what he does in the greenhouse is to try to confine and control the unruly tomato.

Remember he said: "I like to eat tomatoes, but not to grow them."

This dichotomy is acceptable—we are, after all, talking about the always dichotomous tomato. And acceptable, too, because in the end we know that what's important and relevant is that Chapman loves to eat tomatoes. So he's then driven to meet the challenges and grow the sweetest, most flavorful tomato. He does it to satisfy his passion, and, lucky us, ours then is gratified too.

{ CHICKEN MARENGO }

Julia Child gives a wonderful description of the origins of chicken Marengo in her book *From Julia Child's Kitchen*, in which she describes how Napoleon's chef invented the dish in the battlefield "with whatever was to be had in the neighboring Italian countryside. What the 'whatever' was, besides chicken and tomatoes, no one can really say since it was never formally catalogued." This leaves the lid off for all cooks to concoct their own version of chicken Marengo; which is what I've done here, with strong reference to Julia's recipe and *The Joy of Cooking*. Be creative with this dish; just remember that to be a chicken Marengo it must have chicken and, of course, tomatoes.

Serves 8.

1 small onion, thinly sliced
½ cup olive oil
1 large frying chicken, cut into quarters
1 pound shrimp
½ cup vermouth
2 cloves garlic, pressed
1 tablespoon chopped fresh thyme
1 bay leaf
Parsley sprigs
1 cup chicken stock
2 cups coarsely chopped Roma tomatoes
1 pound mushrooms
16 or 20 small white pearl onions
4 tablespoons (½ stick) unsalted butter
Juice of 1 lemon
1 cup pitted olives
Salt and freshly ground black pepper
Splash of cognac

In a skillet over medium heat, sauté the sliced onion in a bit of the oil for 3 to 4 minutes until translucent. Add the chicken and more oil and brown the chicken on all sides for about 8 to 10 minutes. Remove the chicken to a plate, add more oil to the pan if necessary, and sauté the shrimp until just pink, about 3 minutes.

Return the chicken to the pan and add the vermouth, garlic, thyme, bay leaf, parsley, stock, and tomatoes. Cover and simmer for about 1 hour, until the chicken is cooked through.
Remove the chicken and shrimp to the plate, strain the sauce

through a fine-mesh sieve, return it to the pan, and cook over high heat for 5 minutes to reduce the sauce.

Preheat the oven to 350 degrees. In a separate pan, sauté the mushrooms and pearl onions in the butter and lemon juice until softened. Arrange the chicken, shrimp, mushrooms, onions, and olives in a large earthenware baking dish and season with salt and pepper. Sprinkle with the cognac. Add the sauce and bake for about 15 minutes, until heated through. Serve with rice.

{ SUN-DRIED TOMATOES }

Sun-dried tomatoes are, of course, simply tomatoes that have been dried in the sun. Historically, in Italy, this has been accomplished by halving Roma tomatoes (or any other meaty tomato), seeding them, and then drying them on a screen, very often on a rooftop. In this country, where the hot sun can be less predictable and intense than around the Mediterranean, the drying is often done artificially in an electric food dehydrator or in the oven. If you would like to experiment with making your own sun-dried tomatoes, here's how:

If you can, use tomatoes from your garden or a farmers' market. Besides Roma, the cherry tomato varieties of Sweet 100s and Red Currants are good for drying. Halve each tomato or cut them into $3/8$ -inch-thick slices. Spray a wire rack with nonstick cooking spray and place the tomatoes close together, but not touching, on the rack; sprinkle with a bit of kosher salt.

Dry in the oven at 135 degrees for 6 to 8 hours if they are slices, 10 to 15 hours if they are halves.

Let the tomatoes cool, then store them in the freezer or let them dry for another week in a glass jar—to eliminate any further moisture—and then pack in air-tight glass jars and store in a cool, dark place.

Alternatively, the dried tomatoes can be preserved in olive oil, which has the pleasant bonus of producing tomato-flavored olive oil—a nice addition to many recipes.

Here's what to do: In a small jar, put 3 garlic cloves, peeled and sliced, along with a bit of white vinegar—enough to cover—and let stand for 12 hours at room temperature.

Rinse about 2 cups of the dried tomatoes in a colander with more white vinegar, drain them well, and pat dry. Sprinkle the tomato halves with 1/2 teaspoon dried basil and 3/4 teaspoon dried oregano, then pack them in a sterilized pint jar, cover with olive oil, and seal.

Keep in the refrigerator for a week or so before using; the tomatoes will keep, refrigerated, for up to several months.

LEAPING GOAT CHEESE

{ VERMONT BUTTER & CHEESE }

BURLINGTON IS VERMONT'S only true city, and a small, faraway one at that, yet its proximity to Montreal and Quebec's French influence, along with the cosmopolitan effect of the University of Vermont, makes Burlington gastronomically quite sophisticated. So despite the fact that I'd not met Allison Hooper or tasted her goat cheese, I accepted her invitation to dinner at a Burlington restaurant and looked forward to a good meal. The drive north to the top of Vermont is a spectacularly beautiful hour-and-a-half drive from my home in New Hampshire and is the stuff of summer sightseer and autumn leaf-peeper dreams as the highway passes through fields of bucolic majesty and the foothills of the Green Mountains. The ride reminded me that Vermont is indeed still dairy country, and supports not only family farms but encourages, through state organizations and tax benefits, craft and rural businesses-makers of artisanal foods. Maybe there was potential for cheese artistry here, and maybe Allison was one of its practitioners. But I confess I had some deeply ingrained doubts about Vermont cheesemakers.

As a born and bred Midwesterner, I was very provincial when it came to cheeses. I grew up eating exclusively Wisconsin cheese and then as an adult spent time deep "behind the cheddar curtain" writing about what I considered to be the very seat of American cheesemaking. Wisconsin was then, and is still, this country's largest cheese-producing—natural and processed—state. Wisconsin's cheese production and reputation is closely followed by those of California, where as early as 1979 Laura Chenel was championing the art of making fine goat cheese.

I first heard about Allison Hooper when I met her husband at a fund-raising event in Vermont, and he'd said to me simply, "She makes terrific goat cheese—and she's been doing it since 1984." It was the mid-1990s when I met Don Hooper, and you could count the number of Vermont cheesemakers, of any type, on one hand—well, maybe two. A good goat cheese from Caolifornia or Wisconsin I could see, but it seemed improbable that a goat cheese made by a first-generation Vermonter could possibly approach cheese artistry.

The small, white-tablecloth restaurant was in downtown Burlington, on Lake Champlain's waterfront. It was crowded when I entered. I asked for Allison and was told she'd not yet arrived, and was handed a menu and a press kit about Vermont Butter & Cheese. Every course—from hors d'oeuvres to dessert—was thoughtfully designed around one of Allison's products: phyllo flowers of smoked salmon and herbed mascarpone; shrimp, impastata, and quark (similar to a yogurt) crepe; Grand Marnier rolled chèvre; and a pecan-crusted pork tenderloin with a cranberry and pear crème fraîche sauce, served with a goat's milk cheddar risotto cake.

In short order, a pretty, fair-haired woman appeared; she was not large but had a strong sturdiness to her build. Somewhere in her mid-thirties, she was clearly the star of the show. As bright and natural-looking as her cheeses, Allison had packed the restaurant with her adoring cheese fans—and me. Soon I learned what there was to adore: I grazed first on the straight cheese samples of bonne-bouche (an ash-covered aged goat cheese) and fontina and then moved happily on to the set menu. Everything was exquisite. There was a subtle intensity in Allison's cheeses that I hadn't experienced since, when? In Wisconsin? Maybe never? "Artisanal cheeses," Allison said, "have distinctive flavors depending on where they're made." Yes, her cheeses are made in rural Vermont at Vermont Butter & Cheese, where aged cheeses are ladled into molds by hand and fontina is washed with salt water and turned by hand as it ages. But it's not *just* about the place—I know, I've been to cheese-Hollywood Wisconsin—it's also about the cheese creators. And

I clearly was just beginning to understand the depth of Allison's passion for cheese.

In 1980 Allison spent the spring term of her junior year in college abroad, studying French and living in Paris. At the conclusion of the term she decided to stay the summer, which meant attempting to cover living expenses without work papers. Through the French organic farmers' association, she contacted several farmers and asked them to put her to work in exchange for room and board. She spent six weeks on a tiny Brittany farm—returned the following summer as well—where the floor was dirt and refrigeration primitive but where she learned to make great goat cheese and more.

Her time in France was truly formative: she was staying with people who not only lived off their land, but lived very close to it. The woman of the farm made a cornucopia of cheeses—crème fraîche and quark—while her husband made pâté and tended the twelve Jersey cows, twelve ewes, a herd of goats, and chickens and pigs. With access to homemade cheese and a kitchen garden, their fabulous meals were nothing short of culinary art. What Allison saw in her French hosts was that lovely meshing of food with everyday life, a connectedness to that which nourishes, and nourishes more than the body.

After her summers in Brittany, and then another summer of cheese-making apprenticeship in the Alps, Allison returned to her New Jersey home and for a time kept goats and made cheese for sale in New York City. The New Jersey period hardly satisfied her desire for that world of connected food, but it did demonstrate that producing goat cheese was a viable business. She moved to Vermont—where she'd summered as a child— because "it seemed like a cheese-friendly kind of place." To her dismay she found that, despite its reputation as a dairy state, in Vermont that meant only cows. There were no commercial-size goat herds.

Allison took a day job working for the Vermont Department of Agriculture, as a dairy lab technician, and it was there she met Bob Reese. As marketing director, one of Bob's jobs was to connect local farmers and food producers with chefs who would incorporate Vermont-made products into their menus. Bob was putting together a special dinner event at the restaurant at the Top Notch resort in Stowe, Vermont. The chef there, Anton Flory, needed goat cheese and, of course, it had to be Vermont-made. Allison made a small batch of her chèvre. The chef raved; the guests raved. "Everyone was drunk," Allison laughs modestly. "That was our first market research." Just as Alice Waters's very first specialty purveyor, Laura Chenel, was a producer of fine, local Sonoma goat cheese, so too, for Allison Hooper, it was a great chef who opened the door of acceptance for her chèvre. (About three-quarters of Vermont Butter & Cheese products today still go directly to professional kitchens.)

Bob remembers that his wife, Sandy, turned to him at the dinner and said, "Why don't you and Allison go into business together?" Although Allison admitted that when Bob first approached her with the partnership idea, her first question was: "And what's your last name again?"

Allison was twenty-five, Bob was twenty-nine, and she confesses, "In 1984 we were young and could take many more chances than if we started it today. Cheese making is a very tiring job, long hours, quite physical. I was very single-minded. I didn't have any other responsibilities." Each partner committed $1,000. They got $4,000 from the agricultural loan committee of the United Church of Christ and an $8,000 loan from the local bank to start Vermont Butter & Cheese. And they worked very hard.

Finding an established and good-quality source of goat's milk was the first problem. Don Hooper, who had a small farm in Brookfield, Vermont, did keep a hobby-size herd of goats, bottling some of the milk, and he wanted someone else to use what was left. "He allowed us to set up operation at the farm for free," Allison said, "and I could finally make a little goat cheese." (She later married Don, of course, and the farm became her home.)

Yet back then only three goat herds existed in Vermont. Allison was forced, if she wanted to make a business out of her goat cheese, not only to help develop commercial-size herds but also to spend a whole lot of her time in a pickup truck. In order to get enough goat's milk she was driving twice a week from one end of the state to the other to pick up about fifty gallons of milk from hobby herds. Each trip produced just sixty-five pounds of cheese. They boiled the milk themselves in the milk house and chilled the cheeses in an old soda cooler.

Goat's milk, besides its rarity in Vermont at the time, had another problem: it's a seasonal commodity and, of course, bank loan payments are not, which meant that Bob and Allison needed to find a year-round product line. In classic small, Vermont family-farm fashion, a local dairy, Booth Brothers, offered Allison the cream that was separated out in its skim milk process on an "extended credit" basis. Vermont Butter & Cheese expanded to include cow's milk-based products like crème fraîche, quark, mascarpone, and fromage blanc, and today the cow's milk products constitute 68 percent of the business.

Allison *loved* her life as a cheese maker. She loved the entire process, from getting the animals' milk, to making the cheese, to selling it to someone who appreciated eating it and cooking with it. It had that circular, connected sense she'd been searching for: "It's thrilling for me when my cheese can succeed in creating a presence in someone's mind. And then when the connections become so far reaching that a company like Bread & Circus [a Boston-based chain of natural and gourmet food stores] says, 'We want to buy cheese from her.'"

Allison and Bob's venture was blessed with some near-perfect timing. There were a few good natural cheeses being made in Vermont, New York, California, and Wisconsin in the 1960s and '70s, but the artisanal cheeses were so few in number as to be invisible. In the early 1980s goat cheese was difficult to find, and what could be found was a product of France and usually expensive. But then Alice Waters, whom Craig Claiborne called "that great American rarity, a deservedly celebrated native-born chef," and famous for championing the use of good, fresh, local products, helped to change that: in one of her earliest cookbooks, *Chez Panisse Pasta, Pizza, and Calzone*, published in 1984, she validated the fledgling California goat cheese industry by calling for both a French *and* a Sonoma (Laura Chenel's) goat cheese in one recipe, implying equality with differences, and creating a demand for the domestic cheese. Waters and Chenel inspired the use of specialty, natural, and local cheeses and gave American-made goat cheese credibility. It was the same year Allison and Bob started Vermont Butter & Cheese.

However, for most of us American cheese still meant *processed* American cheese. It could come in powdered form, either flagman orange or lint white in color, or rubbery squares that were always overpackaged—in multiple cellophane sheets or foil envelopes in a box—and often required no refrigeration. But in whatever form, it was processed and usually carried the Kraft label. Kraft was synonymous with cheese and growing up in America. After all, Kraft sponsored a TV show, *and* manufactured "mac and cheese," every American kid's favorite lunch-in-a-box and often their first entrée into cooking. Kraft also revolutionized the cheese business and in so doing made cheese history.

In 1918 Swift, Armour, Wilson, and Cudahy were the largest cheese distributors in the country until J. L. Kraft patented his cheese-processing formula in the early 1920s. With a greatly extended shelf life and user-friendly attributes, it's no wonder Kraft's cheese quickly became the rage. Technically, processed cheese is bits of pasteurized cheddar and other natural cheeses combined with emulsifiers and turned into a smooth fluid with all bacterial curing completely arrested. The processing makes the cheese very stable, and without the curing its flavor never develops or changes. By the 1930s, Kraft had become so big that the natural cheese business had to acknowledge the importance of processed cheese. More than 256 million pounds of processed cheese were being produced, 40 percent of all cheese made in the United States. (Today about one-fifth of all cheese produced in the United States is processed.) More important than volume was that the processed stuff established cheese as a food staple, causing an increase in per capita consumption and elevated sales for all—both processed and natural—cheeses. Kraft had used technology to industrialize cheese and make it very big business.

Kraft was headquartered in Chicago, an hour from the Wisconsin border, and that was not an accident. Wisconsin is dairy central and has been for generations; more important for Kraft, however, the state excelled in making the cheeses most appropriate for processing, cheddar and Swiss. Yankee farmers from New York, Vermont, New Hampshire, and Connecticut had come to Wisconsin in the 1830s and brought with them their cheese-making skills, which tended toward the cheddar line. In 1841 Anne Pickett established the state's first cheese factory; in 1874 Joseph Steinward, from Colby, Wisconsin, developed colby cheese; and around 1875 John Jossi created from Limburger a new cheese he called brick. In 1890 Stephen Babcock, of the University of Wisconsin, developed the milk-fat test to determine the richness of milk, a critical element in cheese production. By 1922, Wisconsin had 2,800 cheese factories and was poised for what Kraft was going to do to the business of cheese. Today, the state ranks third in the world for total cheese production. Wisconsin produces more cheddar than any other state—or any other country—in the world.

Certainly Kraft's cheese-processing technology contributed to Wisconsin's ability to produce cheese in this kind of volume. But processed cheese is by design predictable. While predictability—that cornerstone of all processed food—may be comfortable, it also imposes a kind of universal sameness. And sameness in food makes it so you simply don't consider it. In my childhood of the 1950s, cheese was just benignly there—maybe melting into a pizza or dusting the spaghetti or adding bulk to a ham sandwich—but cheese rarely moved radically left from its intrinsic blandness.

Natural cheeses, on the other hand, are the complete opposite of bland or benign. Sid Carr, of Carr Valley Cheese in LaValle, Wisconsin, a fourth-generation cheese maker, speaks of his naturally bandaged aged cheddar with a quiet reverence in his voice, whispering as if in church, "Cheeses are living, and so they constantly change." And as he tastes his favorite aged cheddar (a hefty six-monther) his eyes water slightly and roll toward the ceiling. "You should feel the tingle around your eyes," he says dreamily. It's all about taste.

Certainly it's about taste with Limburger cheese. I once went to visit the last remaining U.S. producer of Limburger cheese, Chalet, in Monroe, Wisconsin, which makes over a million pounds of Limburger each year. Limburger is a very strong cheese that has the unfortunate reputation of smelling like dirty socks. This does not deter the lovers of Limburger, whose appreciation of the sock smell and the cheese's flavor is at best considered enlightened, and at worst bizarre. Monroe boasts not only the lone remaining Limburger plant, but Baumgarten's Restaurant, which specializes in a Limburger, onion, and mustard on rye sandwich that definitely means to challenge the blandness of a grilled American cheese. Again, it's about flavor.

One time I asked Errico Auricchio, of the Italian-based Auricchio cheeses, why he had brought his family and five Italian cheese makers to Denmark, Wisconsin, in 1979 to make Italian cheeses. He said, "If you want to make movies you go to Hollywood; if you want to make cheese you go to Wisconsin." But probably more pertinent than reputation, Errico admitted, was the quality of Wisconsin milk, which is considerably better, higher in fat and protein, and therefore has a more pleasing flavor.

Certainly Allison Hooper would agree: quality of milk is a determining factor in a cheese's taste. Now Allison buys milk from some twenty-five different family farms and is adamant about supporting "Vermont's working landscape of agriculture." She devotes one day a week to quality issues such as herd health, genetics, and ultimately the fat and protein levels of the milk. She rewards those farmers who supply her with better-quality milk by paying a premium for it.

Goat cheese became popular not only because of its fine flavor, visual appeal, and versatility, but for comparative health reasons, too. *Health* magazine stated: "Stacked up against other soft cheeses, like cream cheese and Brie, goat cheese is a far healthier choice. It's significantly lower in calories, cholesterol, and fat, and it's an equally good source of calcium."

Vermont Butter & Cheese grew 25 to 30 percent each year of the company's first decade. For the first nine years Allison made all the cheese alongside just a few employees. Today twenty people work at Vermont Butter & Cheese, four as cheese makers, and they use about two million pounds of milk and make 450,000 pounds of goat cheese—and they moved out of the farm and into a new building in a Vermont version of an industrial park. And they're still expanding.

In 2000 the company began churning its own butter— "Well, we had to," Allison said, referring to the company's name. Already it's one of the finest cultured butters available, immediately ribboning at the 2001 American Cheese Society conference in Louisville, Kentucky. And more recently the company's Vermont cultured butter was the winner of the 2004 Summer Fancy Food contest in the category of "Outstanding Cheese or Dairy Product." Allison Hooper says that despite her multiple awards from various competitions she realizes that these honors have little or no effect on the individual consumer's opinion of her products. "Contests are more helpful to the distributors," Allison explains. "It validates the product if it does well in a contest." Perhaps, then, the better compliment paid to her butter came from the Breton chef who was hired by Vermont Butter & Cheese to consult on the first batches. "This is the butter of my childhood," she said, "Don't change a thing."

Competitions are a way of life in the cheese business, and interestingly it was at a cheese competiton in Wisconsin that I first became aware of the "struggle to mimick Europe," as Allison describes the plight of American cheese makers. On a March morning cold enough to make Vince Lombardi proud, I trudged through Green Bay to the Luv-It Creamery to attend the 1996 World Championship Cheese. There, in a long and narrow refrigerated warehouse, the judges had been divided into ten teams of two, one U.S. and one international judge each. Eighteen countries and twenty-three states had sent cheese entries. It was the largest number of entries in the thirty-nine-year history of the contest—787 cheeses, over eight thousand pounds—all needing to be assessed. At the end of the fourth day of tasting—which involves only tasting and spitting, no swallowing—the judges announced the winners. It was an international sweep: a Danish blue, a cheddar from Quebec, and a Gouda from the Netherlands won first place. I wondered what deficiencies the judges saw in the American cheeses? Later at the airport when I sat waiting to board for my return to New England, I happened to recognize two of the competition judges, also waiting, and decided to query them about the contest results. They looked suspicious of me, perhaps because I was clutching my foam-rubber cheesehead hat—versatile enough to convert into a serving caddy for beer and potato chips in the hollow where your head normally goes. But with my complimentary acknowledgment of them—and the promise of anonymity—they told me that the United States was at least twenty years behind Europe in the skill and technology of cheese making, and both totally dismissed all possibility of American cheeses ever approaching the realm of art.

Since the source of Allison's goat cheese expertise began in Europe, I wondered what her opinion was of French goat cheese versus her own. She thought for a moment: "Yes, I think the French is probably better, but I think that's probably because I'm overly critical of my own. My cheese has a place and I embrace the differences. I feel we are successful when we can present what's real. But in America we have to constantly reassess our market to better understand what the American palate is looking for. Americans have come a long way in their cheese-eating habits—for example, they'll consider eating the rind now—yet still the French cheese maker has the advantage. He doesn't need to make adjustments to his product, or be concerned about distribution; his market is established and constant. There is a small town in France, Selles-sur-Cher, and the local cheese maker produces enough goat cheese weekly for eight thousand people, which is the exact population of the town, and he sells out every week!"

Allison explained to me that in France there is tremendous attention to detail. Every step in the cheese-making process is very precise and disciplined, and the artisans are knowledgeable and have great respect for the effects of time on a cheese. The cheese makers' knowledge is their legacy and is passed on to other generations. "I made mistakes," she said, "because I had to learn by trial and error. And if you start wrong, your mistakes get compounded in the aging process and it can be very costly. I had to stop making the bonne-bouche and the fontina because, as it turned out, I was making these aged cheeses too near the fresh cheeses—they were getting contaminated."

Allison will return to making her bonne-bouche soon—it means "good mouthful" and it is that—once they have completed building a separate area for the aged cheeses at Vermont Butter & Cheese: "Where it is warm and dry and can ripen the eight to ten days it takes to make a good rind, to eat. Now we are moving into a new level in America." She smiles.

This year I drove to Websterville, Vermont, to visit the Vermont Butter & Cheese operation during our northern New England mud season—or, as the rest of the world calls it, springtime—and when the company was in mid-construction. Not a pretty time, but as I opened the door to the plant I found myself standing in a tiny, cramped office where three women were holding a meeting; they were happy enough to multitask as receptionists and find Allison.

I've known Allison Hooper for more than ten years now and we greeted each other as old friends. We donned hairnets, booties, and white coats for a quick tour of the new plant and I immediately fell comfortably back into the realm of food processing—a realm I've known in one form or another all of my life. It is this cheese-making world, however, that I find particularly pleasant. The receiving room has large, fat hoses to carry the milk into a huge stainless-steel vat, culture and rennet are added, and then the milk begins to coagulate. Deep tubs sit nearby, where, after the culture has grown overnight, the curds and whey are separated. The curds are poured into bags with holes to allow the water to drain out. What rather magically remains is cheese. Of course, everything is spanking clean and, because it is a cheese factory, it smells warm and sweet and is small and simple in design. Whether here in Vermont or in Wisconsin, the world of cheese looks the same—always modest and homey. We pass through to the butter-churning room, where they can make eight hundred pounds at a time, and then to where they hand-pack—with a bit of help from a machine—

the logs of goat cheese. We end the tour with a look at the not-yet-operational aging room and the attached gallery for school-children to view the process. Back in the office she shares with Bob, Allison and I talk.

"I want to make the best goat cheese in America," Allison says. "I don't need it to be on every table, maybe just in every New York restaurant," she laughs. "Mostly I want to have the confidence that it will always be good. I know I can't truck Vermont to people, but I can truck cheese to them and bring them the character of Vermont."

Cheese does have a way of making those who love it rather chauvinistic about the place where it's made. As Errico, Allison, and others tell us, quality milk is vital to good cheese flavor. So then a contented, bucolic place—easy for cow, goat, and farmer to love—becomes critical too. Author Clifton Fadiman once described cheese as "milk's leap into immortality."

But it is the cheese maker who ultimately causes the leap. It is her ability to connect us with the place, create a flavor profile for us that is sublime, that has character and is distinctly her own—that is the art. I taste Allison's chèvre. It is not the tingle of Sid's aged cheddar. Nor is it Chalet's Limburger, with its vapors shooting from taste buds into sinuses to effect a "cheese high." Nor is it the extremely subtle, substantial, and expected French goat cheese. Allison's goat cheese is clean and clear in flavor, distinct, and, yes, it has a "real" quality to me. Actually I like to think that Allison made her goat cheese American, bright and new in taste, but reminiscent of the Old World, too. To me, Allison's cheese has made the leap.

{ GOAT'S MILK CHEDDAR-RISOTTO CAKES }

Serves 2 as a main course or 4 as a side dish.

½ cup minced white onion
1 small carrot, minced
1 teaspoon minced garlic
1 tablespoon olive oil
1 cup Arborio or long-grain rice
¼ cup white wine
¼ cup Marsala
2 cups chicken stock
2 teaspoons fresh thyme leaves
2 teaspoons minced fresh chives
1 teaspoon minced fresh rosemary
½ teaspoon salt
1 teaspoon ground white pepper
⅓ cup grated goat's milk cheddar
All-purpose flour for dusting

In a heavy skillet over medium heat, sauté the onion, carrot, and garlic in the oil until the onion is translucent. Add the rice and cook, stirring constantly, for 2 minutes. Stir in the white wine and Marsala and cook for 3 to 5 minutes, stirring occasionally, until reduced.

Add the stock and bring to a slow boil. Lower the heat, cover, and cook for 15 minutes, stirring occasionally. The risotto is done when most of the liquid is absorbed.

Remove from the heat and stir in the herbs, salt, and white pepper. Sprinkle with the goat's milk cheddar and stir gently to combine. Let cool to room temperature.

Dust your palms with flour and shape the risotto into small cakes. Reheat the cakes by placing them on a baking sheet in a 350-degree oven for 15 minutes or frying with butter until brown on both sides, about 3 minutes per side.

THEIR ONCE IN A
BLUE MOON SORBET

{ BLUE MOON SORBET }

ON A HOT June evening, dining at an outdoor café on the banks of New Hampshire's Mascoma River, I had my first taste of Blue Moon Sorbet. Eating Mango Passion that night was such a fabulous food event—a flavor explosion of jungle fruit, so tropical, sweet, and refreshing—that I can remember exactly where I was sitting, who I was with, the soft air, and how fun it was to be surprised by this sensational taste. Here was something that fulfilled my desire for end-of-the meal sugar, yet didn't even begin to make me regret I'd eaten the whole thing. The next delight came when the waitress told me that the Blue Moon line of sorbets—which then featured Mango Passion, Blackberry Lime, Grapefruit Campari, and Strawberry Daiquiri—was in my local grocery store. Back in the mid-1990s a supermarket's idea of frozen dessert was still predominantly the big blocks of ice cream, sometimes an expensive pint of vanilla with nuts and cherries in it, a lemon sherbet, or something cold on a stick. This stuff was different, or as it said clearly on the label: "Only in a Blue Moon does something this good come along." The Blue Moon label also told me the sorbets were made not far away, in Quechee, Vermont. I would pay a visit, and more than once.

Quechee is a tiny village perched along both sides of the Ottauquechee River, a few miles west of its natural wonder, the Quechee Gorge. It was founded in the 1760s as a mill town, back when mills were, by Industrial Revolution standards, relatively small. And like many very old towns, hints of why it came into being are still in evidence, and help to sustain its original personality. Unlike the neighboring town of Woodstock, with its

Rockefeller resort and perfect charm, Quechee is still an unpretentious place. Its most prominent business, the nationally known glass designer Simon Pearce, is housed in the one remaining old brick and wood fabric mill that sits peering over the Ottauquechee waterfall. On the other side of the falls is a row of small homes, one of which belongs to John Donaldson and Pamela Frantz, the inventors of Blue Moon Sorbet. John was the pastry chef at a Woodstock restaurant and Pamela worked there too, as a bartender, when they started the sorbet business—in their basement. It was in that basement that I first met John, a tall guy with a relaxed stance and eyeglasses that defied stylishness and looked like he'd owned them since the 1970s. Dressed in a thin flannel shirt, he was grinning as he told me how the idea of Blue Moon Sorbet came to him:

He was standing in front of the freezer case at the grocery store in 1994. "No one knew what sorbet really was then, and it was just all raspberry and strawberry, raspberry and strawberry, strawberry and raspberry. They were just so simple and boring. The first thought that came to my mind was why doesn't someone make something more interesting, like I make at the restaurant? And then the light bulb went on, 'Hey, we could do that!' I came home and told Pamela about it and she thought it was a great idea."

At the time, John was making desserts at the elegant Prince and Pauper restaurant. He said, "That's were I learned—experimenting with different flavors and combinations of fruits and liqueurs—to make a certain style of homemade sorbet and ice cream. I even made a saffron ice cream, which I thought was fabulous, but no one else did. Well, almost no one. It didn't go over especially well with the waitstaff, and if the waitstaff doesn't like it . . . well, the saffron ice cream sat around a couple of weeks and it became a big joke. So then it was Halloween night and the kids showed up at the back of the restaurant trick-or-treating and Chef gave them a big bowl of the saffron ice cream and finally got rid of it. I think they enjoyed it. It had good color."

When John initially started his ice experiments it was in the 1980s and the serving of sorbets was confined to fancy restaurants like the Prince and Pauper, and rarely a home event. It was still pretty unclear what course in the menu a sorbet would claim. Sometimes it wasn't served as dessert but between the escargot and the Dover sole to cleanse the palate. The etiquette of using sorbet as cleanser originated with the nineteenth-century French icon Chef Auguste Escoffier, and seems to have gone in and out of favor in America at various points in our haute cuisine timeline—the 1980s was an in-favor period. I remember first experiencing sorbet back then at an elegant hotel restaurant in Dallas. But for me the revival of the cleansing protocol was simply not on my Miss Manners or culinary radar. I wondered that night why I was being served sherbet—a dessert I'd not ordered—when I'd just finished the appetizer? The haute waiter detected my confusion—perhaps he'd seen it before— and whispered, "Sorbet. For the cleansing of Madame's palate." Ah, so this was not a sign that the meal was ending, but that there was something about the meal that demanded palate housekeeping. For a long time after that when I thought sorbet, I thought mouth cleaning, never dessert. Certainly this was not what John intended with his sorbets or for that matter what the inventors of sorbet had in mind for their delicacy.

Nearly a thousand years before the first ice cream, there was sorbet. Nero, that Roman emperor with a propensity for burning things, was not only into hot stuff but clearly appreciated cold: in the first century A.D. he had runners along the Appian Way bear buckets of snow from the mountains to his banquet hall, where it was mixed with honey and wine and served for dessert.

Fruit-flavored ices probably originated in China and were brought to Persia and other Asia Minor countries. When Richard the Lionhearted conquered the Saracen leader, Saladin, during the Third Crusade (1191), a peace offering was presented to Richard. It was a "charbet," which Saladin had made from snow brought from the mountains of Lebanon and flavored with fruit. And when Marco Polo returned from China at the end of the thirteenth century he brought recipes for concoctions of snow, juice, and fruit pulp.

Many food historians believe that Catherine de Medici, upon her marriage to the French dauphin Henri of Valois—he became Henri II in 1547—introduced *sorbetto* to the French. As the story goes, the fourteen-year-old Catherine brought her chef from Florence with her to Paris, and he made a different-flavored ice for each day of her wedding celebration. However, at least two noted food writers, Elizabeth David and Esther B. Aresty, point out that for various reasons—the least of which being that all of Catherine's kitchen staff was originally *from* France—it is unlikely that the gastronomically advanced French were introduced to sorbet by a teenage Italian girl. Nonetheless, royal support for sorbet vaulted it to dessert sensation status, and by 1576 there were 250 master ice makers in Paris. French cuisine—focusing on, perfecting, and almost obsessing over all that was *gastronomique*—defined and refined sorbet over the next two centuries.

Sorbet is French for "sherbet," but there is a difference between the two. Sorbets never contain cream or milk, but sometimes use egg whites to smooth the texture. An ice, or *granita* in Italian, is just that: a grainy-textured sorbet, which occurs because the water, sugar, and flavoring—usually a fruit, herb, wine, or coffee—are simply frozen. Sorbet, on the other hand, uses the same fruit flavoring—although often a more pulpy consistency—and in the freezing process is churned or whipped, much like when making ice cream.

William Blake recorded one of the first American ice cream experiences in Maryland in 1744. And ice cream appears throughout our early history, but there's never a mention of sorbet: from George Washington, who in the first summer of his presidency in New York, finding the heat unbearable, ordered $200 worth of ice cream; to Thomas Jefferson, who brought a *sorbetière* back from France not to make sorbet but to churn custard surrounded by ice and salt—ice cream.

Ice cream fed our love for dairy products: in 1924 an American's average annual consumption included 17.8 pounds of butter, 6.8 gallons of ice cream, and 350 gallons of liquid milk. Frankly, nondairy sorbet didn't have a chance against our passion for ice cream's fat and sugar content. Well, not until ice cream manufacturers, in a fit of cost-cutting measures, eliminated the very essence of what makes ice cream great. Using cheap ingredients such as stale-dated milk, returned then repasteurized and pumped with air, they cut out the very best part—the heavy, sweet cream—and with it went taste. Airy, bland ice cream was what became the standard and certainly what I grew up on in the 1950s and '60s. But when a generally more health-conscious public targeted fat and dairy intake as a problem (adding to the ever-present weight-watching issues), the stage was set for sorbet's surge in popularity.

John mentioned to me his own weight-control issues and the hazards of being a professional dessert maker: "I was eating my work," he confessed. "As a pastry chef I had to taste everything. And then sometimes one was left over and I couldn't just throw it away. I *had* to eat it. I ate a lot of mousses and tortes and heavy desserts. I was getting really fat and kept looking for something light to make for dessert. That's when I got interested in sorbets."

We were sitting at the dining room table in the Donaldson house, a pleasant, cozy home. Pamela was in the adjacent kitchen making coffee and could easily hear our conversation—adding to it now and then. John was talking about his life and how much of it had been spent in and around the food world. His dad worked for Standard Brands—a food company that eventually merged with Nabisco—and the family moved a lot. John was born in Peoria, Illinois, then moved to various suburbs of Chicago, went to high school in Montreal, and ended up going to Grove City College in Pennsylvania. After he finished college in 1973, he went to visit friends who were starting a restaurant in Bellows Falls, Vermont.

"They were just a bunch of hippies," he said. They found a building that was up a little set of stone steps. Twenty-five years earlier, it had been a restaurant, so John and his friends cleaned it up and turned it into the Stone Step. "We were good at cleaning," John laughed.

Like the others, he'd never been involved in a restaurant before, but he started working there as the breakfast cook. "We didn't know what we were doing and weren't making any money. We made everything there, baked our own bread. I was the bread slicer because I was the only one who could slice it straight. So I guess it was at the Stone Step that my interest in food and restaurants got piqued."

But the Stone Step didn't last long. John ended up working at several other restaurants until he decided in 1976 to attend the Culinary Institute of America. After CIA he went to work at Houlihan's, which then was only a small chain of twelve restaurants, and John ended up having to work in four different cities in three years. He'd done enough moving around in his life and so decided to quit Houlihan's and head back to Vermont. There he managed an egg roll factory in Putney—Mimi's Egg Rolls— a tiny company run by a Korean woman. John said, "All we did was make egg rolls all day long. We'd come in each morning, chop up some vegetables, throw them in woks. Wrap 'em in egg rolls, fry 'em, and sell them fresh all over Vermont from the back of a station wagon."

John's next job took him mid-state to cook at the Norwich Inn, where he met Pamela. She'd grown up in San Diego and left when she was eighteen to visit friends in the East. Pamela, a no-makeup kind of woman, with pleasing looks and long brown hair, spoke softly from the kitchen doorway: "I thought it was really great here and stayed." John left the Norwich Inn for the Prince and Pauper, and Pamela followed him there a few years later. This was the early 1980s: "When everyone went out to eat," Pamela recalled, "and before the big crash of no one eating out."

But Pam and John, after a decade of working at the Prince and Pauper, grew tired of working for other people and began discussing the idea of starting a home business. They researched the idea of a family specialty-food business, and then John had his epiphany in front of that ice cream case at the grocery store. They had a friend of a friend who owned a scoop shop and invited them to come down a couple times to see how he made ice cream. John said, "He was so open with us and told us everything. We mixed up some batches, experimented with different flavors, and went down and used his equipment."

Next they had to determine whether or not they had enough electric power to run the equipment and if the zoning permitted commercially producing sorbet in their basement. Then they bought, through an ad they'd seen in a trade magazine, a used Taylor 121 sorbet maker and hardening cabinet from an ice cream equipment dealer in Florida. "He sort of ripped us off because he sent us a smaller hardening cabinet than the bigger one we'd paid for. But since the machine is still working today, eleven years later, we've really gotten our money's worth there, so it sort of worked out," John said.

They spent a year experimenting with different flavors. Using as their base the French fruit purees that had been the key to the successful flavors John made at the Prince and Pauper, they settled on three sorbets to start off with: Mango Passion, Grapefruit Campari, and Red Raspberry. "We tried to make a tangerine and a cantaloupe ginger," Pamela explained. "Cantaloupe was really delicious, but we couldn't get consistently good fruit. And we had to squeeze the tangerines ourselves to get the best juice—everyone else oversqueezed the fruit, which made it taste of pith. We thought we'd eventually find good juice to buy, but never did."

Finally in 1995, they were ready to make their first batch of sorbet. John told me they went down in the basement, aprons on, and mixed up three batches of red raspberry—they can make two to two and a half gallons at a time in the machine—intending to make six or seven gallons of sorbet. "It took us all day long and was such a mess," he said. "We had no idea what we were doing and it was spilling all over—on the floor, all over walls, and all over ourselves. You don't remember that?"

John was looking at Pamela, who had a quizzical look on her face. "I don't remember it being that bad!"

"I remember it taking forever and ever. We started out so happy and at the end of the day, grrrrrr," John laughed. "It was a pretty loooong learning curve. Back then we were so concerned about every single pint being cleaned off and absolutely perfect. Now it takes ten minutes to make a batch. In a day we make forty batches—eighty to a hundred gallons—eight hundred pints in an eight-hour day. Well, yes, we still do care about that, but I guess we're just better at it."

"No, actually *we* don't do it anymore," Pamela said dryly. Their employees make the sorbet now.

"So *that's* why it works out so much better now!" John grinned.

In 1995, after the first year of basement production, they decided to take the next big step: John quit working at the restaurant. "It went to the point where you couldn't be doing anything else," Pamela recalled. "My memory's not so good on this, but one thing I won't forget is John saying, 'Just give me three months and then everything will be fine and then we'll be rich and famous.' But then three months went by and you were in so deep you couldn't turn back and you'd say, 'I better make this work' and you'd keep going. And it just keeps working and working and slowly working."

"I loved it, how about you?" John said.

"I kept my day job. And I still have a day job!" she answered.

They grew the business carefully and slowly, adding nine more flavors, two of which are seasonal—Apple Cider and Cranberry Orange. Most of their sorbets are made from the French fruit purees, with the exception of the Lemon Zest. "Only California lemons worked," John said. "Who knows why? We tried lemons from all over the world and nothing else had the right flavor."

In 2000 they were able to move production from their basement to a three-thousand-square-foot cinderblock building in White River Junction, Vermont. John gave me directions to the facility: "It's just up from that store 1,000 Gifts, next to the dog grooming place Raining Cats and Dogs that replaced the barbecue restaurant."

The space was on two levels, with the entire ground floor containing only a stairway and three large refrigeration units. Names had affectionately been given to the two freezers—Little Henry and Bessie. One of them is the same size as their whole operation in the basement. A climb up the stairs took us into the office space, decorated with a painted red floor and yellow trim. In one corner was a desk, a poster of the moon pinned behind it. The opposite corner was what John referred to as the art gallery. "We found all of these paintings at the dump," he told me incredulously. Next to the stack of paintings was an exercise machine—their "work-out area"—and a loom belonging to Christie, one of the two Blue Moon employees.

John took me into an adjoining area, where the sorbet is made. A clean, white room with the old Taylor standing prominently near the new Taylor. On a counter sat a big juice squeezer with crates of lemons nearby. And a huge kettle for mixing sat by the far wall; leaning against it was a giant wire whisk nearly as tall as I was. John walked immediately to the corner of the room and pulled back a massive wooden door to reveal what was clearly his prized possession: a dumbwaiter that was large enough to double as a freight elevator. John beamed as he made it go up and down. "It's like something out of a Frankenstein movie, but it certainly makes it easy to get the sorbet down to the ground floor and into the freezer. It comes out of the machine at twenty degrees and then goes into the walk-in to take it down to minus twenty. And then we put it in the truck."

Clearly, they had grown. Distributed throughout New England in places like Whole Foods and high-end grocery and gourmet shops, much of Blue Moon's growth had come from word of mouth.

As John put it, "We didn't really market it—it marketed itself. So I'd go out on the road with samples and spoons and try to get people to eat it. I found if they didn't actually taste it then they were reluctant, but once they tasted it they generally wanted it. Eventually people loved it so much, I'd walk in and they'd say, 'Oh, the sorbet guy. Great!' It was a boost to my ego."

"It seems to me it's better to do it this way," Pamela said, "to market slowly, stay in control. Do you know how much this stuff costs? I still do the books and am based in reality and the more mundane. But I get the same thing, 'Oh, I can't believe you *make* this stuff.' It's great having your own thing, I wouldn't trade that. That must be the addictive part of being an entrepreneur—it's yours. That is, if it's good."

Like all successful entrepreneurs, they also had a bit of luck. Emily Balducci, from the family of the famed New York gourmet shop, was skiing at Vermont's Stratton Mountain, bought the Blue Moon Blackberry Lime, and feel in love with it. She called and asked how she could get it in New York. "Well, it's in Dean & Deluca's (a Balducci competitor)," John told her. "Ahhh," she replied. "You're already going to Dean but not to Balducci!" It's now also carried at Balducci's.

John explained that their current distribution goes as far as he can drive. Though the next step would be to go to a distributor, there are advantages and disadvantages to that: unlike other frozen desserts, Blue Moon Sorbet doesn't have stabilizers in it. It needs to be closely watched and can't be left out of the freezer for long. Distributors handle so many products they can't keep an eye on it like John does, keeping it fresh and rotated. Of course the advantage of using a distributor is that they'd get a lot more business.

"But then we'd have to hire more people, buy more equipment, more storage, everything," John said. "And we'd be right back to where we are now financially. We'll try to grow into new markets—maybe drive as far as Washington and Baltimore, get more Whole Foods stores to carry us, and keep looking at the idea of getting a distributor—but there's still a huge market in New England and a lot of potential there."

"We'd like to grow the volume, too, by adding flavors," said Pamela. "We'd love to do a pomegranate, but you have to be cost efficient, and pomegranate juice is very expensive, so it's difficult to make it work. We might do a pineapple."

John added. "We'll stay with fruit flavors. Sorbet is traditionally a fruit product. Tea sorbet, for example, is not really sorbet to me. I've experimented with chocolate sorbet, but that's not really a sorbet either. But if we could make a good chocolate, I'd do it. Coconut's another flavor I'd like to try. But sorbet is supposed to be fat-free, that's its big advantage, and chocolate and coconut both have fat in them. You could make a fat-free chocolate sorbet, but what's the point of fat-free chocolate? It just doesn't work."

The conversation turns to what they would like to see happen with Blue Moon. Pamela said, "I always envisioned being a successful company when we could gainfully employ other people and could go on and create another business. Not always be the driver and bookkeeper and be more directing. I have no idea what that other business would be. I just want Blue Moon to be more self-sustaining."

"You mean you want to work less," John laughed.

"No that's your dream," Pamela retorted.

John added, "I want it to become successful enough so when we're ready to retire we can sell it or pass it on to the kids. I don't think either of the girls is interested, but you never know. It's more likely we'd sell it."

"It would be hard to let go," Pamela said softly.

"But we can't do it forever. We have to retire sometime," John returned.

"I guess you have to have things change so that they can continue," Pamela said, mostly to herself.

John turned to me and said, "We would hate to see it changed. We've always made it just like in the restaurant. You can't really charge what it's worth. Someone else might cut the amount of fruit and add coloring or flavoring. We put a lot of heart and soul into it and we like it the way it is. The quality of the product is really what we've been mostly interested in, producing a quality product. That's what gives us the most satisfaction and pride. Hopefully, we'll find someone just like us—crazy enough."

Yes, I would hate to see it changed too. I'd miss the heart and soul in it—and the craziness? Perhaps you do have to call John and Pamela—and others I write of here—a little crazy. But let's just refer to them as passionate instead—certainly it is a passion that produces an extraordinary taste.

{ MANGO LASSI }

Serves 4 to 6.

1 pint mango sorbet
1 quart vanilla yogurt

Let the sorbet soften slightly at room temperature. Place in a
blender with the yogurt and blend until smooth. Pour into
glasses. The lassi is best with spicy Indian food.

{ EASY ELEGANT DESSERT }

Serves 8.

1 pound cake (homemade or store-bought)
Raspberry sauce (see Note)
2 pints sorbet (such as Blue Moon's Red Raspberry and Lemon
     Zest or any two contrasting colors)
Raspberries and a few fresh mint leaves for garnish

Cut the cake into serving portions (wedges, squares, or circles).
Put a small amount of raspberry sauce, just enough so the puddle is larger in size than the cake portions, on serving plates and
place the cake on the sauce. Use a melon baller to scoop out the
sorbets, arranging the scoops around the cake. Garnish with
raspberries and mint and drizzle more raspberry sauce over
everything. Serve immediately.

Note: To make raspberry sauce, combine 1 pint raspberries with 1
tablespoon sugar. Mix well and press through a fine-mesh sieve.

THE FELLOW WHO
PLANTED THE TREE

{ POVERTY LANE ORCHARDS }

CAN YOU SPELL that for me, please?" I asked in my most journalistic, businesslike voice, concealing, I hoped, the fact that I couldn't even pronounce the word. "Sure, I can spell it. I can spell them all," Steve Wood grinned. He is tall; his thick, dark hair shows threads of gray, and his auburn eyes pierce just enough to make the connection feel real. His old work jeans are barely able to hang on to his hips, and an unbuttoned, faded red shirt is thrown over a T-shirt, in an apparent attempt at warmth. In spelling-bee mode, he repeats the word and then rattles off the spelling of the apple variety he's explained was reputed to be Thomas Jefferson's favorite: "E-S-O-P-U-S-S-P-I-T-Z-E-N-B-E-R-G—Jefferson grew it at Monticello in the late 1700s when it was the hot new variety from Esopus, New York."

It's a cloudy-cool September day in Lebanon, New Hampshire, and Steve and I are driving around his Poverty Lane Orchards—once four farms now combined to form nearly a hundred acres of apple orchards—in a small truck whose every spring has clearly sprung. And we're not driving roads, we're driving the fields. The bounce that is set up reminds me of a trampoline—out of control—and we chat while I try to take notes. At the top of a hill the truck hesitates, but before we plunge down a grassy lane through the orchard I catch a glimpse of the vista: old, rounded mountains stacked in waves back to the horizon, each line beginning to show fall's yellow, red, orange, and evergreen. As I hear a distant eighteen-wheeler shift gears, I'm struck momentarily by what I know to be a truism of New Hampshire: that stunningly rural beauty does exist less than ten minutes from the Interstate. We waddle down the hill in the pickup and then stop. The backdrop to our parking space is what Steve calls "the R&D section" of his orchards: it's where cuttings of antique apple trees have been grafted onto the root stock of the more prolific and common-to-New England McIntosh tree. Suddenly the truck door bursts open, spewing Steve, who then bounds in huge, tall-man steps up the orchard's hillside lane, talking fast and enthusiastically as he goes. Fumbling for the door handle, I try first to catch up—catch, too, what he's saying—and then to grab the different apples passed back to me: Ashton Bitter, Westfield Seek-No-Further, Cox's Orange Pippen, Ashmead's Kernel, Wickson, Calville Blanc d'Hiver. The names are like sweet nonsensical nursery rhymes— word games of bare explanation that hint at the fruit's character or place of origin, the discoverer's name, or all of the above. Steve handed me a small apple the matte color of tan suede blushed with rose, a Pomme Grise with a pedigree of over 150 years of growing in the St. Lawrence River valley and likely to have derived from a French apple during Louis XIV's time. Its flavor was "brilliant," as Steve said. Rich, complex, and wonderful, I added. After an hour of conversation there was no doubt he knew how to spell—and also spellbind with his extensive knowledge of the art of growing apples.

Poverty Lane Orchards was purchased in 1965 by Steve Wood's father, a physician in small-town Lebanon who wanted to teach his four children about hard work and living on the land. Steve worked at the orchard—which then grew primarily McIntosh and Cortlands for the wholesale market—from the age of eleven through high school. Departing in 1973 to attend Harvard, he tried managing the orchards from afar during his first years at college: "I spent a lot of time commuting from Cambridge." He assumed that with graduation the infatuation with the orchards would pass, that he was probably bound for graduate school, and would leave the apple business forever. But he came back in the late 1970s to "settle some land affairs" for the family and somehow never left. In 1984 he purchased the orchard.

At first Steve stuck with selling, primarily wholesale, Cortlands and Macs (McIntosh) and only dabbled with the antique varieties—"I was sort of an apple gardener. It was a hobby for me the way clock makers collect old clocks." But then in the early 1980s the apple world began to change: new technology for machine packing and cold storage of the fruit plus the fashion of waxing apples all added to the apple growers' production process—and production costs. Simultaneously there was an apple glut on the world market, which drastically lowered the price to growers. Hand-packed apples could no longer be sold at a premium, cold storage units were expensive, and waxing, in Steve's view, was merely a method of disguising inferior apples. For many growers it was a question of get big or get out.

But Steve and his wife, Louisa Spencer, approached the situation differently. First they asked themselves, Should we keep doing this? And should we keep doing it on this particular land? Steve said, "I realized that this is what I do. And to try and duplicate the intimacy I already have with new land would take another lifetime. I realized that if we couldn't find a way to produce a viable crop, it wouldn't survive as farmland when we're done." They decided to sell quality, not quantity, to not get big, but get niche. The hobby—heirloom apple propagation—was to become the business.

Apples are as old as Adam and Eve, but beyond Eden the tree probably originated in an area between the Caspian and Black Seas. Evidence of dried apples dating from 6000 B.C. has been excavated in the stilt-built homes of Swiss lake dwellers, and as early as 2000 B.C. apples were cultivated in India's Indus Valley. Around 750 B.C. Etruscan nurserymen planted apple orchards across the Italian countryside; later the Romans, perhaps the greatest agriculturists of any early culture, established thirty-two varieties of apples there. By A.D. 1271 apples were a major component of the Chinese diet, and in 1296 one of the first cultivated varieties, the Costard, was being sold on English streets, twelve pennies for a hundred apples.

The apple's history is dotted with celebrity—from England's Richard II's inclusion of the apple, and apple cider, at his infamous two-thousand-guest banquet to Isaac Newton's apple-inspired conclusions about the nature of gravity in 1666. There are the famous old apple sayings, "An apple a day keeps the doctor away," which comes from an old English adage "To eat an apple before going to bed, will make the doctor beg his bread" and certainly confirms the long-held belief in the health and nutritional value of apples. Only about eighty calories each, apples are free of fat. Because they are so high in pectin they also are a great source of fiber; one apple has five grams. There is also my favorite saying, "As American as Mom and apple pie," although America's identity claim on apples is actually a bit erroneous, since it is truly a fruit of the world.

Surely the apple's importance and popularity in the world is confirmed by its constant and pervasive migration: when Spanish conquistador Pedrode Alvarado invaded Guatemala he introduced the apple; the pilgrims planted our first apple trees in the Massachusetts Bay Colony; and when English colonists came in 1632 to what is now New Jersey they planted apple trees. Because most apples can be grown farther north, in colder environs, than other fruits—and they blossom late in the spring, which minimizes frost damage—they can be found in both the Southern and Northern Hemispheres, from Australia to Sweden; seventy-five hundred varieties of apples are grown throughout the world. In the United States apples are grown today in all fifty states, commercially in thirty-two of them, and we grow over 2,500 varieties, 100 of them on a commercial basis. Worldwide the apple production in 2004 and 2005 is estimated to be about 42 million metric tons. Apples are everywhere.

Certainly the apple of the American folklore eye is Johnny Appleseed, the king of wanderlust. Born John Chapman in Leominster, Massachusetts, the rather eccentric Johnny Appleseed started traveling westward in 1797 selling or giving settlers seeds he'd collected at cider mills. In 1806 he loaded two canoes full of apple seed and floated Ohio's Muskingum River. By the time he reached the river's White Woman Creek he'd run out of seeds but had managed to plant thousands of acres of apple trees in Pennsylvania and throughout the Ohio Valley, Indiana, and Illinois. In 1821 Johnny Appleseed befriended a Jeromesville, Ohio, settler named Conrad Fridline and as a gift planted nine apple trees on the Fridline Farm. Johnny Appleseed died in 1847, but in the 1950s Fridline's grandson could recall seven of his grandfather's trees designated as the "Johnny Appleseed Orchard." The last of those trees survived until 1965, living to be over 140 years.

Gone but not forgotten, and in the tradition of great heirloom apple men, Fort Collins nurseryman Scott Skogerboe—who'd already obtained a cutting from the Isaac Newton-descended Flower of Kent apple tree—went in pursuit of an apple tree derived from a Fridline-Johnny Appleseed cutting. In the mid-1990s, after a year of truly investigative work, he finally found one, obtained a cutting, and grafted it to one of his trees. It takes between five and ten years for an apple cutting to bear fruit, and Skogerboe wasn't expecting much in the way of taste from the Appleseed descendent. "I've run a knife through thousands of apples," he recalls, "but there was just a little different feeling when I took a slice from one of these trees. I guess the quality was not exciting, but I can't remember. I was thinking about the fellow who planted the tree."

Just because an apple tree is old doesn't make it better, of course. There is often a reason a variety has melted into obscurity. Steve Wood realized he couldn't afford to be a museum for apples. "We're not a nonprofit apple museum, trying to save old apples. Contrary to popular belief old apple varieties aren't really endangered. We're a business trying to find and establish a niche." In his quest to make more money per fruit he focused on antique or, as he has now labeled them, "Uncommon Apples."

He knew he'd have to select varieties carefully, given the lead time from cutting to fruit. He set criteria for choosing and hoped it would be a formula for success, too: grow apples that indeed have a story to tell, a history, but also have the stamp of the land on them, and do well in New Hampshire.

He said, "I want our soil and weather to put their signature on the character of the apple. Empire and Red Delicious taste the same, no matter where they are grown. I want fruit that tastes like it could only have been grown here."

Poverty Lane had to produce apples, in Steve's mind, with some "point of amusement—unusual appearance, brilliant taste, or perhaps a good cider apple."

As often as not, many of the old apples were cultivated not for eating but for drinking. Some of the earliest apples—bitter crabapples from Asia—were actually inedible. And many of the colonists stuffed their pockets full of apple seeds that would produce cider—not eating—apples. One such variety, Hewes' Crab, is still grown at Monticello and valued for its high sugar content—important to fermentation—and juiciness. On a trip to England in 1983 Steve had become interested in the apples there that produced cider, particularly the fine English hard ciders. Steve's first planting of antique apples was in 1987, and he planted some again in 1989, and they actually were a cider variety. When he handed me an Ashton Bitter apple he suggested I taste it "carefully" because I wouldn't like it. True enough, I spit it out—it may make great cider but it certainly didn't taste like it could.

At the conclusion of that first orchard tour at Poverty Lane, we headed for the old barn that housed the cider press, the floor-to-ceiling rows of barrels, and the 1999 vintage cider. Steve disappeared to find wineglasses for an impromptu tasting. I waited and realized that it was not just the lingering bitter taste in my mouth from the Ashton that was putting me off the cider tasting; a bad hard cider memory was bubbling to the surface of my sensory perceptions. Back to that time during my father's year of believing he could make hard cider at home. For months he carted many gallons of not-yet-fermented apple cider in huge glass containers in the back of the family station wagon. Until one day a sharp turn clanked the glass jugs together and brought a cider-fall of slightly chunky, sticky apple juice over the back seat onto my short self. I was washable, of course, but the car for all eternity smelled of sweet-rotting cider. The aroma was indelibly pressed into my mind—and was making the cider tasting less than positively anticipated.

"You're either going to really like this or really hate it,"
Steve said, pouring a glass of his very-limited-production 1997
Kingston Black cider. I drank. This very dry, subtle—not a hint
of apple saccharin—cider was fantastic! Yes, a truly wonderful
wine, but different from wine. Yes, the cider was certainly a good
idea, but there was still more to be done with antique apples.

In 1991 Steve planted the first of his uncommon eating
apples, dwarf trees like Lady and Wickson that would bear fruit
sooner, and some of the Spitzenbergs, which, as with Jefferson,
are Steve's favorite because they are versatile, good cider *and* eating apples. In 1993 Steve and Louisa stopped hand-packing the
Macs and Cortlands. In 1995 they had their first drinkable cider
yield, and by then Steve and Louisa had become convinced that
all the uncommon apples could make a business, so they quit
selling McIntoshes and Cortlands to the wholesale market. In
essence they bet the farm. "The gamble," Steve said straightfor-
wardly, "is for the land; if we fail, we're the last ones on it."

There were a thousand gallons of cider being fermented by
1996. Steve continued to plant more antique apples in 1997 and
1998. By 1999, there were enough fresh uncommon apples to
pack and sell wholesale and five thousand gallons of cider produced. In 2002 Poverty Lane stopped selling Cortland and
McIntosh apples altogether—except through their U-pick
operation. And since then, from October through December,
Poverty Lane Orchards has sold uncommon apples—those
lovely Pomme Grise, Wickson, Ashmead's, Golden Russetts,
and, of course, the Esopus Spitzenbergs and many more—and
terrific hard cider under the Farnum Hill cider label.

On my most recent visit to Poverty Lane it was unusually
warm for late September and it didn't seem like apple time yet.
As if to confirm that, when I parked my car next to the long
tractor shed and looked out into the orchard, I saw one, just one,
perfect-looking red apple hanging from the tree. Dogs saun-
tered around, moving from the large white farmhouse to the
smaller of the two barns, past a pile of long wooden beams, and
then they lay down near the cart of pumpkins by the big weath-
ered, once-white barn.

Somewhere from inside the barn Steve appeared, and suddenly we were galloping down the dirt road toward the area that held the Calville Blanc d' Hiver and the Hudson's Golden Gem. Again, I was trying to catch up—writing notes while walking through grassy orchard lanes is a difficult feat, and I remain bad at it—and again, I was passed apples to sample. The Calville Blanc is a French cooking apple that is green in color and has a lumpy shape, but even just one bite—we would bite once and throw the rest on the ground—was enough to let me know how fabulous its tart, intense flavor is. Then we were into the next row: dwarf trees, their limbs staked and wired for support, with clusters of small red apples; one bite here takes half of the apple.

Steve spoke into his walkie-talkie, "The Wicksons are ready. Can we get a crew up here to pick this afternoon? Well, yes, if it's supposed to rain maybe we pick right now."

For years, Jamaican pickers have come to work in the fall at Poverty Lane and Steve told me the tiny apples are their least favorite: "Wicksons are good for cider, for cooking, and fresh, but they're slow to pick." We crossed an old, slightly damp spring and walked into the next orchard, where only cider apples were growing. I sampled just one, but Steve tasted several of the varieties. These cider apples are gathered after they've fallen on the ground, no picking necessary.

Around the whole orchard was a twelve-foot (maybe higher) wire fence to keep the deer and porcupines from eating the fruit. "Apples have lots of enemies; this over here is to get rid of the maggots." Steve pointed to a Christmas ornament-like ball painted red—an imitation apple—hanging from one of the tree limbs. Attached close to the "apple's" top is a small vial of yellow powder that smells like apple candy. He explained that the smell attracts the maggots and they get trapped in the ball and die.

"It's a pinpointed, and therefore better, solution than spraying the whole orchard with pesticides. And it's a hundred percent effective." But pests are just one of the problems with the orchard.

"It takes a decade with apples to learn if you've made a mistake," Steve said. "We fluctuate between growing a hundred to two hundred different varieties, and sometimes you just end up with a real jerk tree that won't behave. Plus propagation sources aren't consistently reliable—you buy one variety, put it in the ground, and get some entirely different apple than what you thought you bought. So we're in the business of grafting scions onto existing trees, tasting the apples once they've fruited, and if okay then sending the grafting wood to a commercial nursery. A year later the nursery sends us the young tree and in four or five years we get a dependable crop. This coming year we'll be planting fifteen hundred trees."

He bounds ahead, talking as he goes. I run, trying to keep up and hear what he's saying: "It's actually unusual for one orchard to grow both the cider and eating antiques together, but since I'll ferment anything once, I like to experiment by adding different apples to my cider. I've gotten now so I can tell with one bite how it'll ferment. But cider is a tricky business because the laws for selling alcohol vary from state to state. The fresh uncommon market is getting better—it used to be that brown apples were out of favor, for example—but the Golden Russets are very popular now. It's fine if an apple is spectacularly ugly as long as it's distinctive. When storekeepers taste the apples they're usually thrilled, and want to carry them immediately. Still we need to help them differentiate the apples for the consumer."

Lulu, as Steve refers to Louisa, handles much of the marketing. "She's deeply immersed in the cider now," said Steve, "but she did design a beautiful set of point-of-purchase cards for the eating apples." Each laminated card pictures the apple in color and gives a brief history of the variety, tells how it's used, and provides a description of the apple's flavor: "Tompkins King—A husky fruit, literally heavy with sprightly sub-acid flavor and its own elusive perfume. The original tree sprouted in Washington, NJ, before 1800, but large-scale grafting for market began in the mighty orchards of Tompkins County, NY; and spread to most of the colder U.S. apple regions over 100 years."

And each of the descriptions made me want to buy and try. Eleven varieties of apples are marketed under Poverty Lane's "Uncommon Apples" label in select markets from New York City to Houston.

"In so many ways we're like a start-up business," Steve said, "with concurrent gambles going on, the cider and then the uncommon fresh apples. Failure is not really a fear of mine, and I don't have any illusions about the apple orchard. For me it just has to make sense as an orchard. I don't want money to come from selling the land. We just want to be able to look Harry and Otis, our sons, in the face and say what we're doing is not a lie—that we're not just fooling around with an aesthetic orchard to someday sell the land and retire to Florida—that what we're doing is a worthwhile and noble enterprise. And we are, I think, moving in the right direction."

There is a pause and then Steve continued, "I do have an addiction to the trees. I just love the years of hopefulness they promise."

Tree men have a different sense of time I think—that very long view.

Weeks later it is a cold, damp Saturday in late October—now it is apple time. I have the sublime pleasure of an afternoon to myself with the one assignment of cooking dessert for the dinner party we are to attend that evening. Since I was sixteen and just learning to bake such weather has tempted me and brought on the desire to make an apple pie. There is so much comfort and straightforwardness to an apple pie—maybe it's that inference of being about Mom and so all-American. This afternoon I make my slightly morphed version of apple pie, an apple and Calvados tart. The apples are Uncommon—Calville Blanc d'Hiver—from Poverty Lane, a lovely green blushed with pink. I take my time, and when pulled from the oven the tart smells of cinnamon and the apple's own spicy tartness. It looks divine, but, better yet, when it's eaten that evening the flavor is simply wonderful. And as I have the second slice and wonder what it might be that makes this apple tart taste so exceptional, so uncommon, I realize that I, too, "am thinking about the fellow who planted the tree." And that makes all the difference.

{ APPLE COBBLER }

Steve Wood says of this recipe: "Otis Wood, our sixteen-year-old son, has made this cobbler for us many times. While putting it together the other night, he remarked, 'Hey, this is completely fat-free, except for the stick of butter.' Otis's favorite apples for this, in descending order of preference, are Calville Blanc d'Hiver, Esopus Spitzenberg, Baldwin, and Cortland. He's tried it with various combinations of cinnamon, nutmeg, vanilla, sugar, Calvados, and other booze added to the apple mixture, but prefers the apples cooked on their own—his family beneficiaries agree." As is not surprising for someone who has grown up with heirloom apples in his backyard, this apple cobbler of Otis Wood's is particularly dependant on using very good apples; otherwise it would seem a tad bland without cinnamon or Calvados. When I tested the recipe (in early September), the Calville Blanc d'Hiver, Esopus Spitzenberg, and local Baldwin and Cortland apples had not yet come in. On Steve's advice, I used Ginger Gold apples, and Otis's cobbler was, indeed, sublime.

Serves 10.

4 teaspoons cornstarch
3 ½ to 4 pounds apples, cored, quartered, and sliced thickly
1 cup all-purpose flour
½ teaspoon baking powder
¼ teaspoon salt
½ cup unsalted butter, softened
1 cup sugar
2 egg yolks
½ teaspoon vanilla extract

Preheat the oven to 375 degrees. In a small bowl, dissolve the cornstarch in ½ cup water. Toss the cornstarch mixture with the apples and spread the apples evenly in an 11-by-15-inch pan.

In a bowl, combine the flour, baking powder, and salt. In another bowl, cream the butter and sugar. Beat the eggs and vanilla together and add them to the butter-sugar mixture. Add the dry ingredients to the butter-egg mixture and stir just until combined.

Distribute the batter over the top of the apples by big table-spoonfuls. Bake for 45 minutes to 1 hour, or until the topping is lightly browned. Serve with cream, yogurt, or ice cream.

WILD MUSHROOMS AND DREAMS

{ EARTHY DELIGHTS }

I DON'T SEE any, do you?" I said to my husband. "No, must be too late for them," he said. We were standing in a forest, a hillside of tall, mature trees, open just enough to let the sunlight penetrate the green canopy and splash about on the messy, leaf-covered ground. It was May in New Hampshire and our second season of learning to forage for wild mushrooms; we were looking for the distinctive yellow morel.

It had been easy to find our first-learned—the golden-colored chanterelle-mushroom, always brightly peeking through the pine needles; you could spot a chanterelle in a dark woods wearing sunglasses. But the morel had proved frustratingly elusive. We stood staring, our eyes sweeping back and forth, invisibly raking the forest floor. Deciding there weren't any morels to be had here, we turned to climb back up the hill and to the dirt road leading home. "Wait! Here's one! Here's another... and another!" It was the grown-up version of an Easter egg hunt and we were suddenly filling our basket. It is the oddest thing about mushrooming: seeing them doesn't happen until your eyes get accustomed to the seeing—or maybe it's your brain that must do the adjusting. You think you've looked hard, you think there's nothing there. And then suddenly, like mirages that come true, they are there and everywhere. There is nothing like foraging for wild mushrooms.

There is also nothing like the taste of wild mushrooms—earthy, pungent, unusual, and so wonderfully wild.

Of course, the world's wild mushroom eating goes back many centuries. It is truly ancient: hieroglyphics dating back 4,600 years detail how Egyptians believed that mushrooms would ensure immortality. So intrigued were the pharaohs with the flavor of mushrooms that fungi were proclaimed royal food and commoners were banned from even touching them.

Surely the wild mushroom's status as prized edible must have inspired the concept of cultivating them. Actual mushroom cultivation first began in China in A.D. 600, but became more formalized by the French in the early 1700s. In the regions around Paris the quarrying of stone to make Parisian buildings created a network of large caves. The cool, dark, and empty caves were ideal "fields" for mushroom growing. Given these perfect environs in conjunction with France's burgeoning mastery of the culinary arts, it's no wonder the cultivated mushroom business would flourish throughout the next two centuries. In 1867 a single cave in France contained twenty-one miles of beds with *daily* mushroom yields of three thousand pounds.

Mushroom propagation didn't even start in the United States until the mid-nineteenth century with spawn imported from Britain, but by the 1890s the business of mushroom growing was well established on Long Island. Next, Pennsylvania flower growers discovered that they could supplement their incomes by raising mushrooms under their greenhouse tables. By 1914, their mushroom profits were outstripping flower profits—it cost a grower as little as fifteen cents to grow a pound of mushrooms.

Other areas began to cultivate mushrooms—Massachusetts, California, Michigan, Illinois—yet Pennsylvania remained dominant, in 1924 producing 85 percent of the mushrooms grown in the United States. Today mushrooms are produced commercially in virtually every state. Pennsylvania, however, still accounts for over half of the total U.S. production.

Globally mushrooms are cultivated in eighty countries, but Campbell's—of soup fame—is the largest grower of mushrooms in the world. For use in their soup or for packing into cans, they propagate primarily button (*Agaricus*) mushrooms. So over 90 percent of all mushrooms cultivated in the United States are buttons, although two decades ago that number was closer to 100 percent.

Expanding beyond the buttons began in the early 1980s when Campbell's, along with Phillips Mushroom Farms in Pennsylvania and several others, began to grow "exotic" fresh mushrooms. Exotic mushrooms are cultivated, but flavor-wise more like wild; they include shiitake, oyster, portobello, cremini, and an increasing number of other mushrooms. Phillips first added shiitake mushrooms, about two thousand pounds a week, to their button crop. Today Phillips grows exclusively exotics—thirty-five million pounds of specialty mushrooms annually.

Certainly the exotics' popularity mushroomed because they're more flavorful, but also because a glut of shiitakes in 1988 suddenly made them very affordable for many restaurants. Chefs began to experiment with all kinds of mushroom recipes and, since exotic cultivated mushrooms aren't seasonal, they could include them on their menus year round. Also, mushrooms—all mushrooms—fit into that ever-increasing interest Americans have in low-fat, healthful foods.

Mushrooms are actually a fine nutritional source. And although somewhat atypical for a popular, tasty food, mushrooms are the ultimate light food. One serving (five medium-sized white mushrooms) has only twenty calories and is free of fat, cholesterol, and sodium. High in protein, mushrooms are a good source of vitamins B, C, and—rather ironically given their dark beginnings—the sunshine vitamin D, and of minerals such as iron, potassium, phosphorus, and folic acid. Recent findings suggest that mushrooms could also turn out to be an important ingredient in a cancer-fighting diet. When it comes to their selenium content (selenium is an element that has been found to reduce the risk of prostate cancer), mushrooms surpass all other items in the produce category.

My own first major culinary brush with anything other than white button mushrooms came when I traveled to France in the early 1980s and visited those ancient caves where exotic mushrooms were growing in profusion. Unfortunately, back home availability was still often an issue except in special places such as the Seattle-type open-air markets, where I might find fresh portobello, wood ear, and enoki mushrooms.

Sympathizing with my mushroom obsession, a friend on a vacation in Italy risked the scrutiny of customs agents and smuggled home a gift of dried porcini. They were wild and better than any exotic I'd had. I was in love. I hydrated the dried porcini in order to add their essence to—everything! (I think I may have even splashed some of the hydrating, porcini-laced water behind my ears.) Now I was thoroughly hooked on the wild—well, actually re-hooked.

My father taught me as a child to make lovely spore prints of the wild mushrooms he'd collected. For me, the prints were pretty pictures. For him, the spores were identifying characteristics that helped determine the mushroom's qualification as edible treat. Unlike many families that pass the secrets of mushroom identification, habitat, and known sites from generation to generation as if they were heirlooms, my father's knowledge of wild mushrooms was derived more from adventuresome exuberance than from actual firsthand experience. We did have many wonderful wild mushroom meals, of which I have fond memories.

But then there was the bad one. It was basically an upset stomach, which is the most common side effect of eating poisonous mushrooms. However, it was a poignant reminder that misidentification can lead to far worse consequences than tummy trouble. In later years my father—in a move similar to what was happening in the bigger mushroom world—tried growing shiitakes. Meanwhile, I left home for a city college where mushrooms grew only in funky, dark, and dank places. And the most common consequence from eating one wasn't epicurean in nature, but an adventure to rival Alice's Wonderland.

But fifteen years later came the trip to France, then the porcini, my ever-increasing passion for wild mushrooms, and quite clearly the need to learn about foraging for wild mushrooms. Fortuitously, not long after we moved to New Hampshire, I met Nadia. A Hungarian biochemist researcher at Dartmouth College who grew up in communist Romania, she knew quite a lot about classification and the European tradition of collecting wild mushrooms. Nadia trained me to follow the golden rule of mushroom hunting: know how to identify just a select handful of wild mushrooms—preferably shown to you in the field by an experienced mentor—and know them well. Each year my husband and I add to our foraging repertoire. Some years the wild mushrooms are prolific; other years we call Earthy Delights.

Ed Baker, president of Earthy Delights, a Michigan-based purveyor of wild edibles, told me the first time I spoke with him in 1996, "For me there is one overriding reason to eat wild mushrooms: flavor. Wild mushrooms add incredible complexity and flavor to anything."

Earthy Delights started as one of the first, maybe *the* first, suppliers to offer—initially to chefs, then later direct to home cooks—fresh wild harvested edibles such as ramps, fiddlehead ferns, and wild mushrooms. This was not an easy business. "Finding exotic, fresh, and flavorful mushrooms can be a daunting task, due to the seasonality and relatively short shelf life of fresh mushrooms," Ed explained. "Originally people said we were nuts: 'You can't ship wild edibles overnight. What a crazy idea!'"

This was back in 1986, long before the concept of overnight delivery of fresh foods had become a regular occurrence. In fact it was before wild mushrooms, or even the exotic mushrooms, had gained much acceptability here in the United States. Most of us were still barely out of our white button mushroom stage. "As the American palate became more sophisticated," Ed explained, "we found ourselves searching for new flavors, often looking to ingredients long favored in the cuisines of France and Italy, where wild mushrooms have been used for centuries."

I first found Earthy Delights on the Internet. "We had a website as early as 1995—one of the first in the food business," Ed explained. "It wasn't functional; you couldn't order from it, but you could look at stuff. And by 1997 or '8 it was fully functional. That side of the business grew very fast that first year."

A decade before their website, Earthy Delights had started as a nonprofit marketing cooperative in Lansing, and initially was called Michigan Marketing Association. It wasn't started by Ed, but by Chris Steele and Bob Conaway. Chris had always been interested in plants and unusual foods and food markets, and he realized that there were people out there who harvested or grew some very unique products but didn't know how to get them to market. And there were chefs who wanted and needed these specialty foods and didn't know how to find—much less purchase—them. So right from the start, two out of the three foods Chris and Bob sold were wild: mushrooms, fiddleheads, and edible flowers. Next they added baby white asparagus, hydroponically grown mâche and arugula—all specialty produce items. Chris ran the operation out of his house for a year or two, then took a couple rooms in an old house in downtown Lansing and made them into offices. He hired a filing clerk in 1988 and hired his first salesperson in 1989, his second in 1990. "That was me," said Ed, "and that was the first year we did a million in sales."

They branched out into herbs and goat cheese and called themselves a specialty produce company. "We did a lot with a company that grew hydroponic greens near Detroit. That company actually owned a big landfill, so they could easily heat greenhouses with methane. I'm not sure that they ever really cared about the hydroponics part—they just wanted to pretty up their image a little, I think. I shouldn't say that; maybe they did care," Ed laughed.

Michigan Marketing Association was still a co-op, which meant that the owners were not Chris or Bob but rather the producer members, all of whom had equity in the company. "That wasn't working," said Ed. "So there was an attempt in 1992 to take that corporation private. Something went bad during that period, and Chris got fired; there were lawsuits, and things got pretty ugly for two or three years after that. When I came to work at MMA, it was really just another job. I liked the lack of formality in the office. Actually, I thought in the beginning that overnighting food around was crazy. After a year suddenly everything changed and opportunities opened up—like owning the company. After the first attempt to privatize the company and Chris losing his position and then getting fired, I was just sort of riding over it, keeping it running by the skin of its teeth. I had to make it up as I went along. It was nothing I'd prepared for at all."

Ed grew up an army brat. "My dad was a lifer. We'd moved fourteen times by the time I was thirteen years old." Born in Georgia, where his mother was from, Ed lived on army bases in Japan, Ft. Leavenworth, Pittsburgh, back to Georgia, then went to Ft. Knox, back to Georgia again, and again to Pittsburgh. Fortunately, all that moving around occurred when he was young, "When it was a little easier to take." So he was able to complete high school in the Pittsburgh area. He went to Michigan State in 1969 as a National Merit Scholar and then, as Ed described it, "I ended up wandering down the rosy path, doing the Jefferson Airplane thing for a few years."

He did a little bit of theater and music and then started working in a restaurant in East Lansing. He stayed for ten years, and did everything—dishwashing, cooking, bartending, waiting tables—and was promoted to assistant manager and then full manager. "I hated it; in a year I made less money and worked more hours, so I went back to being a waiter."

At the same time, he began working for several food brokers, "schlepping around Stouffers, Hefty bags, Smuckers, stuff like that, selling to grocery stores. But I still waited tables for a couple nights a week for another six years. It wasn't a very good-paying job, and I didn't know what I wanted to do. I struggled growing up. But I'm sure the experience selling got me the job with MMA and after my first couple years there my story and the company's story became one and the same."

By the mid-1990s, Ed was running what by that time had been renamed Earthy Delights, and several of his friends said they'd be interested in investing and becoming co-owners. Ed put sweat equity into Earthy Delights, no money, but got an equal share in the business.

Ninety percent of Earthy Delights' customer base has always been food services. They have a few executive chefs, like Charlie Trotter and several others in big cities, who want the freshest of the fresh. But most are not in the major cities. "Our specialty is providing fine ingredients to small-town country clubs, restaurants, inns, out-of-the-way places," Ed explained. "Where there may be a chef who trained at CIA, worked in San

Francisco for ten years where he had everything at his fingertips, and now he's in Montana and going, 'Ahh, where can I get this stuff?' That's about ninety percent of the business and now ten percent comes from Earthy.com and the catalog aimed at individual home consumers."

Earthy Delights expanded beyond produce into specialty oils, vinegars, and heirloom beans and rice over time, but its primary business has remained wild and exotic mushrooms and produce—50 percent is mushrooms and truffles, 25 percent produce, and 25 percent all other products.

Ed said, "Chanterelles are our biggest mushroom seller to chefs because it's a longer season. Morels might be bigger per time available, since the season is shorter. But for our direct consumers, far and away morels are the most popular. Morels are really a big thing in Michigan, but there's not enough excess here for them to be sold commercially. Everyone picks their own five or ten pounds and eats them all—or takes them up north to a local chef. The season's only a couple weeks long here. But out west—in Oregon, Montana, Washington, British Columbia— their season goes maybe four or five months. Now chanterelles or hedgehogs or porcini, I can hardly get consumers to even try those. The black trumpets, lobster mushroom, chicken and hen of the woods do okay, and some of the cultivated exotics, too. Well, not the shiitakes or portobellos because they've almost become commodities now—portobellos, after all, are just big buttons—but trumpet royale, cinnamon caps, bluefoot, the ones we supply in the winter do okay."

For me, variety is but one of several reasons for my patronage of Earthy Delights: there's also the perfect quality of the mushrooms, certainly better than I could pick myself. Plus, they can find them!

Earthy Delights' wild mushrooms come primarily from half a dozen companies in the Pacific Northwest whose business it is to send buyers out into the woods and mountains to find people who regularly harvest wild edibles. Also, since Earthy Delights has had a website for a long time many professional foragers contact them directly.

"And I turn ninety percent of them away," Ed said. "I'm not just going to buy from any Joe blow who says, 'Yeah, I've been picking mushrooms for twenty years.' They all want to go around the mushroom companies and sell directly to me because they think they're not getting enough money. They go online and I'm selling them to individual consumers for thirty-nine dollars a pound. They want to know why they're getting only four dollars a pound. Okay, if they're getting four a pound and I'm paying nine a pound, it sounds like I could pay six-fifty and we'd both be better off. But there's no quality control there, it's too dicey. I just can't do that."

Ed also got a call one time from a lady in Idaho who worked for a local health department. She said she was really stumped because she'd gone to the state and the feds and couldn't find the regulations for inspecting wild mushrooms. It is a little under the radar, so Earthy Delights' relationship with sources is important. For fifteen years Earthy Delights has been doing business with the same companies that were checked out quite some time ago. "We don't deal with the Johnny-come-latelys," Ed said. "We've never had a bad experience—knock on wood." They do carry a $2 million liability insurance because many of their big customers, like Disney and Marriott, insist on being named specifically in Earthy Delights' policy.

"Only thing close to something bad happening—and it's just one of those things—was when some guy ate the dried morels without reconstituting them. I think he got the runs; he got really sick. So I guess I have to put something on my dried mushrooms about these *must* be reconstituted and cooked before eating. I never thought I would have to do that, you know what I mean? We all think it's so stupid when we see on an iron: 'Do not iron clothes while wearing them.' Freaky—would you ever imagine someone doing that?"

I laughed out loud as I wrote down Ed's story—and pictured the guy as the mushrooms hydrated in his stomach—but Ed seemed happy to have learned from the guy's ignorance.

"One of my big learning experiences with my website," he said, "is how much more information is needed—recipes, information on the packaging and label—in selling to stores and consumers. I can send just a baggie full of dried morels to a chef and if they're nice morels, he's happy. But selling direct to consumers is different."

Earthy Delights grew rapidly for the four years from 1996 to 2000, but Ed admitted that during the last five years sales had been essentially flat. So now he's looking to expand into stores. A slightly different business than food service—although the product is still wild mushrooms, of course—retail relies more on point-of-purchase information and packaging. "I just got back from the printer these little five-by-eight recipe cards with information about wild mushrooms, recipes, and what to do with them," Ed said. "I think I'm getting in at a good time. I think there's huge future potential for selling a nicely packaged dried mushroom."

In 2005 a California company bought out the last of Ed's investors, which meant that he still owned his half and the California company owned the other half. Earthy Delights is housed in an old shopping center—about six thousand square feet—north of Lansing's airport in DeWitt, Michigan. Ed said, "We've got four people in the office on the phone selling, four or five doing the clerical—billing, answering the phone—and then a warehouse with lots of dried mushrooms. We employ twelve or thirteen people year round, eighteen to twenty during morel season, a lot of temps during Christmas. It's kind of cool: one of our farmers who has nothing to do in the winter comes and works for me in the warehouse."

In the future Ed wants to concentrate on repackaging the mushrooms for retail sales. He commissioned an artist to do a painting of each wild mushroom, and a graphic artist to make the labels.

For now he wants to keep the business small. "We'll never get that big. Even if we could sell thirty times more wild mushrooms in this country we'd still be tiny, tiny by European wild mushroom standards. But if I could be in on some growth that would be nice. I'd like to do mushroom-based products—value added. Mushroom-related, delicious products—that'll be my focus. I don't make anything myself yet, but I hope to soon. First step is to repackage—anything, chiles, spices, dried mushrooms. Then private labeling truffle oil and balsamic vinegar is step two. Step three is inventing and making new products, but developing new product is five or ten years away."

There's a pause in the conversation and then, quite out of nowhere, Ed Baker suddenly bursts into song. Yes, actual song:

You got to have a dream, if you don't have a dream.
How you gonna have a dream come true?

He sang in a quiet, controlled (and probably trained) voice. A quick image of the nice looking, fair-haired and blue-eyed Ed Baker—a musician and always interested in being on stage—popped into my mind. "You know that song from *South Pacific?*" he said. "Well, my dream come true would be to have someone else running the business and to have my main job be finding interesting foods."

Certainly that is my dream too. Yet as I yank on the cardboard clasp (with the pretty label) and pull it from the cellophane bag, the strong, organic smell of Earthy Delights' perfectly formed dried morels floats about my kitchen. And I know I need look no further for the wonderful, the often elusive, and the always wild mushroom.

{ WILD MUSHROOM AND POTATO FLAN }
Serves 8.

8 ounces fresh wild mushrooms, such as chanterelles or oyster
      mushrooms, washed and stemmed
2 tablespoons unsalted butter, plus some for the mold
$2/3$ cup coarsely chopped peeled and cooked potatoes
Salt and freshly ground black pepper to taste
2 sprigs fresh thyme, chopped
1 $1/2$ cups milk
$1/2$ cup heavy cream
3 eggs
2 egg yolks

Preheat the oven to 325 degrees. Have a kettle of boiling water ready to use during the baking of the flan.

Place the mushrooms in a sauté pan and cook over high heat to evaporate any water left from cleaning. Add the butter and lower the heat. Sauté for several minutes, until the mushrooms are softened but still hold their shape.

Season the potatoes with salt, pepper, and thyme. Generously butter a 4-cup ring mold (or 8 individual ½-cup custard cups) and set it in a roasting pan or cake pan.

Combine the milk and cream in a small saucepan and heat until just steaming to scald. Let the mixture cool for 5 minutes or so. It should be very warm but not scalding hot. Slowly pour it into a bowl with the eggs and egg yolks, whisking constantly. Season well with salt and pepper and pour through a fine-mesh sieve into a pitcher.

Pour a bit of the custard mixture into the prepared mold (or custard cups). Spoon the mushrooms and potatoes over the custard and pour in the remaining custard. Pour boiling water into the roasting pan to bring the level of the water about two-thirds of the way up the side of the mold.

Cover the roasting pan with foil and bake for 15 to 20 minutes, until a knife inserted halfway down into the custard comes out clean. Do not overbake; the custard will continue to cook after it is removed from the oven. Let rest for 5 minutes in the mold, then unmold by running a knife around the edge and inverting the mold onto a plate. Serve warm.

REAL POTATOES FROM
A REAL POTATO FARMER

{ WOOD PRAIRIE FARM }

THERE ARE PARTS of America still left where the place itself—the mountains, the sea, the land, the trees, the vistas—will always dominate what you remember about it. Where people and their worldly trappings are less evident, have barely even had an impact, and where the geography is what's important and what determines life. Maine is such a place, and particularly northern Maine, which as the gateway to Quebec and the Maritime Provinces foreshadows the colossal wilderness that is to come. My husband and I travel up to New Brunswick, Canada, once or twice a year to fish for Atlantic salmon or to hunt game birds. We drive through Maine on our way, and after the Interstate ends we make our border crossing in Houlton, Maine, a town some 120 miles as the crow flies from the topknot of Maine. Houlton is in the southern part of Aroostook County, a county with only a handful of towns, lots of pine trees, occasional patches of tough, windswept land, and a climate that must be coupled with such adjectives as *rough* or *harsh* to accurately describe it. And nearly every time I pass through there I wonder to myself, How do people here make a living? Why do people live here? I found my answers in potatoes.

"Aroostook County, Maine, is the best place in the world to grow potatoes," said Jim Gerritsen, of Wood Prairie Farm. "Cool seasons, with mostly seventy-degree temperatures that rarely go above ninety all summer. The rainfall is plentiful, like Ireland, and the soil is sandy loam that has good drainage. Our climate is ideal for potatoes, and with such a short growing season this is important. In 1807 the first potato farm was started in Houlton, Maine, and by the 1950s we were the number-one potato-producing region in North America. There's a real potato culture here."

For thirty years, Jim and his wife, Megan, have grown organic potatoes on ten acres of their 110-acre farm in Bridgewater, Maine, in the heart of the state's famous potato area, where the children are still released from school for three weeks in the fall to pick potatoes. The Gerritsens' is one of the last potato farms to maintain the tradition of hand-picking—their organic and heirloom varieties bruise easily and can't take machine abuse.

"And we actually have a waiting list of kids who want to pick," Jim told me. "Whole families, generations, come out to pick on Saturdays. The older ones remember when they got a nickel a barrel. They talk about it being 'an awful *loom-y* (loam-y) season,' meaning the weather has been rainy and so the potato plants are small. Or in the context of it being a nice fall day, they'll say, 'It's a good day to dig.' Our neighbors here know how to treat potatoes and they're very proud. So we get extraordinary quality. We're actually all a little bit fanatical about it. But Aroostook County is a great place to be a fanatic about potatoes because you don't stand out here!"

The Gerritsen potatoes, in addition to being hand-picked and chemical-free, are selected and then gently dry-brushed clean. (Most potatoes are washed and bagged in plastic, which promotes spoilage.) Packed in the classic, old-style opaque paper bags to shield light and inhibit sprouting, most of the table potatoes—they also produce certified seed potatoes—grown at Wood Prairie are sold via mail-order. They come packaged with an old-fashioned-looking postcard attached to each bag explaining the enclosed variety and how it performs in the kitchen:

ISLAND SUNSHINE
A delightful creamy, golden-fleshed potato originally grown on Prince Edward Island. Wonderful flavor. Best for boiling, also baked.

Appropriate recipes are included on the flip side. Potatoes can be purchased by variety, or as part of a Maine potato sampler-of-the-month plan, or by selecting the "Easter Egg Collection"—blue, red, yellow, purple, and white—assortment of baby potatoes. The varieties selected for the catalog are chosen from scores that the Gerritsens have test-grown and, based on flavor and culinary quality, honed to an offering of sixteen types of potatoes.

I first found the Gerritsens and their great-tasting potatoes when I returned from a trip to England in the late 1990s. In Europe the menus identify potatoes by specific name or place of origin—no, not the Idaho-russet—rather the fingerling *la ratte* potato traditionally grown in northern France. Sautéed in butter, the little *ratte* was sweet and delicate yet so full of flavor I wasn't sure I was actually eating a potato.

So once back home I went on a mission—that is, I went online—to find the American counterpart to *la ratte*. I found Wood Prairie's website (and this at a time when most small food growers didn't even have a computer, much less a website) and ordered a catalog, the cover of which was recycled paper from Aroostook County, Maine. The inside pages had drawings of each potato varieties' label, a map of Maine with a star placed on their location near Bridgewater, recipes, and several pictures. One was a photo of the family—Megan and Jim and their (then) two kids—standing in the field. In tiny blue type on most of the catalog pages were testimonials from all over the country: "There is a difference in your potatoes. They really do have more flavor." A bell sounded in my head—yup, I knew that great potato taste sensation—and I ordered. Swedish Peanut Fingerling, Red Cloud, Russian Banana Fingerling, Caribé, Elba, Butte, and more, their names suggested a past as well as the future.

While I waited for them to arrive, I decided to learn more about their ancestors. The varieties at Wood Prairie Farm are old, and not selected for cultivation because of any requirement for high yield, as is the case with the four or five kinds of potatoes most often grown in the United States.

Or as Jim put it, with "the Texas mentality" of bigger and more is better.

However, for a long time bigger and more *was* better for potatoes—even if the farmers had to chemically treat their plants in order to ensure disease resistance. The world spent centuries securing the potato's position as a basic dietary component. And today potatoes are the world's fifth-largest crop—just behind sugarcane, corn, rice, and wheat—and some 338 million tons are grown every year around the world. We've come to depend on the potato, despite the fact that it's a vegetable that for centuries was much maligned.

With evidence of *papas* cultivation in the Andes dating as far back as 3700 B.C., it can reasonably be assumed that potatoes are indigenous to South America. Spanish conquistador Gónzalo Jiménez de Quesada discovered the Incas eating the *Solanum tuberosum* in 1530 and, mistaking the peanut-size, underground tuber for a truffle, named it *tartuffo*. In 1539 Pope Paul III was presented with a specimen of Spain's introduced potato; he in turn gave it to a Frenchman, who then established it in France as an ornamental plant. With the British defeat of the Spanish Armada in 1588 came another migratory leap for the potato: the tuber is thought to have been introduced to the British Isles when it washed ashore on the beaches of western Ireland and was salvaged from the wreckage of the Spanish fleet.

The potato is easy to grow and harvest, yields more food per acre than grain, requires little equipment, and prospered better than wheat in the often nutrient-depleted soils of European countries. Potatoes are high in protein, vitamins C and the Bs, potassium, phosphorus, and iron. But in spite of all this the potato for decades couldn't transcend the category of animal feed. Even worse, in 1618 it was thought that potatoes caused leprosy, and the planting of potatoes was prohibited in Burgundy.

Yet it was going to be hard for the expanding populations of Europe to ignore this fast-growing and nutritional food source. Championing the potato cause in France was agriculturist-botanist Antoine-Auguste Parmentier. Believing that his survival of a Prussian prison during the Seven Years' War was due to a diet of potatoes, he persuaded Louis XVI to promote potatoes by inviting such notables as Benjamin Franklin to a banquet of only potato dishes. The king encouraged potato planting, even wore a potato blossom in his buttonhole, and with his royal backing the potato was on its way to staple status.

Throughout the nineteenth century the dependence and impact of the potato on Europe's food supplies and populations became critical, a fact most obviously demonstrated in Ireland. The Irish have idyllic conditions for growing potatoes, and they also became partial to potatoes. In the eighty years between 1760 and 1840 the population of Ireland grew 600 percent—an increase that has been attributed to the parallel proliferation of Ireland's potato cultivation, and that despite some periods of low production. None of the low-production periods is more famous than the great potato famine of 1845, which caused over a million deaths and the emigration of the same number of Irish, most of them to the United States.

Although potatoes were indigenous to the New World, this had not made them any more acceptable to the colonials. Introduced—or reintroduced—in Boston by an Irish Presbyterian minister in 1718 and planted in the colony of New Hampshire, the potato remained cattle fodder for nearly a century. Until, as he did with the tomato, Thomas Jefferson heavily promoted the acceptance of the potato as an edible: during his presidency he served french fries at the White House and grew several potato varieties at Monticello. This, coupled with the nineteenth-century wave of European immigrants—all practiced potato eaters—clearly contributed to the potato's becoming a staple in American households.

In 1872 a twenty-three-year-old horticulturist named Luther Burbank bred an improved variety of russet potato that came to be known as the Idaho potato, after Burbank's home state. The exceptionally hardy and prolific Idaho was actually grown from Maine to Washington, and it quickly eclipsed the production of the previously dominant New England varieties.

The next leap in potato popularity came when in 1942 Idaho potato processor Jack Simplot won a government contract to supply dehydrated potatoes to the armed forces. By the end of World War II, Simplot was providing thirty-three million pounds of frozen french fried potatoes to the military. Next Simplot, in 1953, introduced his frozen french fried potato to the commercial market by contracting with several fast-food chains, most prominently McDonald's. And by 1995, the J. R. Simplot Co. was not only supplying half of all McDonald's french fries but processing nearly two billion pounds of frozen french fries, hash browns, and other potato products annually. Processed potatoes made potato eating our national pastime, and Americans now eat more potatoes than any other fresh vegetable—an average of 140 pounds per person per year.

Potatoes are grown in all fifty states; Idaho and Washington are the top producers. Every year across the country homage is paid in the form of food festivals to the mighty potato. On the third weekend in October in Monte Vista, Colorado, they'll be eating potato brownies and spudnuts (doughnuts made from potato flour) and running five- and ten-kilometer "Tater Trots." In Shelley City Park, Idaho, where for over seventy-five years on the third Saturday in September they've celebrated Spud Day, they'll be holding mashed potato wrestling matches and recipe contests. Maine's festival in Fort Fairfield venerates the potato with a Little Miss Potato Blossom contest as well as with the Maine Potato Queen Pageant. In August, in Barnesville, Minnesota, you can attend the Potato Sack Fashion Show. At the festivals there are always games of potato golf, billiards, and bingo, plus contests to see who can peel or pick potatoes the fastest and make the best mashed sculpture.

We've become a nation of potato lovers. But somewhere between Burbank and Simplot, achieving the goal of feeding the masses and making potatoes a basic staple in our diet, we seemed to have lost something—or very nearly lost it. Somehow the potato's inclusion in the ranks of common staple also relegated it to blandness and tastelessness. Potatoes have more often than not served as mere enablers for our national addictions to salt and fat. But in the 1970s, the organic farming movement gained momentum and the propagation, both in home gardens and commercially, of heirloom potato strains boldly began to conquer the old oxymoron "gourmet potato." With the quest for chemical-free food came the notion that potatoes could have real flavor, and a kind of potato renaissance began.

My shipment from Wood Prairie arrived, and I was enthralled by the straightforward, real taste of their potatoes. I was captivated by their genuineness and wanted to know about the farmer who grew these fantastic potatoes—the tall, long-haired, bearded man in the catalog picture who wore a white cap with the Wood Prairie Farm emblem and had a strawberry-blond little girl on his shoulders.

Born in Seattle, Jim moved from Washington to northern California when he was two years old. In 1973, after high school, he entered Humbolt State University to study forestry. But, he confessed to me, he wasn't into book learning.

"I'm not patient enough," he recalled, "and I realized if I stayed in forestry I'd end up working for a big multinational paper company or the government. I certainly did not want to be in a city; the city doesn't have any draw for me. I just felt like a fish out of water and in retrospect I think I was simply a farmer at heart. I'm one generation removed from farming—my dad's parents had apple orchards in Yakima, Washington—and I sometimes worked on a farm when I was in school and loved it. Plus I quickly learned you want to work for yourself. So I saved up in order to buy a farm. But I had very little money, and finding a place I could afford was hard."

Jim learned that in Maine land was going for $150 an acre—that was in 1976—so he got in his one-ton flatbed truck with all his belongings and drove to Maine and purchased eighty acres. He planted apple trees and vegetables, grew potatoes in the garden, sold his produce at the farmers' market, and worked odd jobs for his neighbors.

In 1984 Jim met Megan. She was two generations away from farm life, but her grandparents were from Maine and her parents had a country home with twenty acres where they kept chickens and goats and grew vegetables. Throughout her four years at Middlebury College in Vermont, she worked on farms.

In 1985, a year after meeting Jim, Megan married him, and in 1991 Peter was born. Four years later came Caleb, then Sarah in 1998, and Amy in 2003. The kids all work on the farm.

"For one thing we need the help," Jim told me. "But farm life is also a great way to raise kids. It's good for kids to know what Mom and Dad do, and living and working together is a good lifestyle. We've been farming for thirty years now, and it's really taken a generation to set up the land and we'd like to hand it to the kids; that's my dream. But we need to figure out what this farm is going to be like in ten to twenty years. What's the scale; will there be room for all of us? Hopefully we'll be able to feed all of us and raise more than one family. Megan is more open-minded about making sure the kids get experience off the farm. I'm all for them making up their own mind, but that idea of them continuing on grows on me. I'd be especially tickled to see our kids go into farming."

The Gerritsens start their farming year in April by preparing the fields for rotation planting. Jim explained, "We're on the ground by the tenth of May, planting grain first, then potatoes, so we can harvest the grain in August before we get into harvesting potatoes."

First they go over the field to take out the rocks. Because they don't use a picking machine—which takes out rocks too—at the harvest, they have to get the rocks out while they're turning the soil over. Then they start planting. Jim drives the tractor, which pulls the two-row potato planter, a plowlike machine that makes the furrows and adds fish meal fertilizer. Megan and three other women sit on the back of the planter and cut the seed tubers into four sections. The seed pieces are placed on a conveyor, which drops them into the furrow and then mounds the dirt on top. "Always women. Women are best for this work," Jim said. "Some may tell you otherwise. But men are all thumbs and women work quickly."

The potato plants grow very fast, doubling in size every seven days. Within five weeks "row closure"—when the rows of plants begin to touch each other—has taken place, and getting into the field with any equipment without damaging the plants is impossible. So before complete closure occurs, the Gerritsens and their crew return to the field to mound up the potato plant hills. They go through doing this four times, making large, pointed hills that drain well. "Little tricks like making big hills we learned from neighbors," Jim said. "There's a wealth of information up here and we've been trained by the best potato farmers."

The potato flowers start blooming around the middle of July—white, pink, red, purple flowers. The colors indicate the type of potato and can form clusters, or spikes, and several even look like a peacock. "Some folks don't even know potato plants flower," Jim said incredulously.

Usually the Gerritsens don't need to irrigate much at all. Not in misty, cool Maine. In August, twenty to thirty days before harvest, the potato vines, the green portion of the plant above ground, are killed with a propane flame, rather than chemically as on a nonorganic potato farm, which stops the tubers in the ground from growing. In the second half of September they begin picking.

"Since I've been here, Jim hasn't taken a job off the farm," Megan said. But it took a long time to turn a small organic potato farm into a successful business and make money at it.

"It's not that we had any disasters that set us back," Jim said. "I guess we're just too conservative; we move pretty slow. The idea that Rome wasn't built in a day must have been invented by an organic farmer."

In the beginning the Gerritsens grew a wide range of varieties every year. They'd plant three or four new types, and after three years if a variety was still successful they'd add it to their product line. Now they're working on a Yukon Gold variety that has blush and gold color: it's very beautiful, genetically stable, and, according to Jim, "It does well at the farmers' market. We want to be a quality grower that is reliable, a highly respected delicatessen rather than a Wal-Mart."

Initially, Wood Prairie Farm was very isolated. There were no telephone or electric lines on the farm in the 1980s. "But we were part of the organic farmers' association and back then people who wanted organic would come looking for us," Jim recalled. "We'd ship them a fifty-pound box and they'd come back the next year."

But it was really a combination of the web store and mail-order that made them a viable business. "We're so small we can't sell wholesale," he said. "With only ten acres, we're not even on the radar screen of potato wholesalers. I'm not even sure my neighbors at three hundred and four hundred acres can sell wholesale. Ninety percent of our business is direct order."

When the Gerritsens finish harvesting in October they send out their catalog and ship their crop from October to April to customers all across the country. "And we can ship to a standard," Jim said, "and because we control the shipping, the potatoes don't get all beat up. People appreciate the quality. And most of my repeat customers tell me they've never even conceived of a potato tasting so good."

About that great *flavor*: I wondered if it's because a food is organic that it tastes better? Bingo! I clearly had asked Jim Gerritsen his favorite question, and he was off and running— although preaching to the already inclined faithful—and I wouldn't get a word in edgewise now. Good flavor, according to Jim, is the result of the climate, soil, and plant variety, but the last ingredient is the *quality* of the organic farming.

Jim said, "Organic makes for better tasting only when it's done right. It gets complicated because a lot of companies have jumped into organic and think they can make a killing. There's a big difference in quality between a corporate operation that waits out the thirty-six months and one day after chemicals have been used [to meet the organic certification requirements], compared with my thirty years on land that was an abandoned cattle farm before I got it. Since the land was cleared in the 1920s it has never had any chemicals on it, only cow manure and now the dried fish meal I fertilize with. Its mineral content is managed naturally. And there's no comparison nutritionally between our product and off-the-shelf."

Of course, for Jim Gerritsen being a better farmer is synonymous with being an organic farmer. "It's a philosophical thing," he told me. "The challenge is how do humans interact with nature harmoniously—and not just have a sustained pre-serve. How do we rejuvenate our environment in a way that doesn't degrade it? We need to build up the soil and leave land in better condition than when we found it."

My father's words—about farmers being rural philoso-phers—resonate as Jim's convictions continue to spill out, and I'm remembering Jim's admission that he's a bit of a fanatic about potatoes.

"We believe that family scale is the right scale for food and agriculture and the continuance of democracy. Democracy is founded on widespread ownership of the land, and the good thing about the organic movement is that it is creating markets. Maine now has the youngest farming population in the country due to organic farming—fifteen percent of Maine's dairies are organic. Through organic farming rural communities are revi-talized and people are given self-respect."

For most of us, a farm's scale, whether ownership rests in the hands of many or a few, and how organic farming affects rural communities are not topics that have much relevance. Who would have guessed that farm size or organics could have anything to do with democracy? You have to wonder what in particular about being a potato farmer in Maine would inspire such independent thinking. And then I remembered the place.

I pulled a Rose Gold potato from a Wood Prairie bag—the variety is a Gerritsen family favorite. The brown skin is tinged with pink and still dusted with a powder of rich Maine dirt. The dirt is a reminder to me of that country, the land, and of its sig-nificant power. Potatoes can—and do—grow anywhere and everywhere. But in a region such as Maine, which is light-starved and limited in its growing season, the fact that *anything* can grow there is just short of miraculous. And when you live on such land, when it gives you and your family a life, and creates a culture and an ethic that surrounds you, it surely becomes natu-ral to want to care for it. For the Gerritsens it seems it's not as much about potatoes as it is the stewardship of the land and the place, about being part of the culture of Maine potato farming.

I'm not as convinced as Jim is that quality organic farming is what guarantees great flavor. Organic or not, to my way of thinking, it's really the caring for, the thinking about, what feeds you and, without a doubt, the passion that makes the taste special and different.

I knew enough from reading the catalog to wash the potatoes only just before cooking, and to bake them. The taste—a gentle creamy, very flavorful taste—is wonderful.

{ **MEGAN GERRITSEN'S DILLY POTATO SALAD** }

Serves 6 to 8.

5 medium-sized waxy potatoes, such as Reddale or Caribé
5 thin slices red onion, coarsely chopped
½ cup sour cream
1 tablespoon mayonnaise
2 tablespoon minced fresh dill
Salt and freshly ground black pepper to taste

Boil the potatoes in their skins in a large pot of water until tender, drain, and let them cool. Cut into cubes. Combine the remaining ingredients and toss gently with the potatoes.

EVERY DAY THEY WAKE AND
SMELL THE COFFEE

{ BARRINGTON COFFEE ROASTING COMPANY }

I DON'T REMEMBER exactly how I first discovered Barrington Coffee Roasting Company. This is actually sort of a strange memory malfunction, given that I've been drinking Barrington coffee every day now for eight years—and coffee's very important to me. What I do recall clearly is the first time I visited the little coffee-roasting company in the town of Great Barrington in the Berkshires.

The Berkshire mountains are in Massachusetts, and are what the Poconos are to Pennsylvania or the Catskills are to New York: that place in the mountains where urban dwellers flee to enjoy the country and escape the city's summer heat. The Berkshires are old mountains, worn and unobtrusive, which have down-sized now to the point we should probably categorize them as hills. The range stretches from southern Vermont through the western edge of Massachusetts and remains populated with small towns—one or two of them striving to qualify as city. Yet in southern New England terms, the Berkshires are still rural. Rural, yes, but with their own style of urbane culture: the Berkshire town of Stockbridge is where Norman Rockwell lived and painted, and near the Tanglewood Music Center, where the Boston Symphony Orchestra retreats to perform each summer. Perhaps it is the region's proximity to the great and big cities or the intellectual influence from its many colleges, but it feels very cosmopolitan in the Berkshires. It is a place where good restaurants are expected and where it is not surprising to find a real coffeehouse—or an extraordinary coffee roaster.

A little overconfident about how long it would take me to get to Great Barrington (traveling on more two-laners than expected), I arrived late. But behind a roadside business, I found Barrington Roasting Company in a small structure comprised of two large white and bright rooms, both with a heady coffee breeze floating through them. I was graciously welcomed and, of course, offered a cup of espresso.

"Nice extraction," Barth Anderson complimented his business partner Greg Charbonneau. Happily for me, the ominous-sounding "extraction" meant only that I was about to get an exceptional cup of espresso. Nice-looking young men, my grandmother would say. Yes, but clearly of their hip thirtysomething generation, I would say. Barth is tall and side-burned and has light brown—maybe once blond—hair. Greg, a smaller man, with a shaved head. Both are dressed in the tiny-self-owned-business uniform of sweatshirts and jeans. When I arrived the three of us had moved quickly toward the far end of the roasting room, where various coffee-making paraphernalia sat on a kitchen counter. Barth and I stood reverently before the chrome-plated machine as Greg played the wizard of espresso. First he ground freshly roasted Indian beans and filled the machine's metal filter cup. Turning water pressure knobs, he drew liquid through to the spigot and into a cup, then dumped both grounds and coffee into a trash bin. He repeated the process three times, discarding what looked okay to me, then finally handed Barth and me each a little demitasse of deep, rich elixir foamed over with a creamy chestnut-colored froth. Termed the *crema*, it is the mark of perfectly extracted espresso. It was that.

As I sipped, Barth introduced me to the roasting machine. The kettle-drum belly was enameled a cheery red and held the pale white-green beans. The chrome blending arm in place, it stood elegantly, patiently waiting to do its job. Heat is what releases the flavor complexities in coffee beans, I learned, but the application of fire to beans can accentuate or destroy the flavors and requires skill and a sense of the art form. Because the roasting of green or raw beans ranges ever so slightly between twelve and sixteen minutes, it requires a knowledgeable eye and nose to determine doneness. It also requires an understanding of the beans—their source and *terroir*. So the roaster acts as maestro and revealer of flavor.

It is through a "cupping" that the beans' flavor is divulged, I learned next. Like a wine tasting, a cupping is the protocol for assessing flavor and is used by coffee professionals to evaluate a sample of beans. On a long, wooden-planked table, Barth placed several handle-less white cups coupled with small round-bowled spoons for us. He put an amount of just-ground coffee in each cup and poured hot water from a kettle till the coffee reached near overflow. The next step was "breaking the crust"—or plunging a spoon through the floating coffee grounds—and then sticking your nose close to the rim and sniffing the coffee. The crust is then removed—that is, the grounds are pushed aside as the spoon scoops liquid—and very loudly and emphatically, with a quick inhale, the coffee is slurped from the spoon. The purpose of such a big, noisy slurp is that it sprays coffee over the maximum number of taste buds. Finally, you're supposed to spit the coffee out. All incredibly impolite, but it works.

"This one has a bit less acidity, more body, though, don't you think?" Barth asked. "Do you like the lemon taste of the Costa Rican? Or the body in the Sumatran?" Barth was trying to analyze my likes, trying to determine what would evoke the notion of amazing coffee for me.

You really *can* taste the differences in the various beans with just a sniff and a slurp—we tried a Costa Rican, a Sumatran, and a Jamaican Blue Mountain. The flavor was also affected by the color of the roast—there was a cinnamon roast, a city roast, and a French roast to test. (From lightest to darkest, the roasts are commonly termed cinnamon, city, full-city, Vienna, Italian, and French.) Yet what the cupping for me ultimately revealed of flavor went well beyond the color of the roast or the bean's origin. The taste sensation was exquisite, certainly a testament to Barth's and Greg's expertise and attention to detail. And back then—it was 1998—the scene at Barrington Coffee represented the emergence of a new way of thinking about coffee.

In 1971 Americans consumed half the world's coffee output, and 75 percent of every American over the age of ten drank coffee. Twenty years later coffee drinking had dropped to 51 percent and might have continued to decline if it weren't for Americans' discovery of specialty coffee. In 1990 the Specialty Coffee Association of America reported that there were about two thousand specialty coffee retailers in the United States, five years later there were over eleven thousand, and by 2001 that number had doubled. Of course, way out in front of the specialty pack is the multimillion-dollar-a-year Starbucks.

Started in 1971 as a coffee-roasting company, Starbucks sold dark roast coffee beans (some roasters fondly call them "Charbucks") primarily within their local Seattle market. But in 1985 the company began to expand into coffee cafés, airport kiosks, historic-register hotels—you know where they are. By 2005, Starbucks—whose most phenomenal growth came in the 1990s—boasted eight thousand cafés in more than thirty countries. Although there is a certain amount of disdain among coffee aficionados for Charbucks, few would deny that it is largely because of Starbucks that the whole baby-boomer generation—and now the younger generations—learned about lattes, cappuccino, and full-city roast coffee. And we didn't just learn to walk the walk and talk the coffee talk with Starbucks; more important, we began to pay attention to all the elements that must precisely blend to make a great cup of coffee: aroma, its agricultural heritage, quality control, the art of identifying and accentuating flavors.

To listen to Barth and Greg describe their backgrounds and how they came to be coffee roasters, it's as if everything coffee—American's growing passion for specialty coffee—converged at exactly the right time to help them realize what they were going to do in life.

Barth and Greg both grew up in western Massachusetts but didn't know each other until 1984, when they left their respective high schools and entered Simon's Rock College (a liberal arts and sciences college designed expressly for high-school-age students), a division of Bard College in Great Barrington, Massachusetts.

Barth laughed and said, "When we became friends, that was really when our common interest in tasting and exploring the world of coffee, and food, and wine, and spirits started. That's something that hasn't stopped since. And we became quite passionate. We used to roast coffee in a pan on a burner in our house at college. We did all kinds of crazy things like that."

Barth initially had the coffee background and knowledge. As a teenager living in Worcester, Massachusetts, he'd worked at a traditional coffeehouse called the Coffee Kingdom, and in college he'd bring different coffees back from there to try out with Greg.

"Love of coffee started for me at the Coffee Kingdom," Barth recalled. "At that point in time, in 1980, I had no understanding that coffee was grown in different parts of the world and tasted differently from each place. The more I got involved in the world of coffee, the more I realized the nuance of what I now refer to—similar to wine—as the *terroir*. The inspirational thing for me was that I could *taste* these differences, based upon where they were grown. Where these coffees were grown and how they came to be is something we have continued to explore. And that's kind of the heart and soul of it. That's where things began for us."

It might seem at first incongruous with his future in coffee, but Barth graduated with a degree in environmental sciences. Straight from college, he got a grant in fisheries ecology to work on water quality and fisheries management of the Hudson River. He then took a job as a microbial ecologist for the Institute of Ecosystem Studies in Millbrook, New York, a private research company studying the effects of acid rain.

He said, "I did a lot of field and lab work and pretty much realized if I was going to make more than six dollars an hour I needed a master's or Ph.D. And at the same time I wanted to find a work that was sympathetic with life, that I was passionate about, and could also help me eat."

Greg had taken a year off from Simon's Rock and so graduated after Barth in 1989 with a B.A. in art history. But while finishing his degree, he'd started roasting coffee part time—on weekends and once or twice a week—for a local coffee shop, Berkshire Coffee. After graduation he was hired as an art restoration technician for New York's Department of Historic

Preservation and restored works of art on paper. But he continued to roast coffee on weekends and in the evenings.

"When I was doing art restoration for the state of New York," Greg said, "I was all set to get a master's in conservation, just as Barth was going to get his in environmental sciences. Then the woman I worked under went to Malta for six months and left me in charge of the paper lab. And I got a taste of what it was going to be like sitting in a lab by myself forty hours a week staring at artwork, which was kind of fun, but kind of crazy. I decided: 'You know what, I don't need to get my master's in this. I think I need to see more people on a daily basis.' So I left, went to do French furniture restoration for a while, and then rapidly decided coffee was going to be my thing."

In 1993 Greg moved to Seattle, but only for seven months. Once in Starbucks-land it really became clear to him how big coffee was becoming, and could be. "And since I was already involved I got more fired up about it and moved back home and decided to do it full time."

Greg went back to work for Berkshire Coffee. "Yeah, I was doing most of the roasting there; the owner seemed ready to not be burdened with it anymore. So we made this deal, I'd pretty much take over the roasting in exchange for ownership of the roaster."

Barth laughed. "It was this wacky agreement where we roasted coffee for her for the rest of creation in exchange for a roaster. It was a great deal—sort of."

So Greg got the roaster from Berkshire Coffee and started a tiny business in a space the size of a garage. At the same time, he'd also started a little café in Lenox. "And there was no way I could do that and roast coffee, too. So Barth came in as my partner and did the roasting until we got Café Lenox up and running, and then I was able to pull back from the café and become a full-time roaster again."

I wondered how they'd learned to roast coffee.

Greg said, "I learned a little bit in the beginning from the woman who owned Berkshire Coffee, who, I think, basically learned by talking on the phone with the roaster manufacturer.

She knew enough to get by, and then I took over where she left off and did all the reading I could do, talked to people, and a lot of trial and error. Eventually Barth and I refined our roasting technique, and the end result is we're light-handed with the coffee beans and try to bring out the best characteristics without masking or overwhelming them with roasting degrees."

Barth added, "We knew we had had a number of really heightened, quality experiences drinking other people's coffee which were formative and made an impression on us. The Coffee Kingdom's roasting style influenced us. And a fellow who is now back in the coffee business after a period of being out of the industry named George Howell—he signed a non-compete when he sold his small Boston chain to Starbucks—his roasting style had a huge impact on us."

If you lived in Boston in the 1970s and liked great coffee, as I did, chances are you knew George Howell's Coffee Connection. George had discovered the meaning of coffee in the late 1960s when he was living in Berkeley, California, and was introduced first to the original Peet's. Peet's is a dark-roast coffee similar to Starbucks—was actually Starbucks very first competitor—but was later bought out by the chain. George was entranced with his discovery and the possibilities of what real coffee could taste like. And although Peet's initiated him to the ways of good coffee, he quickly found another Berkeley roaster that had a lighter roast. It was in the lighter roasts that George Howell found inner peace, his genius, and eventual prosperity. He developed techniques, a roasting style that was unusual and exceptional, and took it with him when he moved to the East Coast. He opened his first shop in Cambridge's Harvard Square in 1974, down the street from where I worked. I can still remember the first time I walked inside the tiny Coffee Connection. The aroma transported me to a place and a time—a nearly forgotten coffee memory. My parents were not coffee drinkers when they were in the United States, but when we lived or traveled in Central or South America, my father drank coffee. And even when I was a little girl he gave me sips, then cups, mixed with lots of sugar. It was wonderful, yet coffee was merely a caf-

feine delivery system to me—the coffee of my memories unob-
tainable—until George Howell came to town.

Barth said, "We weren't looking to copy George, just to
learn about his product, about roasting, and some very, very
unique origins that he was exploring. We refer to his style as
'classic full-city,' which is very, very different than full-city in
Starbucks language—that's very dark roast. Classic full-city is an
East Coast style, where the roasting takes a back seat to the coffee. You want the coffee to come first, and so you must find coffees that are so good that you don't have to overwhelm them with
a heavy-handed roast flavor in order to have a dynamic experience. We believe a coffee is only as good as it is grown and milled.
We cannot make a coffee any better by roasting it properly."

Ah, yes, finding the specialty beans—grown in so many
countries now—*is* part of the trick. There is a coffee-growing
belt circumferencing the world that stretches from the Tropic of
Cancer to the Tropic of Capricorn. Interestingly, coffee was not,
as many of us might guess, born in the mountains of South
America, but in Africa. The legend goes that it was first discovered in A.D. 844 when an Arabian goatsman named Kaidi
noticed that his goats were friskier after chewing on the berries
of a certain small shrub growing on the hillsides of Ethiopia.
Coffee came to the Western Hemisphere in 1723 when a French
naval officer, Gabriel-Mathieu de Clieu, stole a seedling from
the French Jardin Royale and then made his way to Martinique,
sharing his water ration with the plant on his long sea journey.
That one seedling was to become the ancestor to most of the
coffee bushes in the Americas—and the propagator of a coffee
industry that would eventually produce 90 percent of the
world's coffee.

Barth said, "When we first got into it we didn't really know
how to source good coffee. There were a lot of people who
wanted to sell us coffees that unfortunately were quite
deplorable. Initially we would try to acquire samples from brokers and importers, roast the small green samples from different
stock lots, and then cup them and analyze them to try to determine if they had any merit or not. In that process we developed
our language. We also tasted many completely heinous coffees."

But Barth and Greg got lucky in 1995 when they established a relationship with Costa Rica, which in the world of specialty coffee was the forerunner of super-quality grown and processed green coffee. The Costa Rican La Minita is the flagship coffee from Bill McAlprin's world-renowned La Minita farm. Through McAlprin's example, other farmers realized they could produce something that was exceptional and sell it for more money.

And in that same year, Greg and Barth started working with the Coffee Source, whose Guatemalan rep helped them negotiate bringing in small amounts of green beans in transport containers. Usually transport containers hold many multiple hundreds of bags, and for a tiny company like Barrington to try and move only a few hundred bags at one time was nearly impossible. The Coffee Source helped them team up with other small, quality-minded buyers and move big container volumes to the United States and then split it up when it got here. Barth said, "When we realized this was possible, we said, 'Hey, can we do this with other origins?'"

"Now when we're in the process of approving a coffee from a farm we've worked with—in some cases eight years—we'll have a whole history of experience with the coffee from that very same plot of land and we'll taste a difference. Our roasting approach is the same, so what we taste is the subtle difference in the weather pattern for that growing region. Or if they changed the way they processed, we'll taste that. It's really exciting. Typically it will be a positive. Sometimes we're thrown a curve ball and we say, 'Wow, what a really unfortunate year it was for XYZ farm!' And that year we'll have to find another exceptional coffee from that region. It keeps us lively."

It also creates a constant need for new sources. "One example," offered Greg, "is East Timor—one of the youngest democracies in the world right now—the revitalization process for the country and government is to revitalize their coffee plantations. We got a sample and it's just fantastic—now we're sort of in love with coffee from East Timor."

Coffee plants must have a cool dry season and a warm rainy season, so equatorial, subtropical countries are optimal for growing. The finest coffee, *Coffea arabica*—named for its original fifteenth-century promoters, the Arabs—grows best at an altitude of between three thousand and six thousand feet. *Coffea robusta*, the dominant bean used in canned blends, can grow at sea level and is cheaper and hardier, but lacks the depth of flavor found in arabica beans. Invariably the best coffees come from Guatemala, Costa Rica, Ethiopia, Yemen, and Kenya. Jamaican "Blue" and Hawaiian (the only state to grow coffee in the United States) Kona coffee have earned gold-standard reputations too, unfortunately with a high price tag to match—so valuable that "counterfeit" scams have arisen. In late 1996 Kona growers were infuriated to discover that an independent Californian distributor had been passing off Panamanian beans as Hawaiian Kona.

Price has affected much of the world's attitude toward coffee. The British turned to tea as their favorite beverage and caffeine source when it was determined that one pound of tea could yield up to two hundred cups, versus coffee's fifty cups per pound. This made it more affordable than coffee—except, of course, for the colonists who'd had a tea tax imposed on them. The high price of tea incited protest not only in the 1773 Boston Tea Party but in the form of a campaign to increase Americans' coffee drinking.

But the price of coffee is more commonly linked to production than taxes. In 1869 the disease known as "coffee rust," *Hemileia vastatrix*, appeared in Ceylon and spread throughout Asia. The resulting sky-high coffee prices destroyed the industry, and tea cultivation replaced the bean's propagation there. In the next century "black frost" would decimate coffee bushes in Brazil—the largest coffee producer in the world—first in 1975 and then again in 1994. Not coincidentally, that twenty-year span was when coffee consumption dropped in the United States by 25 percent.

However, Corby Kummer, the *Atlantic Monthly*'s wonderful food writer and author of *The Joy of Coffee*, suggests an additional contributing factor to coffee's overall decline during that time—and an explanation for the eventual explosive growth in the specialty-coffee industry. Understanding that higher prices meant lower consumption, the big commercial coffee companies put more and more of the cheaper róbusta beans into their blends in order to keep the price down. It was coffee that cost less but it tasted less too, and sent consumers scurrying to soft drinks as their beverage choice. Except for those who knew about the good stuff and figured out how to identify, develop, and promote great coffee to people who would pay for taste. (In the United States coffee was surpassed by soft drinks in 1975. In 2005, however, coffee drinking had climbed back and was tied with soft-drink consumption.)

Greg said, "We grew rapidly in the beginning—maybe tripling the number of pounds we bought after the first year— but soon we settled into a four or five percent growth rate. Growing slowly but steadily has been really great for us. We don't really market; people come to us already knowing that they want our coffee."

"We have standing invitations to Brazil, Africa, Guate mala, the Hawaiian Islands, Costa Rica," Barth said. "But because we do what we do to order, we can't go, we don't leave here. We don't integrate ourselves into the U.S. specialty-coffee world in terms of going to shows, trying to advertise, doing seminars, and working with different guilds. We kind of like to hang out and do our own thing. For a farm to be able to get coffee to us here, and for us to analyze it here, gives us a real base of normalcy in which to operate. We analyze things in the same environment with the same set of criteria rather than being on the road infatuated with the people and the pristine mountain air—which is completely wonderful. I think it's helped us be very, very critical and uniform in our protocol year to year. We have been invited to so many different places. The year before last we passed on an invitation to India. They asked us to help develop an espresso program for the country. We were asked to go to Cambodia to develop that nation's coffee. But we also tell our customers that we're going to roast their coffee to order for them, and that's what we set ourselves up to do."

I thought perhaps, too, Barth and Greg's desire to stay home in the Berkshires might have to do with their growing families. Greg had married in 1996, and when we spoke in 2006 his son was seven years old and his daughter was four. "They're an inspiration," he said. "As well as my wife, Cherisse, who is really into coffee now too. When I first met her she was drinking Chase and Sanborn out of a can and putting cream and sugar in it! She pretty quickly gave that up—not by force. She still puts cream in her coffee, but the sugar is long gone. She runs the coffeehouse in Lenox for us because we're so busy up here."

I remembered that Barth had married in 1998. The week I had visited them back then he was leaving the next day for his wedding. "She left a profession and I couldn't believe she'd do that for me. She does say from time to time—I hope it's tongue in cheek—that she married me for the Indian Mysore coffee that we sell. She was a coffee lover, but had no perception of the world that Greg and I were so deeply ensconced in. She moved out here and we had our son, going on two and a half years ago. It's wonderful to have sane and removed women in our lives—who are willing to put up with our lives."

Looking at Barrington Coffee's new facilities in Lee, Massachusetts, I was struck by how much it resembled an open-plan home. Lots of bright, airy spaces inside—walls painted in white, burnt orange, and a mellowed chartreuse green—and the outside was sided with plain, graying barn-board. A thoroughly pleasant place to come to work each day, I thought.

Barth said, "Everybody who has ever worked for us has always been involved evaluating coffees, source tasting, trying, and giving scores and comments. You try to develop a language—it's not like talking about the weather—and some pretty abstract heady discussions arise when we're breaking apart flavors, but because we all do it together, we select even better coffees. Work has to integrate with life. We had to do other things first to learn that. The business we've created has always fulfilled that dream—integration of life with work—for me."

Greg said, "I was thinking about why I got into coffee roasting and I think there is something sort of romantic about it. That's what lured me into it in the beginning: the whole thing— the aroma, the flavor, the exotic origins. And all the ritual involved, from cupping to the processing methods—drip, French press, Chemex, the vacuum brewers, the Turkish coffee espresso. Each one has its own set of crazy rituals that you can get caught up in. It's great stuff."

"It's our work but it's so pleasing," Barth said, "something we're passionate about. Doing a tasting we all get so excited about it. Genuinely excited at the epiphany: 'I've never *tasted* anything like this.' For me the enthusiasm allows my romantic notion to continue and it doesn't seem to ever wane."

Whew! I thought to myself. They truly are living their dream. And sure enough, when I asked them what their dreams and aspirations for the future were, there were long exhales and pauses. Then Greg spoke: "I mostly see us doing what we're doing now, but doing more of it. Making more happy and fanatical coffee devotees, not compromising the quality of what we do while we grow."

Then Barth added, "This business has been focused on trying to do everything at the highest level of quality that we can. Everything we do, we think about it in those terms and it's not like it's a challenge for us. It's just the way we both think about things. We feel so much joy out of having a quality thing come forth from this brand we've created. I don't know if I have aspirations greater than that. But I just hope I get to do this for a long time."

"Like having you for a customer of ours for so many years," Barth said to me. "You hold regard for what we do, and that makes us feel so great. It's like a miracle! How could what we put together and create have so much of a lasting impression for you? It may sound goofy, but I get a lot of self-respect from that. That we're doing something right."

He knows. Barth said it delicately—"a regard" for what they do and that they "create a lasting impression" for me. But he knows it has gone far beyond just my thinking they are "doing something right." They understand that coffee is very personal. They don't force their opinions, but rather accommodate mine. And I am awed by their powers. They are able to taste a nano-nuance of flavor, and they are so into it, *so* into it. They are fanatics, but what would I do without them? It's as if they know—although I have never told them—that my first sip of coffee came when I was seven and visiting a Guatemala coffee plantation with my family. They know how, through smell, intensity, and complexity of flavors, to give me back ever so subtly, instantaneously, a tiny memory of a wonderful flavor moment in my life. And they do it every day. What a gift.

TIPS FOR A GREAT CUP OF COFFEE, FROM BARRINGTON COFFEE ROASTING COMPANY:

1. Use good filtered or bottled water (heated to a temperature of 195 to 205 degrees).

2. Select good-quality arabica coffee beans and grind them yourself. Use 2 tablespoons per 6 ounces of water (whole beans measure out the same as ground).

3. For either manual or electric drip coffeemakers a metal filter is preferable to paper, as it retains the oils necessary to the taste.

4. Brewing-cycle time should range between 4 and 6 minutes, which is easily accomplished using a manual drip; if using an electric drip, try one with a wattage rating over 1,000 for the correct temperature and brewing-cycle control. The plunger pot produces a different but equally great cup of coffee.

TIPS FOR A PERFECT ESPRESSO EXTRACTION:

1. Make sure that your espresso machine is equipped with the proper water filtration for your area.

2. Adjust your machine to dispense 203-degree water at 8 to 9 bars pump pressure.

3. Rinse the group heads and wipe the portafilters before each extraction.

4. Always grind just prior to extraction, and grind only enough for one portafilter at a time.

5. Use enough coffee! Many people in the espresso trade recommend only 14 grams for a double, while we have found that doubles made with 17 to 18 grams are far superior.

6. Balance your grind and tamp to yield about 1 ounce in 25 seconds for a single or about 2 ounces in 25 seconds for a double. Be a fanatic: use a timer to make sure you're on the mark.

7. Enjoy your espresso immediately! When extracted properly, our espresso features a thick, reddish brown *crema* with a sweet, nutty aroma. You will experience a syrupy mouth-feel with sweet caramel flavors and a smooth finish.

{ BARRINGTON AFFOGATTO }
Serves 1.

1 scoop vanilla gelato or ice cream
18 to 20 grams (approximately 1 ½ tablespoons) espresso
beans, plus additional for sprinkling

Place one generous scoop of the finest vanilla gelato or ice cream available into a 6-ounce cappuccino cup.

Grind and evenly portion the espresso beans into a hot, seasoned portafilter and tamp with 30 pounds of pressure. Balance fineness of grind and tamping pressure to extract 2 ounces of espresso in 25 seconds using 203.5-degree water. Pour over the gelato or ice cream. Dust with freshly ground espresso and enjoy immediately.

{ BARRINGTON SINGLE-MALT AFFOGATTO }

Serves 1.

1 scoop vanilla ice cream
1 heaping teaspoon dark, southern-Italian style coffee beans
4 tablespoons single-malt Scotch

Place one generous scoop of the creamiest vanilla ice cream you can find into a 6-ounce cappuccino cup.

Coarsely grind the coffee beans. Pour single-malt Scotch over the top of the ice cream. (The folks at Barrington have long been fond of the peaty smoke flavors of single-malt Laphroaig. The ten-year-old kind works just fine for this application.) Sprinkle the coarsely ground Italian roast on top.

A CRAB-CAKE UNION

{ CHESAPEAKE BAY GOURMET }

ACCORDING TO THOSE scrutinizers of culinary origins, food historians, it's impossible to determine which individual, or culture, to credit with being the first to eat crab. What historians can tell us about ancient crab eating is that the Greeks and Romans were universally unenthusiastic about it. And over the centuries various societies have viewed crabs unkindly: the word *crab*—in several languages—describes a person with a bad disposition. Cancer is not only the deadly disease, but the Latin word for crab. But surely much of the crab's bad rap is derived from its peculiar appearance: those scary-looking claws and beady, antennaed eyes, and its unpredictable and suspicious sideways walk. So whoever that first crab eater was, he was likely both very hungry and very brave. Of course looks aren't everything, as anyone who likes seafood can attest. In the United States crab is second only to shrimp in shellfish popularity and our seventh most popular seafood.

My own experience with crab was limited by a childhood in the Midwest—handy for recognizing a good Wisconsin Limburger cheese, but not too helpful for encouraging an appreciation of ocean-run stuff, like fresh crab. Adulthood, and a move to the East Coast, brought the chance to catch up. My first taste was the gangly snow crab—just caught off Quebec's North Shore, it was sublimely poached in a wine court-bouillon by my French-Canadian hosts. Next I traveled to Alaska, and in the restaurant atop the Captain Cook Hotel, overlooking Cook Inlet in Anchorage, I ate crab imperial—lump crabmeat in a sherry white sauce—made with king crab. Several years later, in southeast Alaska, I helped the chef from the Glacier Country

Inn bait jerry cans with fish heads to lure in the Dungeness crabs. He delicately steamed the huge crabs, served them with melted butter, his poppyseed bread, and kitchen-garden arugula salad. And then came my introduction to blue crabs—not steamed but as a cake—and true passion was born.

As early as colonial days there were crab recipes in the United States—many calling for crab-cake ingredients like bread crumbs and spices—but usually named something like "crab patties" or "crab croquettes." The phrase "crab cake" initially appeared in print in Crosby Gaige's 1930 *New York World's Fair Cook Book.* Yet it wasn't until the late 1980s, as part of the New American cuisine movement, that crab cakes became the rage. Even la-di-da restaurants such as the Mansion on Turtle Creek near Dallas, Detroit's Rattlesnake Club, and Emeril's in New Orleans added crab cakes to their menus. Crab cakes are quintessentially American, likely invented here and made famous then fancy by American chefs. And although it is not uncommon today to get a crab cake made with China Sea crab, historically the crab of choice for classic cakes has been the American blue.

In 1974 William Warner wrote a book entitled *Beautiful Swimmers.* Warner's book is delightful, and through sheer depth and breadth reveals his admiration for the blue crab, but never really tries to claim for it absolute superiority over any other crab. This is fortuitous, since in the over thirty years since Warner's book, the blue crab has become a less and less reliable resource.

These beautiful, savory swimmers come from the oldest and largest commercial crab fishery in the world. Blue crab ranges from Nova Scotia down through South America, but typically over half of the commercial catch comes from the largest estuary in North America, the 180-mile-long Chesapeake Bay, where the crab season lasts from April to December. Always our most harvested crab, the blue's popularity may be partially attributed to its illustrious 140-year history as Chesapeake Bay's most constant and sustainable seafood product. Most Atlantic blue crabs are caught hard, and named "jimmies" (legal-size males), "she-crabs" (immature females), "peelers" (crabs about to shed their shell), and "sooks" (mature females). If you're eating soft-shelled crabs (crabs that have shed their shell but not yet grown a new one) in this country it will always be a blue crab.

In 1998, when I first talked to Ron and Margie Kauffman, they were eight years into their co-ownership—with Margie's brother and sister-in-law of the family-run Chesapeake Bay Gourmet, based in Baltimore and makers of an absolutely great crab cake. Back then Ron told me, "We buy nearly all blue crab and as much of that as is possible from the Chesapeake because the crabs are steamed rather than boiled from there, producing a dryer crabmeat which holds together better in a crab cake. Plus the bay crab processors employ women pickers with generations of experience—producing very clean crabmeat."

Eight years later, when I spoke again with the Kauffmans, Ron said, "We really have been buying *some* crabmeat from the South China Sea for, I guess, maybe ten years, but not to the extent we do now. Recently there is just not enough jumbo lump crabmeat here in the States—particularly in Maryland. Not to mention the price of the Maryland crab."

What happened? A combination of things: Several other of the bay's seafood options have been disastrously impacted by environmental changes and overharvesting—oysters and striped bass, for example—leaving blue crab to satisfy seafood appetites. This is not to say that crabs have escaped environmental pressures. The blue crab harvest has fluctuated greatly—more often seeing a decline—in the last ten years. There are daunting obstacles to blue crab's sustainability. Certainly the environmental impact of fertilizer run-off into the bay has taken its toll, but also a factor is the increase in the area's human population, over 50 percent since the 1950s, which makes for less crab habitat and more folks eating them.

"And the quality of the blue crab has really diminished since we started our business," Margie Kauffman said. "Not the quality of the crab itself, but the quality in the picking of the crab. I love this country, but what's being produced overseas is beautiful and relatively shell-free. I went out in a pinch last October or November—I was entertaining and on a whim went to a local place on Kent Island near where we live—and bought a pound of jumbo. And I was shocked! First of all by the price—it was thirty dollars a pound—and then I brought it home and I was appalled at the shells in it. I was making a crab dip, I actually made it up, and I looked at Ron and said, 'We can't serve this to our guests.' And I threw it away. The attention to detail wasn't there, it has shifted."

Ron explained that the families who shuck oysters and pick crabs are dying off, and the next generation is leaving the bay area and the picking houses for better jobs. In addition, most of the bay crabs go directly to restaurant steam tables, so what's left for the picking houses is not good-quality crab.

"An awful lot has happened," Ron said, "over the last seven years to the yield of crab that has come out of the bay—and the pressures that are there from an environmental standpoint. We love the bay. We were born and raised along the bay. We fished and crabbed as kids and the clarity of the water was so clear back then. A lot's changed, in my case over sixty-five years, Margie's sixty-two years."

Ron and Margie Kauffman both grew up in Baltimore. Ron went to the University of Baltimore and got his degree in accounting and was a public accountant for a short time, until in 1964 he went to work for Gino's restaurant. "It was the last year Gino Marchetti, captain of the Baltimore Colts, played for the Colts. That's where I met Margie. She was working there as a computer operator," Ron recalled.

Margie said, "I was working at Gino's when I met Ron and we fell in love. That was thirty-nine years ago and we still work together happily twenty-four hours a day, every day. It's pretty scary how we can finish each other's sentences."

"I can't imagine it any other way." Ron smiled. He worked for Gino's for eighteen years before it was sold to Marriott and converted to a chain of fast-food Roy Rogers. "I left and did a couple things with Margie," Ron said. They opened up a full-service restaurant of their own, but got out of that almost as soon as they'd gotten into it. Next he was employed by a Baltimore real estate company while Margie remained at home to raise the kids. Then in 1981 Margie got a call from her brother, Les Isennock, who a year earlier had started a crab-cake company—selling frozen cakes to grocery stores—with his wife. He told Margie he was "having some problems" and asked if she could come help out for a couple weeks, "just until he got his head above water."

"Les never really did come back to work on any kind of regular basis, and Margie has been here ever since," Ron said. "She took over and ran it, and I came about a year later. We have really been the ones who had the passion and the foresight to take it beyond just selling to mom-and-pop shops."

In the 1980s, with crab-cake popularity raging, the Kauffmans decided to expand by making a premium, very elegant crab cake using jumbo lump crabmeat and selling it via mail-order. "We saw an ad in *Bon Appétit* or *Gourmet* for Eastern Shore crab," Ron said. "Trying to be coy, we had one of our employees order something from there. They brought it in and we looked at it and said, 'We do things much better than this!'"

By now both the Kauffman sons had joined the business. The younger son, Ron junior, was in charge of operations and put together a four-page catalog for the 1994 Christmas season. It was Chesapeake Bay Gourmet's first attempt at direct sales and the company nearly broke even with it.

But the Kauffman's big break came the following spring when the Maryland Department of Business and Economic Development sent a flyer out to small businesses. It was a request for applications; by completing the form a company would have the opportunity to show their product to QVC, the cable shopping channel. They applied.

"So we showed up at a big open warehouse building with folding tables," Ron said, "and we got a number, and we put our product out. There were two hundred or two hundred and fifty small businesses all showing their wares. A buyer went past and tasted our crab cakes and said they'd be in touch within two weeks, if they liked them. Well, a couple days went by, they contacted us and said, 'We want you to be one of our twenty best products from the state of Maryland.'"

It was the year that QVC was doing a series of shows entitled "Fifty in Fifty," in which reps toured fifty states in fifty weeks and picked the twenty best products from each state and then asked those companies to present their product on a three-hour, live TV show. "We'd never been on TV before," Ron laughed, "we'd never even seen QVC because we lived on the Eastern Shore of Maryland where we didn't have cable or satellite. So we thought we'd just show up and watch and see what the other people who came before us did, and then we'd do the same thing. Well, guess who got the short straw? We were first out there! Margie was scared to death, very nervous. I wasn't really nervous, I just didn't know what to expect. We got a ten-minute sell and within seven minutes we had sold out of two thousand one-dozen boxes of crab cakes. It was the biggest sale we'd ever had in our life. And from that point, it just grew exponentially and it's just continued to grow."

Sales today are almost five times greater than what Chesapeake Bay Gourmet was doing prior to their exposure on QVC. Eighty percent of their business is mail-order now—QVC and their catalog and website—with the remaining 20 percent coming from traditional food-service channels.

Margie added, "Just a sideline to that story is that when we first went on the air we had very little experience with fulfilling a customer's order, delivering the product to their door. So we were challenged after that show to get two thousand units out in two days. We had everybody helping us—our suppliers, our dry ice company—because we thought we'd never get it done. Now in less than an hour we can move two thousand packages. We have grown that part of the business with blood, sweat, and tears. Now we actually do it for other people. They come to us— they have an opportunity to be on QVC or on some website— and they don't have the knowledge or don't want to be bothered with fulfillment—and they really look to us as experts."

The success and popularity of Chesapeake Bay Gourmet crab cakes came not just because of a lucky ten minutes on TV, but from their hard work and, of course, an exceptional crab cake. The first time I had their cakes they arrived in a pretty green tin with a map of the Chesapeake Bay etched on the lid. The cakes were packed with jumbo lump or backfin meat, as opposed to the claw or flake meat (and lots of breading) that I'd seen used in some restaurant cakes.

Ron explained how they make their cakes: They buy crab-meat that's already been picked and processed by a processing house. It can be frozen, pasteurized, or fresh, but since they now use so much crab from overseas, it's either frozen or pasteurized with just a small amount of fresh. CBG workers repick every pound of crabmeat; trying to get absolutely all of the shell out. "We feel that even though our actual name is not on that box of crab cakes we don't want people to get shell-y crab cakes. Now once in a while our people miss some, but we take the extra step and repick every pound." Most of CBG products contain exclusively jumbo lump crabmeat, which is the most expensive but the easiest to find shells in.

Next the repicked crab is blended with all-natural ingredients such as mayonnaise, mustard, Worcestershire sauce, egg, and a binder. For most of their crab cakes a soda cracker crumb base is used as the binder, although bread crumbs are occasionally substituted. CBG crab cakes are hand-formed using an ice cream scoop for portion control, and then finished off by hand. They are cryogenically frozen and then hand-boxed into a variety of package configurations. Very little mechanical machinery is used in the operation, with the exception of a ribbon blender, which combines all the noncrab ingredients in the recipe. The crabmeat is actually folded in by hand so as to reduce the amount of breakage. Crabmeat is very delicate, whether it's blue crab from the United States or swimming crabs from overseas.

When I asked Margie where the recipe for the CBG crab cakes came from she said she'd culled through hundreds of old recipes, handed down through generations of watermen, and once they'd settled on it the company's recipe had changed very little. But with crab cakes it's probably not just a recipe that makes for greatness, I thought; rather, it's the crab itself. So I wondered, with this classic Chesapeake Bay—and therefore blue-crab—cake recipe, what was the effect of substituting the Asian crab?

"I believe in a blind taste test it would be hard to distinguish between the two species of crab," Margie said.

For the Kauffmans other changes, not just their conversion to Asian crab, had taken place in the eight years since our previous conversations: their elder son had gone on to different things, as had their original partners, Margie's brother and sister-in-law. Then Margie fully explained, "We actually sold the company to investors about two and a half years ago. That's why my brother and sister-in-law are no longer here. The new owners tied Ron and me into a contract for seven years to stay on because we're the spokespersons for QVC—I'm sure they didn't want to lose that. I think as long as there is an association with QVC they will want us to stay. Plus we're so knowledgeable about the business; they really needed that for the transition period."

The new owners brought in a CEO who works with the Kauffmans on a daily basis, hired more administrative staff, and did many of the things that Ron and Margie had wanted to do for the company. They also opened up a restaurant called Chesapeake Bay Crab Cakes and More in Hunt Valley and will likely be opening an additional one in Annapolis.

"We love working with QVC," Ron continued. "It's the day-to-day—the coming in here running the show [that's not as appealing to us]. We sold the company to get out of that, and that is occurring. Margie is still involved much more than she'd like to be, but slowly but surely that's being farmed out to some new people. Margie still makes the recipes. She came up with a crab quesadilla; we do lobster cakes now. We do crab fluffs and shrimp fluffs as an entrée, which is sort of a handmade ball, if you will, that surrounds a very, very elegant and rich shrimp or crab. They're to die for."

Fifty or sixty items have been developed and added to their product line for QVC in the last eight years. "Some of them fail," Margie said, "and then you just don't make them anymore. I'm constantly coming up with new recipes and am challenged to come up with new ideas. It's not that I don't like doing it. I love the job I did here—and do here. But there's only so much time you have in a day and if you're involved in a lot of meetings and dealing with production problems, then you can't be involved in R&D. The passion we have for our business is the same passion we have for our sons and grandchildren. We want to spend time with them, so it made sense to sell the business so we could back off a little bit and concentrate on the things that we really wanted to be concentrating on."

Ron said that selling the business has brought more talent into the operation so the company can continue to expand and grow—CBG uses over a million pounds of crabmeat a year, and about a quarter million pounds of lobster—without putting too much additional pressure on the Kauffmans. They now have five grandchildren. "So there are other things Margie and I want to do."

I smiled as I remembered seeing a picture of Margie and Ron basically draped in grandkids—babies in their arms, small children at their side—the bay bridge and ocean in the background. But the Kauffmans are not abandoning the business. "We don't plan on leaving anytime soon. I don't know what the good Lord has in mind, but I'm telling you *we* don't plan on checking out of this building anytime soon. Every day is exciting, every day's a challenge."

"I hope," Ron said, "we continue to be good stewards of this resource—the crabs. There's an effort down here called 'Save the Bay,' a pretty big effort, and we're staunch supporters. Between the developers and the politicians, there's pressure to take more and more of the wetlands away. All of this we're very sensitive to, we get tears in our eyes about some of this stuff. We care, and that's part of the dream for the future." And with the bay being in such a delicate ecological state, perhaps it is fortuitous that the crabmeat CBG uses from Vietnam and Thailand is the better picked and higher quality. This is another way to save the bay as well as make the best crab cakes.

Then Margie said, "The business is like a baby to me. I've spent a third of my life nurturing it, growing it, protecting it. I'd like to see some member of the family involved, to continue the passion, the legacy of it. Our boys grew up with it. They couldn't help but grow up with it, because that's what we always talked about! So I think I would like to see some member of the family still strongly involved with influencing where it goes and the quality of the product."

"Plus there are a lot of crab processors out there," Ron said, "a lot of people that try to copy what we do. And I'm almost ashamed of some of the things we see in the stores that people are calling crab cakes. We think there isn't anyone out there we've seen that does it any better than we do, and that's not boastful. I'm really reading back what people have said to us. As long as we pay attention to what we do, and we have the passion to do it the way we do it, that's the legacy we want to continue. It almost sounds corny to say it the way I just said it, I guess, but we really believe it from the bottom of our hearts. And if Margie is next to me, I'm happy. If it's in the crab-cake business, that's fine; if it's doing something else, that's where I'm going to be. Right now the crab-cake business has been very, very good to us and we hope and pray that most think we're good spokespersons for it and good guardians of it. My vision for where we take it from here is that Margie and I, whatever we do, we continue to work together as we have been and that we get to spend some additional time with interests outside of the crab-cake business but never really lose touch with it."

It had been a while since I'd last dined on Chesapeake Bay Gourmet crab cakes. So I was delighted when Margie's gift of six perfectly formed cakes arrived. The crabmeat was, as Margie had described it, beautiful. I cooked them in the oven with a slice of real butter from Vermont Butter & Cheese (see page 101), and the crab cakes went from smelling of the sea to giving an aroma that recalled the memory of a great taste. Sweet and delicate, yet powerful, they seem to be made purely of crabmeat. I'm sure they were even better than when last I'd had them. Ed and I enjoyed them together for dinner after a long day of our writing life together. It seemed only right. And I thought how much I hoped Margie and Ron would continue to work together and, indeed, never lose touch with the crab-cake business.

{ CRAB IMPERIAL }

Fills about 15 to 20 mushroom caps.

1 pound backfin crabmeat
1 tablespoon butter
1 tablespoon flour
1 cup half-and-half
Sherry to taste
Salt and pepper
1 teaspoon Old Bay or other seafood seasoning
15 to 20 mushroom caps, cleaned and stemmed (or 4 ceramic
    crab shell dishes)

Preheat the oven to 350 degrees. Clean the crabmeat and set
aside in the refrigerator. Melt the butter in a medium-size
saucepan over medium heat and stir in flour. Blend to make a
thin paste. Slowly add the half-and-half. Cook mixture, stirring
occasionally, until hot and bubbly. Add sherry, salt, pepper, Old
Bay, and crabmeat.

Remove from the heat and fill either the mushroom caps or the
ceramic shells with the mixture. Bake in the preheated oven until
lightly browned on top, about 15 to 25 minutes.

GUARDIAN OF THE GOLD

{ L. L. LANIER TUPELO HONEY }

SOLD OUT" IS what the L. L. Lanier Tupelo Honey web-site told me. Well, I knew what to do about that—how to satisfy my craving. Surely there was at least a little bit of tupelo left. I'd phone Ben Lanier directly. But getting through to him wasn't as easy as it had been in the past. I was told each time I called that he was out hunting—then it was fishing—until weeks later we finally spoke: "I lost a hundred and fifty hives so far and probably going to lose another hundred. No way out of it. I just talked to the state bee inspector, to get a letter from him, saying my bees hadn't any mites in the samples. I asked him what he personally thought killed my bees and he said insecticides. I knew what it was, pretty doggone sure of it." This was a stressed voice, a different Ben Lanier than I'd spoken with years ago, back when I'd just discovered tupelo honey.

My passion for tupelo got its start in the late 1990s, on a fly-fishing trip for redfish, when I went to Florida's panhandle for the first time. Ed and I drove from my grandparents' home in Sarasota up the west coast to Apalachicola, a small town situated on the Gulf of Mexico between Panama City and Talla-hassee. Our seven hours on the road took us through low-lying lands of orange groves and cattle farms, gave us glimpses of salt water and long, flat vistas of dry country. And there were the occasional hints along the way—the smell of burning trees, clouds of smoke, ash in the air—of the big forest fires that plagued Florida that summer. The Gulf Coast barely keeps itself above water, seeming at times to hover just below the horizon, and is linked by bridges and causeways that crisscross one hun-dred thousand-plus acres of estuarine sanctuary. Much of the

real estate boom, the urbanization, the money from northern
snowbirds and retirees passes over the Panhandle. It looks and
feels, I'd heard some say, the way the rest of Florida did fifty
years ago. Often it is referred to as the "real" or "old" Florida, and
to me—perhaps because it is still rural—it's decidedly the more
interesting section of the state.

Our mission was to fish by day and eat the region's famous
oysters by night. We arrived in the evening, oyster time, and
headed to the Boss Oyster restaurant; motto is "Shut up and
shuck." Boss prepared oysters thirty different ways—clearly a
gauntlet for us oyster eaters on a short vacation. Fortunately,
there was also the Gibson Inn. The inn's wonderful breakfasts of
toast and tupelo honey were the perfect antidote for my oyster
hangover—and the beginning of my infatuation.

It was June, the week of the summer solstice, with temperatures budging past a hundred degrees on a daily basis. It
was that type of scorching hot that is unknown up north. We
covered our pale skin with light cotton shirts and pants,
donned Foreign Legion-style hats, and lathered SPF-gazillion
on exposed skin, all in preparation for a full day in an open
boat with a beating southern sun. But even with the ashen
haze from the forest fires to screen us, the blistering heat eventually stole my brain, melting it, so that mirages of imagined
boats or tailing fish or birds appeared regularly. When not
casting, I'd try to spot signs of real fish activity, but often my
eyes wandered aimlessly over the backdrop of shoreline. The
flora was deep and thick, dark, and I wondered when, at what
point, a mangrove became a swamp. Yet in that tangle of tropical greenery, I could see from the boat tiny spots of color, for
here was the wild home of the honey flowers. I would remember this place, this mysterious jungle, the "old Florida," and the
flowers when I first spoke with Ben Lanier a few months later
about his magical tupelo honey.

"The only thing I've ever done is play with bees—and build
a couple cypress-wood houses." I heard a grin of satisfaction in
the slow, easy speech of Ben's Floridian-accented words. He's
the third generation of Laniers harvesting tupelo honey in the

Apalachicola River swamps: "My great-granddaddy came down from Birmingham to Apalachicola in 1848. He was some kind of doctor—horse doctor, I think."

In 1898 Ben's grandfather, Lavernor Laveon Lanier, started the tupelo honey business in the blossom-laden lowlands around Wewahitchka, Florida, with a five-hundred-dollar loan from a local farmer. Ben recalled, "Daddy told me L. L. lost the first two or three hundred bees and had to go back and get some more. Died of foul brood or one thing or another, but he didn't give up. He made it the second time he tried, he and his brother Arthur."

Since Granddaddy L. L. had apprenticed as a beekeeper, he recognized the distinctive flowers—ti-ti, black gum, willow, gallberry, and black tupelo—that were ideal for building up bee colony strength and stores. But it was the abundance of the swamp's white tupelo—special because pure and unmixed it's the only honey in the world that doesn't granulate—that prompted a viable business. Even today it remains the only place where white tupelo honey can be produced commercially.

In the midst of the huge state forest, Ben owns an eleven-acre parcel in one place and a seventeen-acre piece in another section, both along the river. "And the only reason I have 'em," Ben said, "is Granddaddy bought 'em for bee yards in the late 1800s, maybe 1901. The first camp was built in 1949, but the one that's there now, it's just an old tin shack. Some of my family hunts and fishes out of it. It's a wonderful place, beautiful there along the Chipola River. There's a cypress tree on the edge of the river and I have a picture of a steamboat tied to that cypress tree. The steamboat is long gone—wasn't there in my lifetime—but the cypress tree is still there, and the river's still running. I don't keep bees down there anymore. The only access to this place when the river's up a little bit is by boat."

Initially, in the days of the elder Laniers, there weren't any roads into the swamp, which is why they used steamboats to access the bee yards. They'd have to put the honey, the bees, everything on the steamboat. Later they built small flat cypress barges, but neither the steamboats nor the barges are used anymore, in part because of the expense. "And it's too much trouble," Ben said—and then suddenly asked me, "Have you ever tried tupelo honey?"

"Yes, in Apalachicola at the Gibson Inn." I'd never forget it.

"Well, chances are it was counterfeit," Ben said. "Ninety-five percent of the honey labeled as tupelo is. It has to be at least fifty percent white tupelo honey as sample tested under the microscope to be certified. Mine is closer to ninety percent white tupelo." White tupelo honey is chemically distinctive because it has a high levulose and low dextrose ratio, which also makes it acceptable for some diabetics to use as a sweetener.

For me, the word *counterfeit* certainly recategorized honey from mere toast topping to very-favored and precious status, and perhaps given the golden liquid's illustrious history it deserves such standing. It was Europe's first—and for a long time only—sweetener, found in prehistoric cave drawings in France dating back to 38000 B.C. Gilgamesh, the hero of the first known written legend, mentions honey in roughly 2000 B.C. And the Jewish dietary laws of 621 B.C., which prohibited eating any winged insect, specifically exempts honey since it isn't actually part of the bee.

When Alexander the Great returned to Greece from the Middle East, he brought back the Indian reeds "that produce honey, although there are no bees." But this cane sugar came from faraway India and China and was so limited it was used in Greek confection recipes only in combination with honey. During the eleventh century, German peasants paid their feudal lords with honey and beeswax, while in England monasteries produced honey as a by-product of their candle wax.

The New World's approach to the business of sweeteners was different from Europe's: first came sugar cane—the chief crop of the Caribbean, introduced from Brazil in 1635—and then later, in the eighteenth century, beet sugar. Both were ready and viable alternatives to honey. Plus sugar cane had two by-products—sweetener *and* rum—to drive its popularity. Although honey, too, can produce a fermented alcoholic drink, mead seems to have caught on only with Vikings.

Honey's lower status here as third-tier sweetener may also stem from the likelihood that the honeybee is not native to the Americas. In 1683 European settlers brought honeybees to New England, and Native Americans referred to them as the "white man's flies." Washington Irving in his *A Tour of the Prairies* states: "The Indians consider them [bees] a harbinger of the white man, as the buffalo is of the red man; and say that, in proportion as the bee advances, the Indian and the buffalo retire."

Honey processing has always been less mechanized and yields are smaller than the other sugars—this combination makes it expensive—plus it's bulky and difficult to handle. Honey got a bit more manageable in 1852 when a Massachusetts schoolteacher invented the first practical moveable-frame beehive, which made large-scale production easier and more economical. Then in 1921 five men from Sioux City, Iowa, pooled two hundred dollars and three thousand pounds of their honey and created a marketing association. Within twenty-five years, Sioux Bee—the name changed in 1964 to Sue Bee—had grown to more than four hundred members and produced about 20 percent of the honey in the United States. Yet hobbyists and part-time beekeepers—those with fewer than three hundred hives—still today produce about 40 percent of our honey. This is likely due in part to the fact that honey is a commodity that's associated with a specific area. With over three hundred unique, local honey flavors just in the United States, honey remains appropriately confined to regional and mail-order distribution.

Ben told me, "I don't sell any of my tupelo in bulk. Just mail-order and a few grocery stores and produce stands in Tallahassee is as far as we go. The Piggly Wiggly in Port St. Joe sells more honey than anybody else locally. They get all the snowbirds and tourist traffic coming off St. George Island."

But L. L. Lanier Tupelo doesn't need broader distribution in order to achieve a national reputation. That actually happened through a honey sale at Lanier's own produce stand in downtown Wewahitchka: award-winning film director Victor Numez passed by and bought a jar of tupelo. He was planning his 1997 movie, *Ulee's Gold,* starring Peter Fonda and ended up setting the movie on the Laniers' swamplands and bee yards. Ben provided beekeeping expertise, and his wife, Glynnis, and both his parents were cast as extras.

I admit that when I was looking for tupelo honey producers and found the L. L. Lanier website with its *Ulee's Gold* connection, I was impressed. But the Hollywood honey wasn't the only reason I first contacted Ben. I liked the website photos: the old black-and-white of the honey-making operation, the beehives and the cypress trees, the picture of L. L. Lanier, Jr., and his wife, Martha, a close-up of the tupelo flower. I liked the picture of Ben and Glynnis—she, with her long, dark, Loretta Lynn hair holding the strong, muscular arm of sandy-haired Ben, both smiling. And years later when I looked again at the site, I found baby pictures of Heath Benjamin Lanier.

"It's all I've ever done—honey—but I'm not going to pressure Heath. He can do what he wants. Daddy didn't pressure me, he gave me an out. Congressman Henry Bishop was like a brother to Daddy and he got me an appointment to the Air Force Academy. I don't know if I could have cut it. I turned it down. Mr. Henry said, 'What! After all we done?' I may be making a mistake, I said, but I don't regret it. I did have a couple of airplanes. Yeah, I can fly, Daddy saw to that."

Ben's father took over the honey business from his father, the senior L. L. Lanier, in the 1940s. Now Ben and Glynnis manage the business with the help of two employees—except in the two weeks of the tupelo flow, when ten or twelve people work with them. Ben chuckles, "It's the only thing in the movie that wasn't accurate: how slowly they worked when the honey was flowing. When the tupelo's in, we really move."

Ben's mother taught school for twenty-nine years in Florida and wanted Ben to further his education beyond high school. Ben said, "My cousins asked me when the Florida lottery came out what I'd do if I won the lottery. I said I might go back to school. They said, 'Go back to school? Are you crazy?' I just wanted to be able to sit down and read and absorb something. My favorite thing to read is the *National Geographic*. I'd rather read that than anything, go places. But I write. I write

something down every day in my journal and been writing it for
twelve or fourteen years. I write what I do that day. You find out
almost to the day, year to year, what you're doing with the bees is
the same thing every day—real close, anyway."

According to Ben, his year of "playing with bees" goes
like this: In the fall and winter, when there are few flowers, he
fills five-gallon buckets with corn syrup to feed and build up
the bees. He puts leaves on top, and places the buckets not
right next to the hives, as many beekeepers do, but at a dis-
tance in order to make the bees fly. They think there's a honey
flow and it keeps the queen stimulated and the hives healthier.
Around Christmastime the bees return to the swamp for nec-
tar, going first to maples and then by March to the strong-
scented ti-ti blossoms.

White tupelo blooms around April or May, and just prior
to that the colonies must be cleaned and stripped of all stores so
that when the tupelo is brought to the hive it remains pure and
unmixed. Lanier sometimes has his hives located in forty separate bee yards, and the hives are cleaned not once but twice, the
second time in order to remove the precious white tupelo before
the gallberry blooms and it gets commingled. "I lose a trace of
the tupelo on the second stripping," explained Ben, "and the
timing on all this is critical, but I learned from my daddy to tell
from the smell and taste of the tupelo when the time is right."

Glynnis takes care of all the "communications." She has a
B.S. in accounting and does the books, runs the computer, and
has a seventy-year-old woman helping her sell at the stand. Ben
has a twenty-three-year-old man working with him. In the winter they bush-hog and clean up bee yards.

"There's never without something to do," Ben said. "Plus
we have a two-year-old now—I'm forty-eight and have a two-
year-old, our only child—and Glynnis is forty-one. So she's
kind of loaded down, it's a real small business, a mom-and-pop
operation, literally, now."

Unless there is a hard frost that freezes the blossoms, the
bees start making ti-ti honey the first week in February. "I don't
try to produce that honey; it's bakery-grade honey. Glynnis

crunched the numbers, and for what they give you, it costs you more to produce it. But you have to clean it out of the hives before they make the tupelo."

Ben's dad got out of the business twenty years ago. But according to Ben, "When Daddy was handling a frame of honey, he wore a ball cap and a short-sleeve shirt, and he never wore a veil. I do wear a veil, but a lot of times I just put on a long-sleeve shirt so I don't have to slow down to say 'Ow!' If you put on a bee suit, like these people who handle 'em on TV do— put on gloves, tape all up, and everything—you can make it where you don't get stung. But it takes thirty minutes to get suited up like that. And I've never put a bee suit on in my life. If they're that mean you're not handling them right and you don't need to be messing with them. Don't stay in 'em too long and only work 'em on a bright, sunny day. When it's cloudy or in a drizzling rain they're in *their* house, so they'll eat you up. You want a day when they're out working too—concentrating on going to get their pollen—so they'll leave you alone."

When Ben and I had talked initially he had over nine hundred hives. But in the latest conversation he'd indicated potentially losing some several hundred hives. I asked him how many hives he had left now. He gave a long sigh before he answered.

"I try to keep around a thousand; I haven't had that many in several years. I made a bunch of increase last summer and the government, the county mosquito control, killed my gol-blame bees. They don't want to quit spraying. What they did is they changed the chemicals they use and they stopped spraying at night and spray in the daytime when the bees are out. So I'm goin' to the county commission meeting. I'd rather get beat up than go to the county commission, but I'm going. You ever talk to a politician? Do you know their brain capacity? They don't believe in evolution. You understand what I'm saying? I'm sorry, but it's true."

Ben's description of a politician certainly made me laugh, but the situation was decidedly unfunny. "That's the worst thing I have facing me," he said. "I go to bed and wake up thinking about it. This is the worst I've ever seen."

Ben's bees had been by killed by pesticides before, twenty years ago. Soybeans were planted near his yards and he lost 150 hives from the crop duster. He sued and collected. He'd also lost bees when he trucked them up near the Alabama state line, far from his home county, and where, unbeknownst to him, they'd been spraying. "By the way," he said, "if they're killin' the bees, it's not good for you, neither. The *Speedy Bee* newspaper—for beekeepers—says the Sierra Club will take this new one up. I hate to do that, but I gotta do something!"

I knew that honeybee populations around the country had declined—over the last fifty years the world bee population has diminished by 50 percent. But I thought Rachel Carson and her book *Silent Spring* had managed to limit pesticide use. I asked Ben if insecticides were the cause of the honeybee decline.

"Mites are definitely a problem," he answered. "They keep becoming resistant to what we use to kill them. Granddaddy never had to deal with them, and my daddy never had them. I never saw one up until fifteen or twenty years ago. We keep rotating chemicals—use one for a while until they become resist- ant—and keep changing. Mites are the worst—everyone has to deal with mites. Spraying may wipe me out, but that's just me."

He couldn't let it go. "Tupelo usually blooms around April twentieth. Last year it didn't bloom until the first of May, late. But I had my bees strong, long beards on the hives, hanging out of the entrance all the way up to the top of the first box. Well, you could actually see them dying on the ground, going round and round. I had 'em right there ready to make the honey and then I lost them right at the worst possible time. Tupelo doesn't bloom but two weeks out of the year, and that's the only chance you have to make it. I'm out of honey now. I would have had forty more drums. They killed my bees right when they were making tupelo. I lost almost a hundred hives! And nobody's listening! It's on my mind, can you tell? I killed a deer yesterday and that helps, but as soon as that's over with, it's on my mind again."

I was quiet. His livelihood, way of life, a legacy of three generations, family, survival, it all now had a new fragility to it. But it went beyond honey and the Laniers.

Ben reminded me that 40 to 60 percent of what we eat is pollinated by the honeybee and as he said we could have a famine of biblical proportions if we lost all of the bees.

He sighed deeply. "The people like to see these trucks going around, but they don't do anything. I was looking in a puddle of water and there were a bunch of dead bees and literally a thousand live mosquito larvae in that ditch. It's just a joke, it's all for show. It's not working. It's working on my bees, but not on the mosquito."

This was getting to me. I thought talking with a beekeeper—an introverted Ulee-type—the old Ben, about his exceptional honey, would be a gentle, uncomplicated conversation. Dreams. Dreams are good to talk about, always a favorite question of mine, and very full of hope, usually. "What's your dream—for your future?" I asked.

"To fish," Ben said without hesitation. "I won't live anyplace else in the whole world because I got the best fishing here. We love going to the Keys in our twenty-six-foot Aquasport. But Junior has to get a lot older to do that now. He doesn't have a lot of patience for being in the boat."

Ben also talked about their home at the beach that he'd made out of cypress. Although cutting down cypress trees is prohibited now, Ben gets them through what is termed "river recovery"—or, as Ben called it, dead-head cypress, trees he gets out of the mud. It may have been there for five hundred years or perhaps just sixty years. He made their entire beach house out of dead-head cypress boards—eighteen inches wide by eighteen feet long.

"Nothing between me and the Gulf of Mexico but white sand," he said. "Come see it before the last of the real Florida is gone. It's not the Florida I grew up in. Daddy says all this building down here is progress, progress backward just like a crawfish. I hate being selfish, but I liked my world better in the seventies than now, 'cause all you got now is more people and less freedom. More people you get, the less freedom you have. This is one of the last wild places in the whole U.S."

Ben finally laughed and then said, "You see how hard it is to nail me down!" And then we were back to bees: "I can see me selling off some of my assets to live if I lose all my bees. I don't want that to happen. I'm just going to try and keep the bees alive, keep doing the same old, same old, and try and produce honey. That's all I want. And I'm not going to give up yet. I'm not ready to throw in the towel yet. I don't know what's going to happen, I don't have a crystal ball. I know a lot of things don't look good. It's not easy."

There was a long silence and then he said, "I'm going to go play with my young-un now."

The conversation was over. And I was struck by how, for Ben Lanier, tupelo honey went beyond passion. It was a defining legacy and therefore different for him than for all the other food people in this book. I found myself suddenly craving some L. L. Lanier tupelo honey even more than usual and frustrated that Ben didn't have any. I remembered the last time I'd had Lanier's honey.

Glynnis's carefully packaged squeeze bottles full of pure tupelo arrived early one afternoon in time for my lunch, and I sampled the honey atop a slice of warm homemade bread. A beautiful clear, deep golden color, a sweet stout flavor, its taste and aroma summoned that dreamy, lush place where the white tupelo flowers grow. I could smell the flowers in each bite—or was it that I could taste the flowers in each bite? Both, of course. It had the food attribute I hold most dear—its taste was rare, of a wild place, and as precious, yes, as gold. An edible that tells you with each bite something about the land it comes from and the person who cares for it—qualifies for being a passion in my pantry.

{ TUPELO HONEY OATMEAL COOKIES }

Makes 4 dozen cookies.

1 cup (2 sticks) unsalted butter, softened
2 eggs
1 teaspoon vanilla extract
1 $\frac{1}{2}$ cups all-purpose flour
$\frac{3}{4}$ tablespoon baking powder
$\frac{1}{4}$ teaspoon salt
1 teaspoon cinnamon
3 cups oatmeal (either quick or old-fashioned)
1 $\frac{3}{4}$ cups golden raisins
$\frac{3}{4}$ cup pecans, chopped (optional)
1 $\frac{1}{2}$ cups tupelo honey

Preheat the oven to 350 degrees. Cream the butter together with the eggs and vanilla. Combine the flour, baking powder, and salt and add to the egg mixture. Fold in the cinnamon, oatmeal, raisins, and pecans, add the honey, and mix well.

Drop by tablespoonfuls onto an ungreased cookie sheet and bake for 10 to 12 minutes.

A SOUTHERN DELIGHT

{ TENNESSEE T-CAKES }

THEY CAME PACKAGED in a pretty white tin, and inside they were cellophane-wrapped in an aura of bubble-rainbow translucence. Although named Tennessee T-Cakes, the little confections inside weren't configured like a standard cake, and this extraordinary delicacy went way beyond my notion of what you eat on a birthday. How could something so small and delicate taste so full of flavor, have such might? With a gentle sweetness, the subtle flavors of the light, perfectly moist cake combined to create a taste sensation that was significant. The cakes had come from a friend, a thank-you for her stay in my home as she made her way back to Alabama. A Southerner, my friend Patricia had spent much of her adult life living in the North, yet still harbored many of the attributes of a Southern woman: self-possessed, polite, and poised, an old-fashioned girl's girl—even in womanhood—and forever gracious. The little tea cakes seemed the ideal emissary for her.

Inside my tin was also a small card, which in cursive type explained the legend of the Tennessee T-Cake. "In the polite society of ante-bellum Tennessee..." it began, and went on to explain that every Southern belle knew that the way to a man's heart was through his stomach, and if she didn't have an arsenal of her own secret recipes she was in big trouble if she wanted a husband. One seventeen-year-old beauty had become renowned for her culinary skills, perfecting generations of her family's recipes and making tea cakes her specialty. But the Civil War changed everything for her. With chronic food shortages, she was unable to bake her favorite desserts and she put away her recipes until her brother, a Confederate major, brought home a handsome young captain. It was the captain's birthday, and the smitten belle wanted to bake him a cake but was without the necessary ingredients. She made a small batch of tea cakes instead, and not long after, the captain and the young woman were married.

So tea cakes can function very effectively as birthday cake even though they don't conform to the standard shape or size. But what is cake, exactly? Coming up with a good definition turns out not to be all that straightforward. The *New Columbia Encyclopedia* says, "originally a small mass of dough baked by turning on a spit." Happily we've moved well beyond *that* type of cake. But even when we get to the eighteenth century and Jean Jacques Rousseau's rumored quote from Marie Antoinette, "Let them eat cake!" there seems to be some question about what the soon-to-become-headless Marie really was referring to; the exact quote is, "*Qu'ils mangent de la brioche.*" Brioche is one of the eight basic doughs in French confectionery—also included are flaky pastry, short pastry, and choux pastry—and produces something closer to a light yeast bread. Sweet and delicious, but not exactly the kind of cake you'd expect to show up, topped with candles, for the six-year-old's birthday party.

Certainly one of the major attributes of cake is that it is a confection often used for celebrating. The French had many festival cakes, perhaps the most famous being the Twelfth-Night cake. Baked to celebrate the feast of the Epiphany, the cake contained a hidden silver coin in it and was served to family members with three pieces reserved: one for the Virgin, another for the baby Jesus, and the third for the Magi. If someone was lucky enough to get the coin in his piece, he was named king of the Twelfth-Night celebration. In the Cajun regions of the United States this cake is now served with tokens or charms in it and is appropriately called a king cake.

There's the English wedding cake, designed not so much to taste fine and delicate but to be monumental, a huge cake that in order to achieve its massive size must be made non-crumbly and not very light. It was traditionally sliced into hundreds of pieces and put into tiny, lavishly decorated boxes and shipped to relations living in all parts of the British Empire—not so much a tasty treat to eat as a souvenir to celebrate the marital union.

And perennially there is the birthday cake. Usually layered and covered with icing, it is still, of course, made as a scratch cake from Grandma's recipe, though now, as often as not, the birthday cake is store-bought and ready-made, or cooked at home from a boxed mix.

Although single-flavored cake mixes had been introduced in 1949 by General Mills and Pillsbury, it was Duncan Hines Cake Mix, out of Omaha, that in 1951 changed home cake baking forever. Called the Three Star Special, it was a three-in-one-box mix: you could use it to make a white cake, or add whole eggs rather than just whites for a yellow cake, or add cocoa powder to make a chocolate cake. It was created by a Nebraska Consolidated Mills chemist named Arlec Andre and captured 48 percent of the new cake-mix market in three weeks. Within a year, the company was preparing thirty-eight thousand boxes a day. Owned since 1956 by Proctor & Gamble, Duncan Hines has remained in the number-one or -two position of top-selling cake mixes to this day.

Yet the box cake was created by a chemist, and so, of course, can never taste as if Grandma's loving hands made it. But then, too, some grandmas wouldn't have the time or inclination to make a cake from scratch. Ah, how to find a cake made with care and where fresh eggs and butter are just the beginning of uncompromised ingredients for the perfect cake. I was happy that Tennessee T-Cakes had come into my life.

The owner of the Nashville-based Tennessee T-Cakes, Inc., and the more-than-a-century-old recipe is Frances Barkley, who started baking the cakes as a business in the early 1990s. I spoke several times with Frances first in 1997 when I reordered more of her cakes. And then more recently—as I was ordering more cakes—she'd asked me to call her at home early on a Saturday morning. I could imagine her with coffee mug in hand, not yet dressed for the day, perhaps still without her make-up done or her blond hair combed. We chatted—her words spoken in that soft, casual Southern accent—as if we were old friends.

"It's actually an old Southern recipe someone had given me. I had to play with the recipe because when you're baking at home in your oven, as compared to baking in a big commercial oven, it's totally different. The oven temperature is critical to keeping the cake from sinking and looking a mess, and the consistency can be a problem. We lost a lot of T-Cakes to the sinking in the middle. I changed the shape of it, and that made a big difference; the original recipe was done in bars. Well, how pretty is that? It's not pretty if you want to sell them. They tasted good, they just didn't look good."

Frances spent at least a year adapting the tea-cake recipe. And not just the recipe had to be altered in order to make the tea cake presentable for sale. Originally she'd tried spraying the mini muffin tins with vegetable oil to help ease the cakes from the pan. She'd put the mixture in the tins, bake them, and then knock the cakes out. But sometimes they wouldn't come out, so she started using little paper cups to line the tins. That method had problems too. "Because," as Frances explained, "you don't want to get a tea cake and take the paper off and have half the tea cake go with it. You've had muffins like that before; people get really upset with that. Finally I went to a trade show in St. Louis and I was telling a paper company my problem, and they sent me some samples and it worked. So the little cups are not your ordinary little muffin cups, this is a special paper. They're specially done and only one place in the country carries them. It's expensive, and you have to get so much at one time. And it was all very labor intensive, particularly in the beginning."

Frances started her business with another woman in 1991, but within a year the woman died and Frances was forced to rename and therefore restart the business. She started it up three times: first it was Tennessee T-Cakes, and then when her partner died—and a question of trademark ownership came up— she had to change the company name to Southern T-Cakes. Then she legally got Tennessee T-Cakes back again.

Frances grew up in Birmingham, Alabama, and was Class of 1966 at Auburn University, with a major in home economics, "because that's what you did back then." She got married, moved to Virginia, and then moved to Nashville, where she's now lived for over thirty-eight years. "So I have three children and now grandchildren. Oh Lord, they're comin' by leaps and bounds. My daughter, who works with me, is expecting. So now it's nine. Lord, who can afford all these grandchildren?"

Before starting up her tea-cake company, Frances worked for her husband in his Nashville copy-machine company; worked at a travel agency; sold plants before that. "I did different things," she said. "And I worked for Native Americans, the United Southeastern Tribe, for about five or six years as an assistant to the executive director. At the time we had only about twelve tribes; now they have twenty or some-odd. I'd travel all over the U.S., go to D.C. to testify on conditions.... But I'd always wanted my own business."

Tennessee T-Cakes was initially located in the Incubation Center in Nashville—where small, start-up companies pay reduced rents and can receive guidance on practical issues in business. According to Frances, "You can only be there for six years and then you have to graduate. So I outgrew it. The bad thing, which I told them, is you make friends with people there and then you have to leave. That's the downside. But I still see some of them because they're in the food business."

Her current facility is off of Interstate 24, near the Murfreesboro Road exit, with easy access to the Nashville airport. The building has six one-level suites, and Tennessee T-Cakes occupies about 2,500 square feet of it, with offices in the front and mixing and baking plus shipping in the back.

From the beginning, Frances sold her tea cakes almost exclusively through mail-order, marketing her cakes by exhibiting at the Junior League and other high-end shows during October, November, and December—shows geared toward the holidays.

"Networking is a big thing too," she said. "I was active in the chamber of commerce and the City Club. But I just got burned out on networking. So my main thing now is my shows, because you get that taste out there. You give samples out and people buy at the show and turn around and order more."

But Frances confided that the company's growth had been up and down. Corporate gifts, a mainstay for Tennessee T-Cakes, had made the company vulnerable to stock market swings, 9/11, and natural disasters—anything that adversely affected the economy. "What people really cut out is corporate gifts," Frances said. "And then, of course, with Katrina some people actually lost some of their branch offices."

Frances has another problem with tea cakes: because of those wonderful natural ingredients, their shelf life is relatively short. So she developed a new product called T-Cake Brittle, which stays fresh longer than the cakes and consequently is more attractive to wholesale markets. "The shops don't carry us because the shelf life of the tea cakes is like about three to four weeks, unless frozen," Frances said. "With the brittle it's four months, and I think it's going to be our little spurt. It's the same recipe; it's just made real thin and crispy. We break it up like brittle so it's not in even pieces. I took five bags to my girlfriend in Atlanta so she could give 'em to her friends, and she ate them all—*ate them all!* And she was putting peanut butter on top of the pieces. You can crumble it over ice cream or just sit there and eat it. So I'm real happy with this brittle. We might do real well with it."

And she's continuing to work on increasing the shelf-life of the tea cakes: "I'm working with a friend who I met through the shows, he does cookies, and lives in Denver, Colorado and we talk about new ideas."

Shelf life may be an issue for Tennessee T-Cakes, but it's certainly worth the headache, since all-natural ingredients are what make the cakes great, right?

She laughed and said, "Funny thing is, I just found out it might not be *all* natural. For the labeling you have to put exactly what's in there—like your flour and flavoring—and my flavoring is vanilla. Well, it's *imitation* vanilla flavor—artificial. . . . So when I reprint my card I'll just have to say no preservatives. But it's not only the quality of the ingredients that makes the cake so exceptional; the ingredients are actually very simple. The uniqueness is in how the ingredients blend together."

When I asked her to elaborate, she hesitated for a second, seeming more as if she were trying to recall the process rather than that she didn't want to tell me. Then she said, "Melt the butter and brown sugar, that's what you do. Add some white sugar, pour that mixture into the big mixer, and add your eggs, flour, and you mix it up. But you only mix it to a certain stage, because if you overmix it, it puts too much air in there. We have a depositor—a machine that will deposit automatically the exact amount in each little cup—which the bakers for some reason don't like to use. They prefer to hand drip them. Then they bake them and you get it to a look—not a temperature, it's a certain look. My bakers know the look. After they cool, turn them out and put confectioners' sugar on them. I don't know why they don't like the depositor, but after being with me for that many years, I let them do what they want to. We don't want to disturb anything—it's working fine. So there you go—they're hand done."

From the early days, Frances has employed bakers to make the tea cakes, and when I spoke with her first in 1997, most were women from Vietnam. She raved about how hardworking they were, and how they had become so completely knowledgeable about making the cakes that she didn't have much to do with the day-to-day baking. This actually got her in trouble when Al Roker, for his Food Network *On the Road* show, decided he wanted to come film Frances baking her tea cakes.

"Well, guess who hadn't baked those things in about ten years," Frances admitted. "I had to get my bakers to go in on the weekend and show me. And then, well, the mixer is so big I couldn't even pull the lever down, much less lift the bowl. So I had to get my son, who had helped me bake before, and my daughter, and all three of us, were doing it—he did the hard part. I thought, 'Oh Lord, how my small Vietnam bakers lift this thing, I do not know!' We'll usually have just three or four bakers on, but during the holidays we'll bring a whole crew in. In fact, this past year it went crazy, so my son, who works for the water department and gets off at three-thirty, brought a crew of ten or fifteen to work at night along with the Vietnamese. It was like a factory back there. Oh God, I've never seen so many people, but they got it done!"

Since she had TV experience, I asked Frances if she'd ever considered selling on the air. She said she'd been approached about doing QVC and she'd thought about it. "But you ship on pallets and they keep it in cold storage in Memphis," she said, "and what they don't sell they ship back to you. Plus I was going to have to pay my own expenses—airfare, hotel, and all that—and be the hostess on the show. Also, they wanted the cakes packaged like three dozen in a box—or something like that—and I'd have to have that box done special 'cause I don't have that three-dozen size. And you can't have anything in there about reordering because it has to all go to QVC. So, me being a small business, I thought no, that's not for me."

But my query about QVC seemed to spark a question from Frances: she asked me what I knew about getting on TV—and specifically about how to get her tea cakes to Oprah. Frances knew that Oprah had grown up in Nashville and that her father still lived in the area. She thought she'd send two dozen cakes in tins once a week to Oprah and staff. Not knowing if they'd actually eat them, she intended to include a brochure and a little note. "Do you think that will catch their attention?" she asked. "And then Oprah's best friend, Gayle King—as you can tell I watch *Oprah*—who is the editor of *O*, her magazine, I got a copy of that to call and see what office Gayle's in so I can send her some once a week too. And I'm going to say, 'I know good friends like to share good things.' I think Oprah'd like them because she likes to eat."

I confessed to Frances that I didn't really know much about Oprah Winfrey, except that getting on her show or in her magazine could change forever the ups and downs for Tennessee T-Cakes. But beyond Oprah, what else would you like to have happen for T-Cakes? I asked. "I don't know if my daughter would want to take it over completely or not," Frances said, "now with the babies. Of course, it's not really ready to take over yet. I'd like to see it grow and grow, and if she wants it I'd like her to take it over."

Frances laughed and suggested that with her daughter expecting twins one of the offices would have to be turned into a nursery. "I said, 'Jen, you can't leave, honey!' She's due in September—so this is not good—during my busy time. She does my show in Nashville for me. She said, 'Well, Mom, I can do it.' I said maybe we can prop those babies up there at the table and give 'em little T-Cake T-shirts. It's good to have your daughter in there. I'll just turn it all over to her. And if not, I'd like to sell it. I don't want to do this forever. I'll always probably do something—I love to travel—but I always want my finger in something. Even if she took it over, I'd still want to be active. And if I sold it, still I'd want to be in it—maybe."

I knew that Frances had been involved in another food project: she'd published three cookbooks—the first one in 1999 and then two more recently in 2005—and all of them were collections of recipes for tailgating parties. She'd tailgated in Nashville for ten years at Vanderbilt. "Now Vanderbilt, bless their hearts," she said, "this year they had a good team, but usually their football games aren't that great, so the main thing is tailgating. I know more about tailgating than I do about football, so tailgating became like a business. We'd have like seventy or eighty people at a tailgate party, which is a lot. And I'd be looking for recipes all the time and I couldn't really find anything very apropos. So I started collecting recipes, years ago now."

With her first book, Frances asked a girlfriend—who'd been in publishing and was very savvy on the computer—to help. They wrote to alumni in various college associations in both the Atlantic Coast and Southeastern conferences asking for recipes. The book was entitled *Tailgating in the Southeast* and was available only through the shows Frances was attending for Tennessee T-Cakes. And it sold extremely well.

The success of the first book led Frances to write, with another friend, *Eat, Drink & More Eagle* (for Auburn University tailgaters) and *Eat, Drink & More Roll Tide* (for University of Alabama fans). "Because we got the collegiate licenses we could use photos from their archives, and quotes, and all that stuff that we were not able to use before. It really made a nice book."

Less than a week after our conversation, a tin of Tennessee T-Cakes, along with the T-Cake Brittle, arrived on my doorstep. Frances had told me she'd be sending the cakes to "revitalize you on what they taste like." The brittle came in a bright red bag, large enough to make me wonder how anyone— much less a girlfriend from Atlanta—could eat five bags. One bite of the crisps and I got it. Then they were somehow just gone in a blink. I don't know where they went, but they were gone. Clearly, *we* really liked the brittle.

Meanwhile, inside the tin, the little cakes, these days wrapped in gold-starred cellophane, now came in an assortment of flavors—lemon, key lime, truffle, and plain, although hardly plain. They were as heavenly as memory recalled, a Southern comfort, this cake, good for gifts to girlfriends, to find the way to a man's heart, and even though they arrived on a weekday, they made our lunch a celebration. This wonderful passion certainly deserved to keep its place in my pantry.

{ CHUTNEY-NUT-STUFFED BRIE }

Frances, of course, would never part with her secret recipe for
Tennessee T-Cakes, but she did send me a recipe—almost as
decadent as the tea cakes—from one of her cookbooks on football tailgating parties. This is from the section entitled "1st
Quarter" and is a wonderful appetizer.

Serves 16.

2 (8-ounce, 4 ½ -inch) Brie wheels
1 (8-ounce) package cream cheese, softened
2 tablespoons unsalted butter, softened
2 tablespoons prepared chutney
⅛ teaspoon freshly ground black pepper
½ cup toasted sliced or slivered almonds
2 tablespoons chopped fresh parsley
Crackers
Red and green seedless grapes

Split the Brie wheels in half horizontally; set the bottom 2 halves
on a serving plate and set the top halves aside.

Combine the cream cheese and butter in a bowl; beat with an
electric mixer on medium-high speed until fluffy. Add the chutney and pepper; continue beating until thoroughly combined.

Spread half of the cream cheese mixture on the bottom layers of
Brie; sprinkle with half of the almonds and half of the parsley.
Top with the remaining halves of Brie and press lightly. Spread
the remaining cream cheese mixture evenly over the tops and
sprinkle with the remaining almonds and parsley. Cover and
refrigerate for at least 1 hour. Serve with crackers and grapes.

THE GINGER MAN

{ REED'S ORIGINAL GINGER BREW }

I'VE NOTICED THAT in California whenever you ask for driving directions, you're first told—often in kind of a gloomy, Eeyore voice—how long it'll take to get there. Then several routes are offered up—just in case the traffic wears you down and you need an alternate. I know traffic weighs heavy on the California mind, and with reason, but multiple ways to reach a single destination have never proved helpful to me. So to avoid any possible confusion, I didn't even ask Chris Reed how to get to his ginger brewery in Los Angeles. Nor was he forthcoming. Instead, when we confirmed the date for the tour, he mumbled something about there not being much to see at the brewery. And for a second I wondered if there was some reason he'd prefer a phone conversation to my visit.

Despite heavy rain, Ed and I managed to reach L.A., east of Inglewood, well ahead of MapQuest's estimated travel time and handily identified the street location for Reed's, Inc. We were early and decided to cruise the area in search of a coffee shop. A scary-looking Jack-in-the-Box—no Starbucks or Friendly's—seemed our only option among the low, warehouse-type buildings of this light-industrial section of the city. We decided to forgo the coffee and returned to Spring Street, parking next to a PT Cruiser with a big Reed's beach-and-palm-trees logo plastered on its side—a two-tone paint job of sunburst orange and yellow. Well, we were in the right place. We darted through the rain for the most likely door in the window-less, faux-wood-sided building, and once inside found ourselves standing in a huge open room. Shabby, colorless carpeting covered the floor and crept through the doorways of various partitioned offices set along the room's perimeter.

Out of the closest office came a tall, dark-haired man who asked if he could help us. I'd not met Chris, but even in short phone conversations I'd developed a distinct mental picture of him, which this ponytailed guy seemed to fit. But this was not Chris; it was Peter Sharama. And as he handed over his business card he grinned and said, "I'm a Gemini." First flashing the front of the card, with the Reed's Original Ginger Brew logo, he flipped it to the other side to reveal his other affiliation: Brookstreet Securities Corporation. That side said his title was Investment Banker; the Reed's side said he was in charge of Corporate Finance & Investor Relations, with an email address of anoracle@pureprophet.com. Reed's, Inc., Peter explained, was in the process of making a public offering of two million shares and he was handling the sale of their common stock. He then went to fetch Chris for us.

We had to wait—Chris was on the phone. So we meandered around the big room checking out the mounds of product para-phernalia: cases of bottles containing Reed's Ginger Brews and Reed's Ginger Juice Brews; in the corner stood a large, gallon-size party keg of Virgil's Root Beer. On a table were packaging sam-ples of a swing-top, sixteen-ounce bottle labeled Virgil's Cream Soda and a couple cans of China Cola, plus several square-shaped tins of Reed's Crystallized Ginger Candy and bags of Reed's Ginger Chews. Propped against the wall, near the sun-colored vending machine, was a trade-show display that announced the three flavors of Reed's Ginger Ice Cream: chocolate, green tea, and (my favorite) original ginger. I began to muse on how I'd dis-covered Chris and his wonderful ginger ale—I mean brew.

Actually I first found Reed's through a root beer, Virgil's. Originally brewed in the north of England, Virgil's was brought to the United States by Crowley Beverage Corporation. Ed Crowley brewed the drink with all-natural ingredients—unbleached cane sugar, anise, licorice, wintergreen, and molasses—not far from me in Massachusetts. An industry icon, Ed had been a great mentor for Chris Reed and many others in the beverage business. In 1999, when Ed got cancer and needed to sell, Chris bought Virgil's. It was a perfect counterpart to

Reed's own line of ginger-based beverages. Prior to Reed's ownership, Virgil's was one of the few "boutique" brews I could get in New Hampshire. But that changed with Chris, and right next to the Virgil's on my grocery-store shelf were suddenly a whole lot of ginger beverages. I love ginger.

Reed's Ginger Brew truly is one of—no, I'm going to say it: *the* best ginger ale. For one thing, it isn't too sweet; plus it gushes with ginger flavor. Not surprising, since Chris's little "ah-ha"—as he sometimes calls the business—is as much about ginger in general as it is about ginger beverages. He believes that ginger's day in the sun is coming: "Just like bran, ginger will become known as a disease preventative with healing, palliative powers. Although unlike bran, ginger actually has flavor." Now combine ginger's healing qualities and taste with the properties of soft drinks—a number of which evolved from medicinal remedies—and you do get a wonder of a concoction.

Soft drinks were originally called tonics. I remember when I moved to Boston approaching a street vendor and inquiring what kind of pop he sold—pop was what we called it, sometimes soda, in the Midwest. It was as if Daisy Duck had quacked the question to him. He looked confused and then out of his mouth came a language I vaguely recognized as English, but by mentally reinserting the R's I was able to translate his Bostonese into something I could grasp. He said: "In Boston if it's fizzy and flavored it's tonic; soda is *club* soda; pop is Dad; and if you want tonic water, you must ask for tonic *water*." (Although, of course, he said "WAH-ta.")

It may lack the onomatopoeia of the word *pop*, but *tonic*—defined in the *American Heritage Dictionary* as a "refreshing, invigorating and restorative agent"—remains truer to the historical derivation of soft drinks: some two thousand years ago the Greek physician Hypocrites suspected that mineral waters had therapeutic qualities (although he envisioned it as bathing rather than drinking water). But by the 1600s sparkling bathwater became a beverage when the Belgium village of Spa, obviously famous for its bathing waters, began bottling the effervescent stuff.

Sparkling waters were thought to cure everything from arthritis to indigestion. And with such healing power scientists, pharmacists, and physicians scrambled to analyze the water's makeup; one of their conclusions was that the gas being released in the tiny bubbles was carbon dioxide. Joseph Priestley, the British scientist credited with identifying oxygen, was the first to invent a method for "pushing" carbon dioxide into water in 1772, and by the beginning of the nineteenth century carbonated water was being manufactured in France and North America. Both artificial and natural mineral waters were considered health products in the 1830s, but believing they could improve upon the curative properties pharmacists began to add ingredients—herbs, flowers, roots, even birch bark—to fizzy water. While no miracle cures were discovered, the "flavored" sparkling water was a big hit; particularly popular were sarsaparilla, root beer, lemon, and strawberry flavors. And, of course, ginger ale.

Actually, Chris's initial reasons for developing his ginger brew had to do with his own health and his search for a tonic.

He told me when I talked with him in 1999 that he'd gone through a number of times in his life where his health wasn't what he wanted it to be. He attributed his physical malaise mostly to being unhappy in his work, and not doing what he wanted. He was always tired, and felt in need of vitamins—in need of something. So he studied up and became proactive about managing his health.

"It's just like what happened with me and taxes," he said. "I figured they're going to be in my life for forty years so I better get smart about taxes. Same thing about the physical body. Having driven it pretty hard as a party animal, I had to get smart. I became a vegetarian, learned about healing herbs, got involved with Ayurveda—an Eastern 'herbology' which originated in India—and began to feel better. I decided I wanted to start a business that promoted a healthy world-alternative energy, natural soaps, solar or wind energy, okay, maybe a food product. I don't know exactly where it came from—ginger and ginger ale—but when it hit, it hit hard!"

Ginger ales were originally created in Ireland in the 1850s and imported to the United States. The first soda to be manufactured here, American ginger ale was initially made by James Vernor, a nineteen-year-old pharmacist from Detroit. He began testing recipes in 1862, but the Civil War interrupted his experimentation. Before he left to serve in the Union army, he placed his prototype ginger ale extract into an old oak cask. He returned four years later, opened the cask, and found to his surprise that the years of aging had actually perfected his recipe—the flavor was terrific!

Throughout the early twentieth century, the pursuit of tastier tonics—often achieved by increasing sugar content—continued, and eventually led to a functional shift in tonics from medicinal to mere soft drink. But as Bostonians continue to remind us, soft drinks can still be tonics. And as Chris Reed reminds us, it can be a tonic and still have flavor. With soft drinks containing ingredients such as sugar, caffeine, ginger, and sarsaparilla, the ability of soft drinks to refresh, provide a lift, settle the stomach, or eliminate headaches is basically intrinsic—and, yes, the little bubbles probably add to the effects. Reed's particular magic is in expressing the robust flavor of ginger. So how did Chris become ginger brew proselytizer and entrepreneur?

We'd at this point moved into Chris's office. On glass shelves running across a long wall sat various bottles of Reed's, other beverages, packaging prototypes, awards, and photos of Chris at trade shows. He sat behind a big L-shaped desk cluttered with papers, computer, phone system, printer, and lots more. I sat close to his desk, not on the back-wall couch—although I didn't have to be close to hear his colorful, gestured story. And as he talked I couldn't help but mentally etch-a-sketch his long, curly hair—yup, captured in a ponytail—into a very short crew cut. Silly, but I'd read that Chris had once been a chemical engineer, an oil and gas man, and I wanted to see if this California dude before me could possibly approach the scientist image. The round spectacles helped, but the tie-dye T-shirt—with the Reed's logo—and stubbly beard definitely brought him back to my original picture of Chris Reed as "New Age" guy.

Chris grew up an army brat, living all over the country—Arizona, Kentucky, Texas, Kansas, New York, and more. "I was actually conceived in Germany," telling me more than I wanted to know. "In Germany, as a kid in the winter, I'd wash cars after school for two or three hours a day—making eight to ten dollars—a ton of money in 1971 for a thirteen-year-old. I think I've always been entrepreneurial."

He bought guitars and amps with the money, learned to play guitar, and had a number of rock-and-roll bands throughout high school. "I wasn't horribly talented," he said. "But I had a big heart and absolutely wanted to be a rock star. So when it came time to go to college, I applied to Julliard and Rennselaer Polytechnic Institute. And I pussyed out. I thought, okay, I'm good at math; I'm going to take a degree I can make money off of and do music on the side. Well, you can't pursue anything on the side at RPI, you just bury your ass in a book for four years. So I came out a chemical engineer and worked in the oil and gas industry."

He told me that in 1985 when oil prices dropped through the floor he had a midlife crisis—this at the age of twenty-nine—and he quit his job. "I'm a dreamer," he explained. "I wanted to create the life I wanted to live. I didn't want to be a chemical engineer sitting at a desk with people who weren't passionate about what they were doing, for whom it was just a job. I wanted to live a big life, a life of passion, and go for my dreams."

He moved out to California, of course, and began studying music at the L.A. Musicians Institute. But, he admits, "Since I'm not a very talented guitarist, at some point I needed something to do for a livelihood." He started working for a friend who had a 1-800-DENTIST franchise. While he was there, he explored several environmental and natural products with the idea of starting his own business, and eventually he began to hone in on food and ginger.

He did his research at the UCLA library initially for root beer, then ginger brew—ultimately moving beyond beverage books and into old recipes. He simmered roots and spices on the stove and sweetened them or added yeast. This was in 1987, and for two years he studied, tested, and developed his ginger brew recipe.

"I talked to a tremendous number of people about my recipe," Chris said, "because I was deeply concerned about the herbal impact of my product. What karma would I get if I put out a food product that wasn't helpful, the wrong blend, for people? I look at herbs as a medicine, not a casual thing to consume. Being into Ayurveda, I believe the cosmic plane has three primordial forces operating through the five energy principles of air, fire, earth, water, space. And according to Ayurveda, different body types require different combinations of these forces. I wanted to put out a drink that was more globally good for people. I wanted ginger to balance fire and cooling. I wanted to know on a deep level I was creating good karma."

He talked to Hanna Kroeger, a German nun turned New Age homeopath, who is well known in the natural food world. "This would be good for you," she told him. In January of 1989 he was ready. He found a small brewer who at the time didn't have a bottling operation but was planning to buy a single-head filler. Chris made a deal to make the first commercial quantity of his ginger brew recipe there.

He described the event to me: "I showed up at this place with ninety pounds of fresh ginger sliced by hand—I had some bad-ass blisters on those hands—and threw it into the kettle with different spices. They go in at different times, some in tea bags, some don't go in all the way—Hanna said it would be *really* good to do it that way—and it does make a big difference. The spices got mixed with pineapple and lemon juice, honey, and then I stirred it all with a canoe paddle. After testing eighty or ninety recipes in the kitchen to see what worked, I panicked and just threw in half of this, half of that. My recipe fell completely apart after all my research."

After mixing up his concoction, the brew bubbled away and then went off to storage tanks to age for several months before it would eventually get bottled. "So it was two o'clock in the morning when I finished, and I was exhausted. It's the end of the night, I'm ready to leave, and the guy comes to me and says, 'Wait a minute, where are you going? Our deal didn't include me cleaning the brew kettle. You climb in there and get that ginger out of the kettle.' And I'm like, '*What*?' So I'm climbing in through the opening, it's still hot, and I don't know this brewmaster very well, and at two A.M. the mind plays tricks and I thought, 'My God, what if this guy closes the lid and fills it with water to make a Chris Reed brew?' So I had to shovel the ginger into pails standing inside the kettle, which was like a sauna, and then finally I got to go home."

His first commercial batch was bottled in June 1989 and was named simply: Original Ginger Brew. It didn't have Reed's name on it for several years. Chris explained to me that one of the people he meditates with—naturally Chris is into yoga— told him that in their meditation they'd seen that the name *Reed* had to be on the product. Chris said to them, "Oh no, I don't want to take responsibility for this! What if they don't like it? But they already liked it."

He washed each bottle of his first batch in his kitchen, labeled them, and put them into cases. "I do hold the Guinness world record for the most number of cases in a VW bug," Chris boasted. "Thirty-six cases, full of twelve-ounce beer bottles, twenty-four cases in the back seat, eight in the trunk. The tires actually stick out at about a forty-five-degree angle with the weight. It's amazing."

He put the brew into four stores—Montana Natural, Rainbow Acres, Zabby's Café, and Mrs. Winston's in Ocean Park. Mrs. Winston's reordered within two hours, and by the end of the year Chris was making a batch every month, forty to fifty cases.

"I was excited about launching my brew and wasn't thinking it would taste that great—it's pretty herbal. I thought more that it would be good for you and real authentic. It tasted kind of funky," Chris said. He was still working at 1-800-DENTIST. He wasn't married—that happened later—and had managed to get his product on store shelves for under five thousand dollars. "I figured in six months," he laughed, "I'd be driving a Ferrari. But I didn't do any accounting. I thought: I did not start my own business to do accounting. But eventually reality set in."

In 1990 Reed signed on with three natural-foods distributors and moved production to a larger facility in Boulder, Colorado, and quickly started producing a thousand to fifteen hundred cases a month. He moved the manufacturing operation again in 1991 to a co-pack plant in Pennsylvania. "But we were always shorting people's orders. My dad put more and more of his money into the business, and at some point I figured I'd better do some accounting. I thought ninety-nine cents a bottle was what we should sell it retail for and still have a reasonable margin. But it turned out we were nowhere near that margin until we moved to the bigger brewery. So we really bit it for a while."

Chris quit his job at 1-800-DENTIST and went on the road marketing his ginger brew at trade shows. He went to the U.S. National Association of Specialty Food Trade and the Canadian version of NASFT, and won top honors at both shows for new product of the year. "I was a one-man show: I set up the booth, threw ginger at people passing by, and held up a big old root and yelled, 'I like big juicy roots' and 'This ginger ale is the way it was made in log cabins!' I was a crazy man and we were a story in 1991 and an overnight sensation. Sometimes my dad would come to shows with me to help out. An ex-army officer and real conservative. I'd watch him deal with the gay guys and the 'natural' women with their beards. But we were on top of the world and I was on this high. It's an amazing thing to be around an entrepreneurial business." By the end of the year, Reed's had signed on its first mainstream supermarket distributor and sales had topped $500,000.

In the mid-1990s he began making more varieties of ginger brew—spiced apple cider, raspberry, and cherry—and in 1997 licensed the China Cola products and began distributing Reed's Crystallized Ginger Candy. Chris had wanted to be in the crystallized ginger business for years and asked the Australians— who are major ginger candy manufacturers—to use raw rather than white sugar. But the Australians didn't think ginger candy with raw sugar was big enough business.

"Then this kid shows up," Chris said, "a surfer dude, and says, 'Hey, man, like, I rep for a candy company in Fiji—I go to Fiji surfing—and I got a great crystallized ginger.' And I tasted it and said, damn, that's excellent. Can you do it with raw cane sugar? I do twelve containers a year of the stuff now. The Aussies had no vision, so they didn't, and I did, and the rest is history."

In 2000 he added ginger chews and also launched Reed's Original Ginger Ice Cream. Chris had the ice cream manufactured by Ronneybrook Farm in Ancramdale, New York—a dairy already famous with Manhattan foodies for making a variety of good, unusual ice cream flavors. "Ronny names his cows, he kisses them, and treats them very well," Chris laughed. "People do say they love the ice cream. It's my best creation. The Original Flavor has no vanilla in it, just cream and ginger."

Also in 2000, Reed purchased the eighteen-thousand-square-foot building—which we were currently in—to house the West Coast brewery, the corporate offices, and warehouse facility. "I haven't learned yet about being a visionary. I decided to buy my facility and have it running by March 2001. It's still not up and running, so I'm four to five years late. Typical, oh, let's just build a brewery. You have to be nuts to do what I do. If someone told you how hard it would be to build a brewery—the health department, FDA inspections—you just wouldn't do it, you'd shoot yourself. We *love* our brewery now; the regrets are all gone."

This seemed like a good time for a tour of the facility.

We left Chris's office, went back into the big room, and passed through a set of large double doors. The immense space housed eight kettles, a pasteurizer, an ozone water sanitizer, nine-station bottle filler and capping machine, a labeler, the candy packing room, plus floor-to-ceiling cartons. As we wandered around, Chris would point to a machine and describe how he rebuilt it, altered another, or repaired it, and I was reminded of the engineer in him. At last he asked if I wanted to look inside one of the brewing kettles. I climbed the stairway to the top of the giant-size (maybe twelve-foot-high or more) covered caldron, and with each step the heavenly smell intensified. I peered inside the opening and let the steamy aromas fill every pore, a facial that soaked not just my skin but all my senses. Chris was listing the ingredients—ginger, spices, pineapple juice, honey, and, of course, the secret ingredient he couldn't mention—but I was lost in the kettle's magic.

He interrupted my aromatic dream and said, "I'm an authentic flavorer. I didn't start this as a foodie at all. I've just absorbed the industry over time and become very food sensitive—now I'm a major foodie. Started as a health food guy, now I'm a full food snob. Well, but underlying that I'm really an herbalist disguising my herbal concoctions as fun food. My products are fun, but it's really important to me that I get a million pounds of ginger into the American diet. It's just fantastic to think of a thing that can be so functional and culinary and still be my favorite, perfect thing. I love the flavor and I love what it does. It's the best."

In food artisans, it is always about their ingredient, it is what truly stirs their passions. And often it's business that bogs down the exuberance of that passion. I think about what Chris said about his ah-ha: "What you learn from being entrepreneurial is it's never as bad as you think it is, and it's also never as good as you think it is. At any one time, I have had the most incredible, and the worst, stuff going on. It's always a combo. You have to do this for more than economic reasons; you have to do it for the passion. If anyone told me what it was going to take to be where I am now, I'd never have done this in a million years. You have to be a dreamer, or be in denial. You have to hold the vision and, like Luke Skywalker, let the force be with you. Or the Death Star is going to get you and drop you through that little hole."

I wish he had stopped there, but the conversation took an unexpected turn. Chris said he wants his brew to be number one in the mainstream stores, not just in natural-foods stores. "I want this everywhere," Chris said. "I'm not saying we'll be Coke, but we're going to be up and down the street. If they can have a premium ice cream industry, they can have a premium soda industry. Our attitude is people will pay extra if there truly is quality."

He talked about the company's public offering and how emails come in every ten minutes with requests to buy stock. "I'm a fired-up guy. I don't want the money—well, I do want the money—what grows is where the money goes. I want my business and I want my money, too. We're getting grassroots financing—selling stock on our website and on bottle necktags—and if we're successful and continue to be passionate about the product and have a passionate consumer, we could revolutionize the food industry. It's empowering to be an entrepreneur with a passionate spirit who's got the goods to go to the customers and say, 'Let's build this damn brand.' And this will change things. I'm telling you, people are looking at me and saying if this guy pulls this off, I can do this too. If we're successful they can point to their customer and say, 'See what Reed's shareholders did?' We're pioneers completely. We're looking at the whole thing and revolutionizing it to the degree we can. We're on fire!"

He stopped for air and then said to me, "Man, you got the true believer, didn't you?"

I wasn't sure that's what I got. Methinks there was a protest-too-much in the number of times he used the word *passionate* in the context of business. In America, making a business out of what you love can have its drawbacks. And I disagree with what Chris mumbled when I had first called him—that there wasn't much to see at the brewery. There was a lot to see! I now believe with certainty that Chris Reed makes the best ginger brew, the best ginger ice cream, and the best crystallized ginger candy. His true passion is all I could ever want.

{ **DARK AND STORMY** }

Serves 1.

3 ounces cold ginger beer
Juice of ¼ lime
1 ½ ounces dark rum
Ginger chews for garnish

In a tall chilled glass or a glass filled with ice, gently stir the soda and lime juice together. Top with the rum. Garnish with the candies.

{ GINGER-MINT ICE CREAM FLOAT }

Serves 1.

10 ounces cold ginger beer
1 lime wedge
1 scoop vanilla ice cream
1 fresh mint sprig
2 ginger chews

Fill a 12-ounce glass with the soda. Squeeze a lime wedge into the drink, add the ice cream, and garnish with a mint sprig. Serve with the candies.

{ STARRY, STARRY NIGHT }

Serves 1.

4 ounces cold ginger beer
4 ounces cold papaya juice
2 ounces cold pineapple juice
Lemon and lime peel
1 or 2 slices of star fruit

In a tall glass (with or without ice), combine the soda and juices. Use a small, star-shaped cookie cutter to cut star shapes from the lemon and lime peels and drop them into the drink. Slide the slices of star fruit onto the glass rim.

Following are two of Chris Reed's favorite ginger recipes that he makes every Thanksgiving.

{ GINGER CRANBERRY SAUCE }
Makes 6 cups.

4 cups fresh cranberries
½ cup fresh orange juice
5 whole cloves
1 teaspoon grated orange zest
5 whole allspice berries
5 tablespoons grated fresh ginger
3 cinnamon sticks
1 ½ cups organic raw cane sugar

Place the cranberries, orange juice, and 1 cup water in a medium-sized saucepan over medium heat. Tie the cloves, orange zest, allspice, ginger, and cinnamon sticks in a spice bag and place in the cranberries. Cook until the cranberries begin to burst, about 10 minutes.

Stir in the sugar and reduce the heat to low. Cook for about 5 minutes longer, until the sugar has dissolved. Remove from the heat and let cool. Discard the spice bag. Cover and chill in the refrigerator for 8 hours, or overnight, before serving.

{ GINGER CARROTS }
Serves 2.

4 carrots, cut into julienne
2 tablespoons olive oil
2 cloves garlic, chopped
2 thumbs of ginger, grated

Combine all the ingredients in a skillet and stir-fry until the carrots are tender.

ON MAKING OLIVES
ALL-AMERICAN

$\left\{\text{ SANTA BARBARA OLIVE COMPANY }\right\}$

THE PREVIOUS NIGHT'S rainfall had ended, yet the streets remained wet and glistening in the morning sun. I felt like I was in a car ad—speeding along the highway, the beautiful Santa Inez mountains ahead, glimpses of Pacific Ocean on the left—as Ed and I drove the thirty miles up Route 101 from Ventura to Santa Barbara. We were meeting Cindy and Craig Makela at the Presidio in the center of Santa Barbara. The fourth and last royal presidio built in California by the Spaniards, it was an appropriate place to meet the Makelas, who, with both time and money, had helped support the ongoing restoration of the over-two-hundred-year-old military fortress. Appropriate, too, because the Presidio entranceway is where the three oldest olive trees in Santa Barbara, likely planted in 1782, still stand. Cindy and Craig are co-owners and founders of the Santa Barbara Olive Company, and Craig's family has been in Santa Barbara County for eight generations, many as olive growers.

I first discovered the Santa Barbara Olive Company in 1996. They'd sent me samples of their wonderful products—I was doing research for a book on mail-order food—and their garlic-stuffed olive quickly became my favorite, good both in and out of gin. Except for the oil, olives had never been a food I had even a vague culinary thought about; in fact, until mail-order made the Santa Barbara olives available to me, even martinis were ordered sans olive—I didn't like the squishy pimento and meaningless green part—and preferred only a lemon twist. Santa Barbara olives were different. They had a purpose in their flavor, and I was in touch with Craig several times again over the years. Our meeting that November morning was our first face-to-face.

Cindy stood by herself on the portico, a pretty, blond-haired woman made taller by high-heeled boots. She was wearing a chic sheepskin jacket that reminded this New Englander that southern Californians think near-seventy-degree weather with an ocean breeze is cold. We introduced ourselves, and then Craig appeared from across the street. With dark brown hair and of medium height, he wore jeans, very white athletic shoes, and a thin, V-neck shell with sleeves pushed up so a metal-banded watch could sit more comfortably on his wrist. I recognized him from photos I'd seen six years back, although the good life had perhaps made him stockier. His greeting was friendly but with intent. "How do we want to do this?" he said.

We started with a tour of the Presidio and learned about the history of the old fort, its chapel, the Santa Barbara Trust for Historic Preservation, the trust's founder, Pearl Chase, about Santa Barbara and the Makela family. The Makelas were rightly proud of their civic-minded efforts to restore the Presidio, careful to show me the reinstated historic "kitchen" and kitchen gardens and to mention awards they'd received for their volunteerism; they joked familiarly with the resident archaeologist, Mike Imwalle. And they pointed out an exhibit about the city's founders, which included a plaque chronicling the role of the Makelas in Santa Barbara history and their family tree, clearly an olive tree.

Craig's great-great-grandfather, Jules Goux, emigrated from France to California in 1848 and brought grapes to start a vineyard. He built the first winery and saloon in Santa Barbara, and married a Spanish woman from Mexico whose dowry included five varietals of olive-tree cuttings. Their next generation, John Emile Goux, became the first commercial olive grower in the United States.

California's earliest known olive grove was planted by a Franciscan missionary at the San Diego Mission in 1769. Then olives were pressed—not eaten—and the oil used for cooking, for medicinal purposes, and for anointment in religious ceremonies. Olive trees, a member of the evergreen family, are amazingly hardy—some trees have lived to be over two thousand years old—and southern California, with its Mediterranean-like climate, provided ideal growing conditions for olives. Over 99 percent of the olives grown in the United States today are done so in California. When father and son Goux started out in the mid-1800s, there were only about five hundred olive trees in California; by the end of the century, there were half a million. And it was still for their oil that the olives were grown.

Then in 1899, David Wesson's development of low-cost cooking oil—made from cottonseed—caused the use of olive oil in America to become nearly nonexistent. Of course, this could have spelled disaster for California's oil-based olive industry, were it not for University of California professor Frederic T. Bioletti, who serendipitously at about the same time invented a method for canning olives. Canning olives meant that they were suddenly available year round. Virtually the entire olive industry in California instantly reconfigured itself and in the early part of the twentieth century started producing olives for the table. Canned table olives have remained the state's primary olive business to this day.

Neither green nor fully ripened olives off the tree are actually edible. They must be treated with lye and/or cured in brine or dry salt to remove the bitter glycoside oleuropein, before they can be eaten. Canned California olives are not only treated with lye but packed immediately in brine and then sterilized. Since the sterilization cooks them, California olives—unlike Spanish olives, and Greek olives, which aren't treated at all with lye and instead are packed in dry salt, or pickled in brine, for six to twelve months to ferment, and then repacked in fresh brine— are not fermented. The absence of fermentation, and particularly the sterilizing, produces an olive fit for frozen pizzas but otherwise pretty bland and uninteresting.

Again, there would come a shift—this time a slow one— in California's olive industry, due to a change in attitude toward food. It started in the 1960s, when natural foods and

the health benefits of olive products became more widely recognized in the United States. The Mediterranean diet—which
includes olive oil (low in "bad" and high in "good" cholesterol)
and the flavorful Greek and Spanish table olives—was
regarded as healthier for the heart and better tasting than the
traditional American diet. Americans had become more cosmopolitan and worldly, and consequently had a greater curiosity about foods from other countries, and there was a desire for
more intense and varied flavors. By the mid-1960s, the United
States was importing twenty-two million gallons of olive oil
annually. The demand for imported olive oil continued to
grow, and by the year 2000 imports were increasing 20 percent
annually, a pace it has maintained every year since. And the
European table olives, particularly stuffed, handily continued
to beat the California canned in flavor.

Less than 1 percent of what Americans consume is domestic olive oil. This is in part because the perception, not unlike the
initial sentiments surrounding French wines, is that European
oils are best. And because olives are a government-subsidized
crop in Europe, olive oil and table olives from abroad can be less
expensive than ours.

Of course, historically Europe virtually owns the olive; it
has flourished in the Mediterranean for some six thousand years
with evidence that olive trees were first cultivated in Crete
around 2475 B.C. Olives even appear in Greek mythology in a
Zeus-inspired competition among the gods and goddesses:
Whoever created the most useful gift would be awarded the
patronage of Attica. Poseidon presented the horse, but it was
Athena who won the contest with her gift of olives. As Thomas
Jefferson said, "The olive tree is surely the richest gift of
Heaven." Sadly he was never able to make his cuttings from
France take root at Monticello.

Admittedly European olives do have their pedigree: the
basic olive, *Oleo europaea*, comes in some seven hundred culti-
vars, producing fruits with different nuances of taste. In Europe
many varietals may be combined to create a specific flavor of oil.
Although the hot, arid climate of California corresponds almost
identically to the prime growing conditions in the Mediter-

ranean, only five varietals are prevalent—Barouni, Sevillano, Ascalano, Manzanillo, and Mission.

"Our climate is better than Europe's, and the California Sevillano and Mission are great olives for oil," said Craig. "But ninety percent of California's olives still are grown for the table and even though we're down to only two canneries they, of course, hold the power and aren't going to promote the California olive oil business. I make about fourteen thousand dollars on two thousand pounds of olives if I make them for the table. If I press that same two thousand pounds I make about nine hundred dollars. But pressing for oil is still cool."

Picking and brining olives for the table may be more profitable, but Craig's right: it doesn't have nearly the cachet as producing a fancy estate bottle of specialty olive oil.

Yet Craig certainly understands both olive oil and the fruit. And the Makelas made some wise concessions to "coolness" by including in their product line the more profitable table olives. The Makelas' initial idea was to produce olive oil, but in 1999, when I first talked to Craig, about 90 percent of their business was olives for the table—today it's more like 50 percent—all specialty, ethnic, usually stuffed olives, all harvested, sorted, and packed by hand, and now certified organic. Their curing methods—Spanish and Sicilian, brined and dry cured—are chemical-free. The olives are packed cold, never cooked, and use only sea salt, cider vinegar, and/or purified water for preservation.

"We use salt and vinegar, the brine, to control the acid level and prevent bacterial growth so we don't need to sterilize. If you don't let the pH get out of whack—above 4.8 or below 3.5—and you have the proper salinity and vinegar, no bacteria can grow. Hot-packed olives are softer, mushier, and cooking changes the color as well as the texture. Cold-packed olives retain the crunch—the flavor has a fresh feel—as well as the nutritional value, which cooking depletes."

Craig explained this to me at his ranch, a hundred acres with five thousand olive trees, a processing plant, the Makela home, a vegetable garden, livestock (Black Angus, cows, chickens, pigs, goats), which overlooks the Channel Islands and the Pacific Ocean.

After our visit to the Presidio we'd headed toward the Makela ranch, twenty or so miles north. We passed first through the city streets of Santa Barbara, many of which are lined with ancient olive trees, some three hundred in number, and old enough to have been planted by Craig's great-grandfather. He told us the trees had become overgrown and barren, and so he'd begun pruning and caring for them. The trees eventually bore fruit, and he harvested the olives and gave the proceeds to the city's homeless people. Craig's Santa Barbara tour was annotated with stories about the city's history, or olives, or the Makelas, or all of the above. But as we traveled—on a glorious day with the California light making everything look clean and bright—Craig's cell phone rang. And when the phone call ended his conversation with us turned to their story.

"It's Cindy and my twenty-first wedding anniversary today," Craig remarked. "I'm kind of a romantic guy. The way I asked her to marry me was I hired a plane to carry a gigantic flag and I took her down to East Beach, and when the plane flew by, the flag said, 'Cindy will you marry me?' A photographer caught her expression on film and the picture appeared in newspapers all over the country!"

Craig had spent virtually his whole life in Santa Barbara County; Cindy was a transplant from out east. They met when they were both working at a health club during college. But it took them five years to fall in love. By then she was divorced and had a daughter and Craig had flunked out of law school. "At least I learned that lawyers are just a big fraternity and aren't really out to help people very much."

In 1982 they decided to start Santa Barbara Olive Company. Craig's dad wasn't a commercial olive grower, but surely that family tree must have provided some of the inspiration for their entrepreneurial efforts. Plus Cindy and Craig saw the potential in a burgeoning U.S. olive oil market and said, "We can do that!"

Cindy was working as the manager of a publishing company, and Craig was an assistant wine maker and marketing manager for Santa Barbara Winery. But they leased seven acres and planted five hundred trees. Their office was in half of a two-car garage that they shared with a little old lady named Ola May. "Ola painted a yellow line down the middle and told us not to cross it," Craig laughed. "But we bought a desk and an old military phone from an opportunity shop, furnishing the office on our side of the line."

Twenty minutes into our trip up the coast we began to catch a glimpse of the ocean. Then suddenly from the highway we took a sharp right turn onto a road that went up and wound along the foothills of the Santa Inez mountains. Passing through a gate, we began to see dark rail fences holding back flourishing olive groves that climbed the arid mountainside. Olive trees can grow forty feet in height, but these were a standard mature size of twenty feet, and so weighted down with heavy fruit they seemed to sag to a shorter stature. Olive trees begin to bear fruit after three or four years and are in their prime at six years. Surely these trees were nearing prime.

It was early November, so the olives were actively being harvested. Here and there among the trees was a worker—olives must be hand picked—and next to the fencing sat hot-tub-size white plastic crates half full of bright chartreuse-colored olives. We parked the car next to a large, metal-sided warehouse-type building and went inside to find boxes stacked high on the right, several labeling and packaging machines on the left, shelves of various products, and a kitchen—all very clean and sanitary. In the rear were Cindy's and Craig's side-by-side offices. Before settling there to hear the story of how five hundred trees got to be five thousand, Craig stopped in front of several opaque plastic barrels and asked if I wanted to taste olive oil that had been pressed just the day before. Not a question. I tasted several drops pulled from the barrel with a long straw. The oil was, I thought, complex, sort of spicy, but satiny and mellow. Craig described the flavor as herbaceous. I was surprised at how lovely it was—mistakenly thinking for some reason that olive oil had to be aged to taste good—but Craig confirmed that one-day-old olive oil is the best. It was a perfect way to begin the discussion.

"Initially, when I was working for Santa Barbara Winery and wanted to go into business for myself, I wanted to make wine," Craig said. "But we both knew that the olive business was wide open and it's cheaper to get into than wine. Wine takes a lot of thought and investment, and you have to be bonded. We didn't have any money, didn't own a home, just a couple of old cars, so economically it made sense to go into olives. Plus the table olive business was full of opportunity. When we got into it only four companies were doing anything similar. Even the foreign olives in the 1970s and '80s were limited to stuffing with pimentos or the occasional almond or anchovy."

Craig quit the winery in 1983, while Cindy continued working for the publishing company. But her boss began to realize she was doing a little freelancing on the side—she kept the books for their new business—and it wasn't long before he gave her an ultimatum and she went to work with Craig at Santa Barbara Olive Company. As Cindy was explaining this, Craig pulled from a desk drawer their first two SBOC paychecks: Cindy's take-home pay was $100 a week, his was $125 in 1986. "Which explains why it was necessary for me to keep working at the publisher for as long as I could," Cindy laughed.

"In the beginning we did everything," Craig explained. "We'd load the delivery van full of product, our sales books, and a hand truck and drive up to Lompoc, where we had two accounts. Cindy would go make a sales call, and then we'd meet in the cheese shop where I'd be finishing the deliveries. Sometimes we couldn't afford a motel so we'd sleep in the van. I'd bring my razor and shaving cream, comb, towel, and swim trunks and in the morning we'd pull into a Motel 6 after sleeping in the van and sneak into the pool. I'd rinse off, shave, and then towel off. I'd smell like chlorine, but at least I was clean—I swear to God we did this! I'd throw on clean clothes, and then Cindy'd jump in with her bathing suit on and then towel off. We'd go to McDonalds, get an EggMcMuffin and a soda, and off we'd go to make more deliveries and sales calls."

"Yeah, those were good times." Cindy smiled. "Every single thing we learned back then came out of blind stupidity and from bootstrapping ourselves."

They were both laughing as they admitted they just stumbled along through those first ten years. "We'd make a mistake, we'd go: 'Oh, shit, this doesn't work!'" Craig said. But despite stumbling, they did find smart solutions and helpful people. Craig purchased his first olive trees from Dominique Delunardes, an old Italian nurseryman and grower, who also kindly spent time educating Craig about olive propagation. "And when the father died the son, Vito, continued to talk to me whenever I'd call to ask about grafting onto mission root stock or what might be good for pest management. He's a real good guy too."

One of the ideas they brainstormed really worked and had a major impact on their growth: they pulled jars of jam off grocery shelves to find names of other small food companies similar to Santa Barbara Olive and sent out three hundred letters asking if they wanted to meet at the National Association for the Specialty Food Trade (NASFT) Fancy Food Show in Atlanta in order to trade information. Eighty-eight companies showed up, and from that they formed the first state food association, the California Gourmet Association. They gathered helpful information— where to get labels for glass jars, freight rates, what trade shows were good—and did consolidated advertising. "One company couldn't afford big ads, but all together we could," Craig explained as he showed me a copy of an ad with the headline: "The Gourmet That Roared" and which pictured Craig in John Philip Sousa-type garb surrounded by a background of American farmers. With the help of such national exposure, Santa Barbara Olive was able by the early 1990s to get nationwide distribution, and more importantly establish a niche category on supermarket shelves for gourmet foods and provide an alternative to imported olives.

"I'm not against European products, but Americans should at least have a choice in their supermarkets. Specialty-food sections in supermarkets gave small companies a chance," Craig said.

But meanwhile, back at the ranch, there was a problem: the individual who had sublet the land to the Makelas lost his lease in a lawsuit and through no fault of their own they were thrown off the land. "I had five hundred nice trees, pretty good size, and I got pissed off and ripped every one of them out of the ground. No one wanted them, but I was not going to give 'em to this guy who screwed us over. So we pulled every single tree out, bagged 'em, and put 'em on a truck. We had no place to plant them, so Cindy and I donated them to the city of Lompoc. We were in a rented guest house—we had two kids by then and were poor as poor could be—and we were out of trees."

They ended up renting a Victorian-style building in downtown Solvang with a top apartment. Their intention was to put a showroom for California Gourmet Association products on the ground floor. But as they were remodeling and stocking the tasting room, people kept knocking on the door and asking when they intended to open. "We decided," Cindy recalled, "what the hell, forget the showroom, we'll go retail. So we bought a cash register and opened the Olive Shop in 1988." And they sold it in 1990 and bought a ten-acre ranch in Santa Inez. They planted 650 olive trees, built an office, warehouse building, and parking, and got more involved in the science of olives. They even hired an expert in pruning to come from Italy. But they wanted to go back to Santa Barbara, so Cindy started looking.

In 1999 she found three hundred acres on the ocean advertised for sale on the Internet. "Nothing had been on this land, it was completely virgin—no water, no sewer, no roads, no anything," Craig said. It was owned by an oil company.

ARCO had originally bought the land for well sites, but had had it on the market for eleven years at a price of $3.5 million. In the dead of winter the Makelas drove up to see the property with the real estate agent, who refused to get out of the car—he didn't want to walk through the mud. So Cindy and Craig walked it alone and then went back to the agent and offered $425,000 for the front hundred acres on the ocean. "Well, he told us that was ridiculous and he wouldn't write it up," Craig said. "So we told him we'd write it up ourselves. Funny thing is, we didn't have $425,000."

And then the miracle: a week after the Makelas' offer was made, British Petroleum bought ARCO. Instructions from BP to the real estate office were to begin negotiating any reasonable offer that had been made on the land. They countered the Makela offer with $450,000, land as is. The Makelas bought the land in 1999 for just over $4,000 per acre. Today it is likely worth over $10 million. "That was a good investment," Cindy laughed. "The best we ever did!"

They lived with their three kids on the property in a 660-square-foot trailer while they built the company buildings and planted trees. It took a year to sell their Santa Inez ranch, so they were financing two properties and really struggling. When it finally sold, they could borrow the money to build a home. Craig built their house himself, with help from a crew of SBOC employees and local tradesman. Ten days before the house was completed and they were scheduled to move in, rags left by the painters caught fire at two o'clock in the morning and the house burnt to the ground. "That morning there were fifteen grown men crying as we looked at the charred remains," Craig said. "But they helped me rebuild that same house in just seventy-two days, and nine days before Christmas the house was finished and we moved in. Our 2001 Christmas card that year pictured us with the crew. Then life got better."

Craig and Cindy drove us up the mountain from the offices to see where life got better, their home: multiple-car garage, large game room, library, wine cellar, recording studio for their concert-piano-playing son, many bedrooms, a large dining room. And of course, there was a kitchen, not just pretty but well-conceived and clearly utilized by real cooks. The back view from the house was of their vineyard of chardonnay grapes, which wine maker Chris Whitcraft, of *Sideways* fame, uses to make twenty-four cases a year of what Chris refers to as his best chardonnay. "He keeps twelve cases and we get twelve," Craig said.

The opposite view from the vineyard, viewed from a wide stone terrace, is just as movie-esque: rolling hills that slope uninterrupted to the ocean. That day, like so many in California, simply sparkled. And as the white puffy clouds drifted by, it seemed the right time to ask the Makelas about their dreams, after accomplishing so much, for Santa Barbara Olive Company.

"We're tossing over all kinds of stuff. We get offers to buy all the time—like the phone call I got on our ride up here was from someone interested in buying us out," Craig said. "Ideally, if we make enough money so the kids can take over and we could still live in this luxury, that would be the best. It would be really cool if we could step out and they step in and it could stay an olive company. The whole family has always been involved in the business. Cindy was doing the payroll taxes while she was in labor with Cody."

"I can remember," Cindy smiled, "when Heather was four years old she insisted on helping us put labels on jars. Then when we got to Neiman Marcus for a sales call we found her little tiny baby fingerprints all over the jars."

"And now," interjected Craig, "her nine-month-old son, our grandson, eats olives like the rest of the family, every day and in handfuls."

I wondered how they'd managed parenting, done everything in the business themselves, and kept the whole family involved. Craig read my mind: "When the boys were young we'd bring them and a nanny with us to do trade shows. We ended up home schooling all our kids and just dragging them along with us. They've been to all the famous museums and landmarks in the country. We could never pay for what the kids learned by being with us and part of the business. Our son, Chad, is a junior in college and his complete, entire design is to take this company over. He'd be kind of sad if it didn't work out. But I don't know, if we got offered many, many millions of dollars . . ." Craig didn't finish the sentence.

And what would you do if you didn't have all this? Without a moment's hesitation, Craig said, "I would build another one of these!"

Olives are not an American food. They can't really be successfully grown here except in California, and in very tiny measure in Arizona and Texas. They are not even indigenous to this hemisphere. Yet if there ever was an American story about a food, it is this one about the Santa Barbara Olive Company and the Makelas. It is about immigrants, and entrepreneurship, ingenuity, gumption, pride in heritage and country, strong character, and, of course, passion.

California olive grower Amigo Cantisano is quoted in Peggy Knickerbocker's fabulous cookbook *Olive Oil* as saying, "You are consuming the place, the microclimate, the character of the soil, and, too, the character of the human who produced it and the care with which it has been handled and pressed."

I think about the fabulous "herbaceous" olive oil I sipped from Craig's barrel, about the wonderful fresh snap of one of he and Cindy's garlic-stuffed olives soaking in my martini. I know, and can taste, the care with which the olive and the oil have been produced. Their olives are, the Makelas have made me believe, actually a very American food.

{ ORANGE, OLIVE, AND FENNEL SALAD }
Serves 4.

1 clove garlic, halved
⅓ cup extra-virgin olive oil
⅓ cup fresh orange juice
Salt and freshly ground black pepper to taste
Leaves from 2 bunches arugula
4 navel oranges, peel and pith removed, sliced crosswise
1 large bulb fennel, halved and thinly sliced
½ cup pitted oil-cured black olives

Rub a large salad bowl several times with the cut surface of the garlic clove; discard garlic. In a bowl, whisk the oil, orange juice, and salt and pepper.

Add the arugula to the bowl and toss with the dressing; transfer the arugula to chilled serving dishes. Add the oranges, fennel, and olives to the bowl with the dressing; gently toss them to coat lightly with dressing and arrange over the arugula on the plates. Sprinkle with additional salt and pepper and serve immediately.

BEYOND BONBONS

{ L. A. BURDICK CHOCOLATES }

IFIRST TASTED Larry Burdick's chocolate bonbons at my friend Mary Lou's house. On Valentine's Day her husband had presented her with a small wooden box. And inside was a menagerie of chocolates shaped like mice—complete with round ears, white-chocolate dot eyes and noses, and pastel-colored, silk-string tails. I was enchanted—and then seduced—as Mary Lou shared her gift. One un-mouselike nibble of the sublimely smooth, rich, and expertly crafted morsel of chocolate both completely satisfied and at the same time roused. Not a connoisseur, yet also not such a chocoholic as to be undiscerning, I was curious, intrigued by the confection that had gone so far beyond Whitman's. Who was this wizard of chocolate artistry? How, and why, were his chocolates so different and exceptional?

L. A. Burdick Chocolates is located in the little New Hampshire town of Walpole. Famous initially for building the first bridge across the Connecticut River in 1785, the classic New England hamlet is tucked in among balding granite hills and old farm hayfields hemming the flood plain of the river. Walpole remains primarily an agrarian community, quiet and insular, and is not only home to independent Yankee farmers but appeals to artists—like filmmaker Ken Burns, as well as chocolatier Larry Burdick—who prefer and need to escape city stress.

The first time I went to Walpole it sparkled with the brightness of a bright early spring day, and the town looked almost too perfect—Hollywood-set quality—definitely topping the list of most charming New England towns. Burdick's then was both a café and a candy-making operation (although Larry would shudder at the thought of his bonbons being referred to as candy). Over the bridge, right at a blinking light onto Main Street, and just past the library, I parked at the white clapboard storefront—perhaps at one time a home—bedecked with striped awnings and painted bench seats out front.

It was the Monday following Easter when I visited, and although I'd expected a lull after one of the busiest times in the year for chocolatiers, there were a couple dozen employees in evidence, moving not only with backcountry slowness, but looking sort of shell-shocked. The clerks behind the counter in particular looked tired, but happy—a bit like they were recovering from an all-night party—and waited on both the café and candy customers with a kind of deliberate concentration. It was nearly ten o'clock and Larry Burdick hadn't appeared yet. But I was early for the appointment and asked to wait, then was given a cup of cocoa while I did so. The cocoa proved a pleasant harbinger of what was going to be an intense morning of chocolate.

When Larry did arrive it was with a small girl in tow. An attractive man, Larry is not particularly big, but not what I'd call wiry either, and on the older side for such a young daughter, perhaps somewhere in his early forties. He asked if I minded walking with them as he took Marietta to school. We ambled the two or three blocks to the church basement where the preschool was housed. And the child—just as my own once-little girl had done—happily skipped in a zigzag pattern a few steps ahead, now and then drifting back to the reassurance of her father's hand. As we walked, he talked about chocolate with a vitality that began to work seductively on my already cocoa-buzzed brain. He's careful to describe his chocolates "not as candy—sugar flavored with chocolate—but as a gastronomic product. Food to be enjoyed at the end of a meal."

Larry was raised near Boston in Dorchester, Massachusetts, under the shadow of the Baker's Chocolate factory. He recalls his uncle telling about smelling chocolate in the air and describing how on an exceptionally windy day a fine cocoa powder dusted the cars of Dorchester.

In his early twenties, Larry and his future wife, Paula, lived in France, where for a year or so he worked as a pastry chef and cook. When they returned to the States he got a job with the accomplished Boston chef Lydia Shear. But Larry wanted greater opportunities to use his French cooking skills, so they moved to New York City. In 1985 he went to Switzerland with the intention of visiting for only a few months. He ended up staying over two years, and during that time his gastronomic attention began to turn to chocolate. He realized that no one in the United States was making handmade, fresh, quality chocolates that were made "thoughtfully," as he puts it. Plus, he'd known for some time that he wasn't really that interested in a career as a chef.

"And you may have noticed," Larry grinned at me, "people really like chocolate." Ah, what a perfectly simple explanation for why chocolate had become his life.

He began making his bonbons in 1987, working out of a hole-in-the-wall kitchen in Brooklyn, and selling them primarily to restaurants. In 1988 he moved the business to slightly better quarters on New York's Upper East Side. But relocating to Manhattan seemed to only increase the near-daily hassles of trying to build a chocolate business. The new enrober (a machine that coats chocolate) arrived with the motor put in backward. A newly purchased tempering machine sat on the docks because customs had lost the paperwork; the delay meant that Larry had no alternative but to do the tempering by hand, "which means my arms fall off." He dreamt about getting out of the city and eliminating some of the stress. Plus he knew Manhattan was not the place he wanted to raise his children. He started building a mail-order business with the plan that he'd someday move his family out of New York and find larger, less-expensive facilities.

Right from the start, Burdick's chocolates gained a reputation of quality and enjoyed the kind of publicity money couldn't buy—the *New Yorker*, *Food and Wine*, *Town and Country*, *Gourmet*, and *Glamour* gave him glowing reviews—and it seemingly came without effort. "I think because it's such a unique product," Burdick said to me. By the early 1990s, his customer list had become extensive. He found an old pizza parlor—that had indeed been a home at one time—in Walpole and renovated it into a café storefront with kitchens for chocolate and pastry making. In 2000 Larry and Paula moved the Walpole café and chocolate-making operation across the street to a larger facility in the old IGA grocery store—a building they co-own with Ken Burns. On my first visit to L. A. Burdick it was still located in the ex-pizza parlor, although with its crystal-clear glass display case and counters and elegant dark wood paneling hardly a semblance of the old pizzeria remained.

Upon our return from school delivery, we sat and drank another cup of cocoa, which I probably didn't need. Then we passed behind the display counter into the back rooms, where Larry began his tour and explanation of how he makes his chocolates. The process of making Burdick bonbons starts by grinding 2.2-kilo blocks of base chocolate, or couverture. This high-grade chocolate comes from beans of superior quality, with a cocoa-butter content of at least 32 percent. Larry uses eight varieties of couverture, each time selecting the one best suited to the type of bonbon he's preparing, and always grinding it just before use so it is at its freshest. To make the interior ganache, he will combine ground couverture with cream or milk, butter, perhaps eggs, a flavoring, or all of the above and then pour the mixture onto a slab and roll it to a thickness appropriate to the type of bonbon being made. This ganache then sits for twenty-four hours before it is cut with a device called a guitar into small squares, triangles, or rectangles. Next the ganache is, by hand or machine, enrobed with tempered couverture. Tempering is a very controlled and critical heating and cooling process—often the test of the chocolatier's true skill—and provides an airtight chocolate seal around the interior.

No candy molds here, just small conveyor belts, pots, a dipping fork, and many hands. As we traveled through the kitchen, skirting trays stacked in racks holding various finished chocolates, Larry generously slipped me samples, explaining the ingredients. With each piece I tasted, the rush of flavor came first from the perfect chocolate, followed less dramatically by a taste of raspberry, or vanilla, or honey, or pistachio, or cognac.

The taste reached a crescendo and then subtly finished with touches of ginger, or lavender, cardamom, cinnamon, or lemon pepper. My complete sensory attention was fully awakened, alert and eagerly awaiting the next series of flavor sensations. Our cruise through the little factory was quick—even with lots of stops for chocolate tasting. Then I was taken to an upstairs office to meet Markus Färbinger, an Austrian pastry chef who was brought to Burdick's in 1998 when the Burdicks opened two additional shops—one in Cambridge, Massachusetts, the other in Edgartown on Martha's Vineyard. (Markus is now gone from Burdick's, as is the Edgartown shop.) Larry left us to our own devices, which for Markus meant giving me a tour of the facilities and sampling their various chocolate wares along the way. As we started the repeat performance, I had a very momentary rush of guilt and thought that I should mention to Markus that I'd already been through the kitchen and eaten quite a lot of Burdick chocolate. On second thought . . . naah.

First he took me into a small room lined with shelves holding bottles of flavor essences—the aroma from each floated in the air and hung there, I'm certain, to entice and make me impatient. Please, please, let's do it again with: an orange diamond, a whipped ganache of dark chocolate and freshly squeezed orange; a porto, dark ganache of chopped hazelnut, cinnamon, lavender, and port wine; or a mocha palet, dark ganache with espresso and kirsch, sprinkled with fennel seeds. First the orange, cherry, almond, kirsch, or nutmeg and then always, always there was the incredible chocolate rushing in, starting from the dark outer shell, and then blossoming as I reached the satin interior.

I succumbed to the symphony of fresh flavors, and the surging, whirling chocolate climax that had moved far beyond anything so simply and often described as a lovely little "lift." I was thinking I needed to sit down, but there was no place to do so. And those strikingly steel-blue eyes of Markus's would see right through me. He'd recognized the fall and knew that despite my professionalism, my usual demeanor of journalistic impartiality, I was in love with Burdick's food.

As I departed for home, Larry handed me an elegant, handled bag full of boxes and cellophane and chocolate. He stared at me momentarily, recognizing, I'm sure, my chocolate intoxication. He gave a sly smile, a Cheshire cat grin, and said softly, seductively, "Enjoy!" I wasn't quite sure what had happened to me. Had a cunning chocolate mouse really started all this?

Of course, the list of those afflicted with a chocolate fixation extends far beyond me. Don't we all have a grandfather, a mother-in-law, or someone in our lives who confess to being a chocoholic—or a chocophile, as Larry more graciously prefers to label those addicted—who influence our chocolate attitude? For me it was my dad, who lives in the walnut-growing region of France for a month each year and apparently thrives exclusively on Valrhona chocolate and walnuts. He taught me to travel with a ready supply of chocolate-covered coffee beans, in case. (In case what? In case there was some corner of the world, some moment in time, in which—oh, horror of horrors—chocolate was *unavailable?*)

But the seeds of chocolate addiction reach back through history, across continents, and names the rich and famous as cocacaospirators and probably initially is less tied to the flavor and more to the buzz. When Spanish explorer Hernando Cortes arrived in Mexico in 1519, Aztec king Montezuma was gulping a drink made of burnt cacao, maize, water, and spices. (Cacao comes from the seeds or beans of the cacao tree and is used to make chocolate, cocoa butter, and cocoa.) Although, suggesting he was drinking *a* drink is misleading—Montezuma, believing not only that cacao was an aphrodisiac but that it possessed medicinal qualities, drank fifty goblets of the stuff a day. His palace staff, equally addicted, went through two thousand pitchers of *xocoatl* daily! The strong, bitter sludge of a drink tasted nothing like today's cocoa. And the conquering Cortes believed that only with the addition of lots of sugar did the chocolate drink have a future in Spain. Cortes had never tasted coffee or tea but recognized chocolate's real potential when he wrote back to his sponsor, Carlos I, describing *xocoatl* as "a drink that builds up resistance and fights fatigue."

Yes, chocolate's ability to fight fatigue is an important part of what makes it popular. I don't think I could have functioned very alertly—even as a twenty-five-year-old—through uncomfortable, sleepless pregnancies without a daily snack of a chocolate candy bar. Although according to U.S. Department of Agriculture data, it's not the twenty- or thirty-year-olds, but the forty-something women and teenage boys who out-choco-chug all other groups in chocolate consumption. The calorie-hungry teenage boys don't really shed much light on the reasons for chocoholism, since they probably out-eat *every* age group in *every* food category. But it is the fact that middle-age women are the big chocolate eaters that reveals more accurately one reason why we all love chocolate—and it goes beyond merely fighting fatigue. Their consumption suggests that it's chocolate's ability to jazz, to lift spirits, and ward off hormonal lows that makes it both necessary and a pleasing experience. A 1.65-ounce bar of milk chocolate has only about 10 milligrams of caffeine (a cup of drip coffee has about 115 milligrams), but chocolate is full of naturally occurring mood-altering chemicals: theobromine, a heart stimulant; and phenylethylamine, called "the mood elevator." Both make the heart beat faster and provide energy. Is it any wonder the ancient Aztecs believed chocolate was an aphrodisiac?

Fortunately for us all, chocolate also has nutritional value, vitamins and minerals, and is considered an antioxidant. But beyond the emotional buzz and the nutritional value there is another and, to my mind, much more important factor in chocolate's universal appeal: taste. Of course, the flavor qualities of chocolate vary greatly, and therefore its popularity is not nearly as explicit or understandable if we're talking about flavor versus its power to create the happy-high. From Montezuma's aphrodisiac to Hershey bars, it's all invigorating chocolate, but the two don't taste even remotely the same.

Columbus actually brought cacao beans back from his fourth voyage to the New World in 1502. But it was Cortes who in 1528 introduced the Spanish not just to the bean's cultivation but the process of concocting a chocolate drink—drying, fermenting, roasting, and crushing. For the next century Spain controlled both the trade of cacao beans and also the production of a popular chocolate drink made from bean extract mixed with orange or rose water. Then in 1615 the Spanish infanta, Anne of Austria, gave chocolate to her fourteen-year-old husband, France's Louis XIII, as a wedding gift. And with royalty back then being the setter of trends, drinking chocolate became the rage with European aristocracy and started the Belgians, Swiss, and particularly the French on the road to making their own couverture and chocolate confections.

When chocolate returned to the Americas, it was produced in such a way as to be good for baking rather than as candy. In 1764 a colonial physician, James Baker, financed a young Irish chocolate maker named John Hannon and started the first American chocolate mill, in Dorchester, Massachusetts. Hannon was later lost at sea while traveling to the West Indies for cacao beans, and Dr. Baker took over the prospering business. Today Baker's Chocolate is still available, still a good chocolate for cooking, and bears what is the oldest trademark on our grocery store shelves.

Of course, for most of the twentieth century, chocolate candy in the United States was synonymous with what Milton Hershey and the Mars family accomplished by mass production. They instilled chocolate confections into our culture—from the chocolate bars supplied to the military in survival kits during the world wars to summer-izing chocolate with a heat-resistant candy coating so there was "no mess in your hand!" Hershey and Mars gave us our national chocolate baseline. However, in recent years our chocolate horizons have broadened and we've begun to understand that there is a whole lot more to chocolate than what Charlie and his chocolate factory offered.

The French and the Belgians are generally considered to be the best chocolatiers in the world, and many of the better chocolate bonbons in the United States are actually imported, although I believe that what European chocolatiers export to the United States is not quite the caliber of their in-country stuff. Probably this is due to a lack of freshness. (Larry recommends eating his bonbons within four days of receipt. I confess I never found this to be difficult to accomplish and really have no idea if Burdick chocolate tastes stale after four days.) Once, in an attempt to find a quality American-made and fresh chocolate, I interviewed a chocolatier who came to my house and made a "presentation" of his chocolate art. It was beautiful to look at—all artfully sculptured into interesting shapes and painted with color-contrasting chocolate—and it tasted pretty good, too. But he seemed rather appalled when I actually ate his art: he clearly missed the point.

There are many chocolate confectioners in the United States but only a handful of people making—selecting the beans, blending, and roasting—base chocolate (couverture) here. It is curious to me that the entire process of producing chocolate—from bean to bonbon—is rarely found in a single chocolatier. They are either roaster or cook but unlikely to be both. It may be that one is a scientist and the other a craftsman, and that the two personality traits are not usually found in one individual. Or that each discipline requires so much attention that it is difficult to do both.

Valrhona has the reputation of being the best base chocolate in the world. It is a blend of cacao beans but is made primarily from beans that come from the island of Guanaja in the Caribbean. It is produced by a small (only 150 workers) eighty-year-old French chocolate manufacturer located near Lyon and the Rhone river (hence the name), which sells most of its products to chefs, confectioners, and other chocolatiers. Valrhona has high (up to 70 percent) cacao content and can contain the rarest and purest cacao in the world, criollo.

Robert Steinberg, a co-founder of one of those handful of U.S. chocolate makers, Scharffen Berger, concurs with something Larry Burdick told me: pure genetic strains of cacao bean disappeared hundreds of years ago due to cross-pollination. Consequently, the relationship of a certain set of flavor qualities to a specific bean type, such as criollo, or forastero, or trinitario, is attributable only in a general sense. Probably Valrhona's superiority is based more on having the best sources for quality beans rather than the best actual variety. As far as fine couverture goes, Valrhona enjoys market dominance, and to some extent this is justifiable. The manufacturer maintains consistent quality and since 1925 has been able to establish relationships, perhaps exclusive relationships, with some of the best cacao plantations and sources. Valrhona makes up about two-thirds of the chocolate base Burdick uses. But Larry believes competition is imperative to sustaining quality in the marketplace and that working with several cacao growers and chocolate makers directly in the development process is critical. He also uses El Rey chocolate—made only from Venezuelan beans—and in recent years he has been consulting with a Swiss company, Felchin, to develop a chocolate with the same standing as Valrhona. Additionally, he tried, in the summer of 2004, to establish a partnership with a cacao plantation and chocolate maker in Granada—until hurricanes devastated the island and postponed plans for a partnership. He still talks of making his own base chocolate and of completing the creative circle—starting with nurturing what the earth bears and finally bringing it to the table as a part of a heavenly culinary experience—by combining great skill, imagination, energy, and knowledge to produce art. Paula rolls her eyes, worries that it would be too much to handle, but hears Larry say that growing cacao and making couverture is an inevitability for them.

Larry Burdick's approach to chocolate—his thoughtfulness—is at least part of why it is so very, very good. "In my imagination, I am the customer." But it is also about his vision and who he is. When next I returned to L. A. Burdick it was with my husband, and we dined with Larry and Paula in their new restaurant. In an effort to convince the American audience that chocolate is a gastronomic product, an integral part of any good meal, Larry felt he needed a venue for his chocolate, and that a restaurant was the obvious solution. For that exact reason, he'd also added—in the same building as the restaurant, the confection store, and kitchens—a fine food shop, all as part of his concept of providing a continuum of good food.

On a cool autumn night, Ed and I arrived a bit late—perhaps knowing that always-working Larry would be late too—

and were seated at a window table with glasses of wine to wait for Larry. Soon enough, he came, removing his ever-present apron and sitting next to me. Older now, of course, but with no graying hair and still amazingly trim. Paula said people are always surprised that Larry, who eats chocolate all day long, isn't fat. She had arrived with their two children, Marietta and Jacob, and dinner began.

We ate as a family—the children politely listening, a parent occasionally bringing them into the conversation—much the way the French do, with attention paid to the food and each part of the perfectly prepared meal. Talk centered on what we ate: Was the foie gras as good as the night before; where do they get such fresh fish? We discussed wines and, of course, chocolate.

"Fine chocolate has as much complexity of flavor as a good wine. Chocolate, however, is a complete food, and doesn't need to be accompanied by anything else. It cannot be made scientifically, from a recipe, but is much more intuitive." Larry stated it and then demonstrated it. We ordered every chocolate dessert on the menu, eight in all, just to sample, but somehow we finished them all. I was getting those Burdick chocolate whirls of giddiness again.

The atmosphere that night was touched by France, but in this lovely New Hampshire restaurant, with fall's colors and crispness just on the other side of the window glass, it was decidedly an American scene, made all the more so by Larry's talk of his desire to make a better-quality chocolate than France's Valrhona, to remind the Old World that the cacao bean is a product of the New World, to build with an entrepreneur's spirit, not only for the sake of extraordinary chocolate, but for the sake of a perfect and total gastronomic experience.

The history and cultures surrounding a specific food are certainly defining elements of its flavor and favor. And there is, too, a food's capacity to evoke a memory. My father's crude but passionate mixing of intense flavors like coffee or walnut with good chocolate was a piece of my past and conjured up by L. A. Burdick's similarly thoughtful, but more artful and subtle, bon-bon blends.

But surely the crucial aspect for approaching perfection comes directly from the extraordinarily talented individual who has the ability to release and expand on one of the world's exceptional flavors, and then to leave his mark on it. I asked Larry one time if I were blindfolded and given a French bonbon of equal quality and freshness as an L. A. Burdick chocolate, would there be a difference between the two? "No, not unless you were already familiar with my chocolate. Then you'd recognize me." Because an artist creates, and stamps it with his character and personality. Larry knows how to draw from Old World craft, blend into it the sensibilities of Americana, stir the dark chocolate pot of memories, and make it his own passion—as well as mine.

{ CARIBBEAN RUM TRUFFLES }

When I asked Larry and Paula Burdick to share one of their recipes, they turned me over to Burdick's production chef, Michael Krug. He sent the recipe below and said: "I wanted to make sure that the recipe that is used is not too complicated, but still thrilling in a culinary perspective." It is, indeed, thrilling!

When I tested the recipe I cut it in half, and it worked perfectly. But as Chef Michal said, "Why go to all that bother for only 75 truffles?" After tasting these luscious bonbons, I understood his point.

Makes about 150 small truffles.

2 pounds Caribbean dark chocolate with at least a 60% cocoa
     content (Valrhona Pur Caraibe, Extra Bitter, Grenada,
     Jamaica, or Trinidad)
2 tablespoons honey
2 tablespoons glucose (if you cannot get glucose, use more
     honey)
1 ⅛ cups heavy cream
Zest of 1 orange

Pinch salt
Pinch freshly grated nutmeg
¼ cup Caribbean dark rum
1 tablespoon unsalted butter, softened
¼ cup unsweetened cocoa powder

Chop half of the chocolate into small pieces and place them in the bowl of a standing electric mixer. (A mixer will make it easier to combine the ganache than a mixing bowl with a hand whisk.) Combine the honey, glucose, cream, orange zest, salt, and nutmeg in a saucepan and bring to a boil. Take the pan off the heat and let the cream steep for about 15 minutes.

Heat the cream mixture up again and pour hot, but not boiling, through a fine-mesh sieve into the bowl with the chopped chocolate. Mix very well with the mixer or a whisk to a smooth ganache. Add the rum and butter and mix again.

Place two sheet pans upside down on a counter top and cover them tightly with plastic wrap. Pour half of the ganache on top of each pan and cover with another layer of plastic. Make supports for the ends of a rolling pin, one on either side of each sheet pan, using two books or magazines of the same height. Resting the ends of the rolling pin on the supports, roll the ganache to a uniform thickness of about ¼ inch. Let the ganache rest for 36 hours or up to 72 hours in a cool but dry place.

After the ganache has rested, cut it with a knife into small, even pieces; the size is your preference. Wearing plastic gloves, roll the pieces into small round truffle-shaped bonbons.

Meanwhile, melt the remaining chocolate in a double boiler over steaming, but not boiling, water. (It is important that the melting of the chocolate is done gently and not at too hot a temperature, as chocolate can be burned if it is heated higher than 130 degrees. Milk and white chocolate are even more sensitive and should not heat over 120 degrees.)

Still wearing the gloves, place some of the warm melted chocolate in your palms and coat each truffle with a thin layer of chocolate. (We like to roll our truffles with a chocolate that is 94 to 99 degrees.) Place the coated truffles on a sheet pan lined with parchment paper and let them rest in a cool room for 30 minutes.

Coat the truffles a second time with another thin layer of chocolate, then roll them in cocoa powder with a fork and let them rest in the cocoa powder for at least 2 hours in a cool area.

Take the truffles out of the cocoa powder and brush excess powder off with a pastry brush. (Do this gently, as cocoa powder is very light and could provide a thin layer of cocoa dust over your kitchen.) Place the truffles on a tray and serve at room temperature. Truffles will stay fresh in a cool room for up to 14 days.

ACKNOWLEDGMENTS

WITH MY DEEP gratitude, I wish to thank the very talented food artisans in this book for giving me their time and their stories, and for their willingness to reveal the joys and troubles of creating something unique. But more important, they have my appreciation for giving the world their magnificent foods.

My thanks, too, go to Jay Heinrichs who during his tenure as executive editor of *Attaché*, the U.S. Airways in-flight magazine, gave me the opportunity to write regularly about food and the people who produce it. I was introduced to many of the people in this book through my research for that column.

Jennifer Unter, my wonderful agent, was also instrumental in this book's becoming a reality; thank you for being a persistent, clear-minded, and strong advocate.

I am very proud and lucky to claim Susan and Ethan Becker as friends and food soul mates now. I enjoyed every minute of my glorious time of contributing to their seventy-fifth anniversary edition of *The Joy of Cooking,* and I greatly appreciate their inclusion of me in their circle of "Joy Friends." Ethan's historical perspective and understanding of the world of food in America is without equal, and I am honored by his willingness to introduce this book. Thank you, Ethan, for being on these pages.

And as said since 1986 in my first book, I give a note of thanks here to Ed Gray—my best editor, mentor, partner, critic, and, of course, my very best friend.

DIRECTORY OF ARTISANS

ALLEN BROTHERS, INC.
3737 South Halsted Street
Chicago, IL 60609-1689
Phone: 800-957-0111
www.allenbrothers.com

BARRINGTON COFFEE ROASTING COMPANY
165 Quarry Hill Road
Lee, MA 01238
Phone: 800-528-0998
www.barringtoncoffee.com

BLUE MOON SORBET
P.O. Box 874
Quechee, VT 05059
Phone: 802-295-1165
www.bluemoonsorbet.com

BROKEN ARROW RANCH
3296 Junction Highway
Ingram, TX 78025
Phone: 800-962-4263
www.brokenarrowranch.com

CHESAPEAKE BAY CRAB CAKES & MORE
8805 Kelso Drive
Baltimore, MD 21221
Phone: 800-282-CRAB
www.cbcrabcakes.com

CLEAR FLOUR BAKERY
178 Thorndike Street
Brookline, MA 02446
Phone: 617-739-0060
www.clearflourbread.com

DANCING SALMON SEAFOODS
P.O. Box 482
Dillingham, AK 99576
Phone: 907-842-4505
www.dancingsalmon.net

EARTHY DELIGHTS, INC.
1161 E. Clark Road, Suite 260
DeWitt, MI 48820
Phone: 517-668-2402
www.earthy.com

L.A. BURDICK CHOCOLATES
P.O. Box 593
Walpole, NH 03608
Phone: 800-229-2419
www.burdickchocolate.com

L.L. LANIER & SON'S TUPELO HONEY
P.O. Box 706
Wewahitchka, FL 32465
Phone: 850-639-2371
www.lltupelohoney.com

LONG WIND FARM, INC.
82 Wilson Road
East Thetford, VT 05043
Phone: 802-785-4642
www.longwindfarm.com

POVERTY LANE ORCHARDS
98 Poverty Lane
Lebanon, NH 03766
Phone: 603-448-1511
www.povertylaneorchards.com

REED'S ORIGINAL GINGER BREW
13000 South Spring Street
Los Angeles, CA 90061
Phone: 800-99-REEDS
www.reedsgingerbrew.com

SANTA BARBARA OLIVE COMPANY
12477 Calle Real
Santa Barbara, CA 93117
Phone: 800-624-4896
www.sbolive.com

TENNESSEE T-CAKES
200 Hill Avenue, Suite 3
Nashville, TN 37210
Phone: 615-256-3950
www.tntcakes.com

VERMONT BUTTER & CHEESE COMPANY
40 Pitman Road
Websterville, VT 05678
Phone: 802-479-9371
www.vtbutterandcheeseco.com

WOOD PRAIRIE FARM
49 Kinney Road
Bridgewater, ME 04735
Phone: 800-829-9765
www.woodprairie.com